the great
DECISION

the great DECISION

JEFFERSON, ADAMS, MARSHALL, AND
THE BATTLE FOR THE SUPREME COURT

CLIFF SLOAN
AND
DAVID McKEAN

PublicAffairs
New York

Published in the United States by PublicAffairs™, a member of the Perseus Books Group.

Printed in the United States of America.

Book Design by Jeff Williams

Library of Congress Cataloging-in-Publication Data

Sloan, Cliff.
    The great decision : Jefferson, Adams, Marshall, and the battle for the Supreme Court / Cliff Sloan and David McKean.
        p. cm.
    Includes bibliographical references and index.
    ISBN 978-1-58648-426-2 (hardcover)
    1. Judicial review—United States—History. 2. United States. Supreme Court—History. 3. Marbury, William, 1761 or 2–1835—Trials, litigation, etc. 4. Madison, James, 1751–1836—Trials, litigation, etc. I. McKean, David. II. Title.

KF4575.S56 2009

347.73'12—dc22

2008046107

First Edition

10 9 8 7 6 5 4

For Mary Lou, Sarah, Annie, and Nick
and
For Kathleen, Shaw, Christian, and Kaye

CONTENTS

PROLOGUE

ON CONSTITUTION AVENUE in the nation's capital, midway between the White House and the Capitol, sits the National Archives, a gleaming, white, marble, temple-like structure with massive Doric columns on all four sides. The Archives features a "Charters of Freedom" hall, a cavernous rotunda on the building's second floor where on any given day a long line of visitors from around the world waits patiently behind hooked rope barriers to view the sacraments of our national identity.

Before entering the rotunda, the expectant visitors file past a thirteenth-century copy of the Magna Carta, the British decree from 1215 announcing the protection of certain "liberties," "rights," and concessions. Upon entering the dimly lit great hall, they see two large paintings depicting the signing of the Declaration of Independence. As the line proceeds, they view America's national treasures arranged in a semicircle and carefully preserved in individual, climate-controlled cases. The very first document on display is an original copy of the Declaration of Independence, with its unyielding commitment to "life, liberty, and the pursuit of happiness."

Then, it's on to an original copy of the Constitution, with its audacious statement that "We the People" create the union, and its historic division of the government into three branches of separated powers and checks and balances.

From there, the visitors witness an original of the Bill of Rights, adopted soon after the Constitution, with its guarantee of basic liberties such as freedom of speech, freedom of the press, and freedom of religion.

The next national treasure on display, after the Declaration of Independence, the Constitution, and the Bill of Rights, is a single Supreme Court decision from 1803: *Marbury v. Madison*. Unlike the other documents, *Marbury* is unknown to many people. The exhibit explains that it is "one of the cornerstones of the American constitutional system," the first case in which the Supreme Court struck down an Act of Congress as unconstitutional.

Why is *Marbury* considered the greatest decision in American law? What is it about, and where did it come from? What impact has the decision had on the nation? Few people know or fully appreciate the story of *Marbury v. Madison*. And it is a rich, complex, sometimes surprising saga—arising in the midst of bitter enmity between a new president, Thomas Jefferson, and a new chief justice, Jefferson's cousin John Marshall; emerging from the cauldron of political warfare between the defeated Federalists and Jefferson's triumphant Republicans; culminating in a triple bank shot by Marshall that enhanced the Court's power and prestige, avoided a futile confrontation between a weak Court and a strong president, and blasted Jefferson for lawless actions without giving him an opportunity for defiance. The case would emerge as the leading totem of American judicial review, inspiring some of the Supreme Court's greatest later decisions.

Marbury v. Madison is perhaps underappreciated because it lacked the drama of a classic courtroom argument: Neither man showed up before the court at all, and, while Madison is heralded as one of the founding fathers, no one now knows who Marbury was. Neither man appeared ever to be personally affected by the consequences of the case. Marbury seemingly never mentioned it again. But what is indisputable is that, framed as it was, the case was a classic struggle between two factions, representing one of the first tests of American civic architecture and determining whether the country could in fact successfully cope with strongly expressed yet divergent views.

The Supreme Court was created by the founding fathers at the Constitutional Convention of 1789. It was conceived as a co-equal branch of the government, on the same level as the president and the Congress. But it wasn't—at least until the decision in *Marbury v. Madison*. This is not just the story of one legal case; it is the story of America at the dawn of the nineteenth century and of how personalities, politics, and law all contributed to completing the dream the creators of the American Constitution began.

Marbury is rightly considered a national treasure, for it is a uniquely American icon that vividly stands for the rule of law. But it is much more. It can also be viewed as John Marshall versus Thomas Jefferson, the chief justice versus the president, the courts versus the Executive, the Federalists versus the Republicans, the advocates of a strong central government versus the proponent of states' rights. As such, *Marbury v. Madison* became a profound public test of the viability of America's new Constitution, embodying political attitudes that still divide Americans to the present.

It's no accident that the case was heard following the country's first truly contested election in which real enmity and acrimony split the Senate and the House of Representatives and reverberated throughout the press. Schism was in the air; the young republic could have fractured. The election of 1801 was the first in which power was transferred from one party to a rival. *Marbury v. Madison* would not have happened but for the extraordinary circumstances that saw the outgoing president, John Adams, still making political appointments late into the final night of his term of office at the White House.

The case, then, is about America's identity. The political and judicial history of the republic was shaped by the outcome of *Marbury v. Madison*, and, even more important, the way that outcome was reached. It is a moment in the life of the nation when the enduring character of the country rested on the narrowest of margins, in the hands of six unelected judges, appointed by patronage, one of whom was too ill to walk from his lodging to the Court. It didn't seem to be a propitious way to determine the future of a country still wrestling with its independent identity, but it worked.

INTRODUCTION

JOHN JAY RECLINED AT HIS DESK in his rented home at 60 State Street in Albany and stared at a letter he had just received from President John Adams.

It was early January 1801. The United States of America, not yet twelve years old, was in chaos. In the election of 1800, Adams had been defeated but it was not yet clear by whom: Vice President Thomas Jefferson or Jefferson's running mate, Aaron Burr. Running as a ticket, Jefferson and Burr had received the same number of votes in the electoral college.

Burr, the running mate, then had shocked the nation by not withdrawing his name, and so signaled that he was prepared to challenge Jefferson for the presidency. Under the Constitution, with no majority in the electoral college, the matter would be settled by the House of Representatives, and the new House, largely filled by victorious Republicans, would not assemble until later in the year, after the new president, whoever he turned out to be, would take office.

As Jay began his day as governor of New York, he pondered Adams's letter. Chief Justice Oliver Ellsworth had resigned from the Supreme Court and the president wanted Jay to replace him. For the first time, the Supreme Court would be required to meet at least a few weeks each year in Washington, DC, a mud-soaked, sparsely settled city that had become the nation's capital only months earlier. Jay was a distinguished American in the nation-building generation, a peer of George Washington, Thomas Jefferson, James Madison, and Alexander Hamilton. Along with Benjamin Franklin and John Adams, he had negotiated the Treaty of Paris, which ended the Revolutionary War. He had served as president of the Continental Congress during the Revolution, and as the nation's first secretary of foreign affairs under the Articles of Confederacy before the adoption of the Constitution in 1789. Together with Madison and Hamilton, he had been one of the authors of *The Federalist Papers*, a highly influential series of newspaper articles urging support for the Constitution.

He had served as the nation's first chief justice, from 1789 to 1795. Appointed by George Washington in September 1789 on the same day that Congress passed the Judiciary Act creating the Supreme Court, he was confirmed unanimously two days later. But Jay hated the job.

Jay especially loathed the work schedule. The Justices sat together only twice a year for two or three weeks. Otherwise, they were out "riding circuit," covering the country in vast geographic districts where they traveled to towns and villages to hear cases during the day and to sleep in crowded inns or rented rooms above taverns at night. John Adams described the taverns as "full of people drinking drams, toddys, carousing. . . . Here the time, the money, the health, and the modesty of most that are young and many old, are wasted: here diseases, vicious habits, bastards, and legislators are frequently begotten." Travel conditions were primitive and difficult, with coarse roads, poor food, and uncertain accommodations. One justice complained of having to share a bed with "a man of the wrong sort." This was all too much for Jay, who was to the manor born, descended from wealthy French Huguenots, and someone who richly enjoyed life's comforts.

In each of the almost six years that Jay was chief under President Washington, the Supreme Court issued only a handful of opinions. Many thought that Congress or the states, rather than the courts, should be the final judge of the constitutionality of a law. Jay was convinced that the concept of a federal judiciary would not amount to much in the American system, and he had jumped at the chance to leave the Supreme Court.

As early as 1793, while still chief justice, he ran for governor of New York and barely lost. At the request of President Washington, he spent the next year in London, negotiating the controversial Jay Treaty for increased trade relations with England. As news of the treaty spread throughout the country, angry anti-English mobs burned him in effigy. While still serving as a chief justice and envoy simultaneously, Jay ran again for governor of New York in 1795, winning this time and happily resigning as chief justice to take the reins in Albany.

Jay considered himself lucky. Many of his fellow original appointees to the Supreme Court had met sorrier fates. One died soon after being released from debtor's prison. Another left the Court after he was maddened by a mysterious ringing in his ears. The man nominated to be Jay's successor as chief justice, John Rutledge of South Carolina, saw his nomination rejected by the Senate, largely because of his vehement opposition to the Jay Treaty. Upon hearing the news of his defeat, Rutledge attempted to commit suicide by jumping into a river in his home state. Passing slaves pulled him out of the water.

By 1801, nearing the end of his second term as governor of New York, Jay looked forward to retirement. He intended to live the life of a gentleman farmer, enjoy his country estate, and stay close to his family and particularly his ailing wife Sarah. But that peaceful future had been interrupted by Adams's sudden summons to return to head the hapless Third Branch of government.

"I have nominated you to your old station," Adams began hopefully. Ruing his defeat by what he saw as a fickle public, Adams emphasized that the chief justice is "independent of the inconstancy of the people" and independent of "the will of a President," an obvious reference to the looming administration of Jefferson or

Burr. Adams hoped the judiciary might provide a crucial bulwark against the imminent Republican takeover of the presidency and Congress. "In the future administration of our country," Adams concluded, "the firmest security we can have against the effects of visionary schemes or fluctuating theories will be in a solid judiciary; and nothing will cheer the hopes of the best men so much as your acceptance of this appointment."

Jay smiled and shook his head. He wanted nothing to do with it.

Jay knew that, in the new capital of Washington, the President's House and the Capitol, both grand edifices, were under construction. But nobody had bothered to include a place for the Supreme Court. By January 1801, the best the Court could hope for was that Congress would allocate a spare room in the unfinished Capitol where it could occasionally meet.

Jay seized his pen and quickly replied to Adams. "I left the Bench perfectly convinced that under a system so defective it would not obtain the energy, weight, and dignity which are essential," he reminded the president, ". . . nor acquire the public confidence and respect which, as the last resort of the justice of the nation, it should possess. Hence I am induced to doubt both the propriety and the expediency of my returning to the Bench under the present system." Jay sealed the letter and sent it in care of Adams's secretary of state, John Marshall, who, at 45, was a decade younger than Jay and had served in the Adams administration for less than a year.

Rebuffed by Jay, Adams was determined to install a Federalist chief justice on the Court who would serve in the new Republican administration. But he was equally determined not to appoint a candidate favored by the extremists in his own party with whom he and his embattled band of moderates had been feuding. He decided not to shoot the messenger but to promote him: He asked his young secretary of state to be the new chief justice.

Within barely more than two years, John Marshall would transform the branch that John Jay had ridiculed, and lead his colleagues in issuing the most important Supreme Court decision in legal history. With one judgment—deciding *Marbury v. Madison*—Marshall would chisel judicial review into the American system. Whatever else would be said of the Supreme Court in the two centuries after *Marbury*, it never again would be viewed as John Jay had seen it in January 1801—as lacking all "energy, weight, and dignity" within American government. Marshall's decision settled that question—asserting clearly and unequivocally that the Supreme Court did indeed possess the power to strike down an Act of Congress as unconstitutional—and laid the foundation for the American rule of law. The country would never be the same.

THE COMBATANTS

John Adams

Thomas Jefferson

John Marshall

William Marbury

James Madison

THE JUSTICES:
JOHN MARSHALL'S SUPREME COURT COLLEAGUES IN 1803

Alfred Moore

William Cushing

Samuel Chase

Bushrod Washington

William Paterson

"THIS GIGANTIC ABORTION"

T he fact that Washington had become the nation's capital at all was a surprise. The first Congress, meeting in
New York in 1789 and 1790, had disagreed for months
about the location of the seat of government. The Constitution,
which had been ratified only a year before, provided for a permanent capital as a symbol of the new government's durability. But it
did not specify its location. Under the Articles of Confederation
adopted in 1781, the Continental Congress had been a vagrant,
moving from city to city, begging and borrowing space in state and
local buildings, once even having to flee its home in Philadelphia
when local authorities refused to protect it from street mobs. In the
newly constituted nation, legislators wanted their own state or region to host the capital and shape its character. Cities jostled to be
the new permanent capital. New York and Philadelphia sought the
honor, as did Baltimore, Annapolis, Trenton, Carlisle, Frederick,
Germantown, and a host of others. President George Washington
had advocated a capital on the Potomac, near his home in Mt. Vernon, but many in the new Congress had ridiculed the idea.

As the stalemate continued, on June 20, 1790, Thomas Jefferson
hosted a dinner with Alexander Hamilton and James Madison at
Jefferson's new residence on 57 Maiden Lane in New York City,

several blocks north of Wall Street. Jefferson was the nation's secretary of state, Hamilton the secretary of the Treasury, and Madison an influential Virginia congressman, architect of the Constitution, and Jefferson's close political ally.

Over a meal that undoubtedly consisted of several rounds of Madeira (the favored wine of the era), the diners agreed to an elaborate political bargain. Jefferson and Madison would persuade their fellow southerners to drop opposition to Hamilton's plan for the national government to assume state debts if Hamilton would approve the choice of the Potomac for the future capital.

Congress assigned the job of selecting the exact site for the capital along the Potomac to the president, much to George Washington's delight. A surveyor by trade, Washington stitched together the new capital on the Potomac from land within Maryland and Virginia. It included the established towns of Georgetown in Maryland and Alexandria in Virginia, and a rambling, murky, muck-filled wilderness that now would be called "Washington City." The fact that others saw the site as a desolate swamp did not deter Washington. Some whispered that his judgment was colored by his personal land holdings within the designated area.

THE BUILDING OF THE NEW CAPITAL was star-crossed from the start. Efforts to launch and build it repeatedly faltered and sputtered. Soon after the selection of the site, Washington and his three appointed capital commissioners grandly announced a public auction of lots of land in the new city. At the rain-drenched auction, with Washington, Jefferson, and Madison in attendance, individual bidders, most of whom had been extended generous credit terms, purchased only thirty-five lots. There was clearly interest; it was, after all, the nation's capital, but few were willing to actually put money down.

A triumvirate of wealthy investors formed a syndicate to construct buildings in the new city. By 1797, the syndicate had declared bankruptcy. The partners went to jail and left half-finished buildings as monuments to their losses. Jefferson, who had overseen the capital building project for Washington in his role as secretary of state, worried that there were so few habitable structures in Washington that the congressmen and senators would have to "lodge, like cattle, in the fields."

Washington appointed Pierre Charles L'Enfant, a noted French architect, to design the city. Although L'Enfant produced a masterful plan that became the blueprint for the capital, he also feuded bitterly with the capital commissioners over everything from financing the enterprise to design issues. Ultimately, L'Enfant refused to report to the commissioners and in 1792, Washington ordered Jefferson to fire his city planner.

By 1800, Washington City, home to the still unfinished President's House and the Capitol, contained only 3,210 people—approximately 500 families, with only 109 brick houses and 263 wooden houses. The entire capital area, including Georgetown, Alexandria, and Washington City, totaled 14,093 people—of whom approximately 10,000 were white, 3,200 were slaves, and 800 were free blacks.

Workers on the Capitol included slaves, Irish immigrants, and other laborers of many nationalities. Their temporary shanties and dormitories sat prominently in the midst of the city. Mud was everywhere, especially on the new Pennsylvania Avenue linking the Capitol and the President's House—the major thoroughfare named after Pennsylvania as part of an ongoing effort to mollify the state for its loss of the national capital. Residents described the street as "a sea of mud." Citizens carried walking sticks, both to provide a foothold in the morass and to ward off wandering animals such as hogs and cattle.

The President's House was little more than a construction site in the middle of a field. The new home for Congress was in no better shape. The Capitol was unfinished, with only the Senate wing ready for use. Construction had stopped in the fall of 1800, once again because of a lapse in funding. A grand ceremonial procession to open the Capitol, planned for November 21, 1800, had to be cancelled, both because of an unusually heavy snowfall and because of squabbles among the planners.

The grapevine-filled field around the new Capitol building, known as Jenkins Hill, contained the bare minimum of services and establishments. As Congressman Albert Gallatin reported to his wife in early 1801, the new Capitol area featured, in addition to seven or eight boardinghouses, exactly "one tailor, one shoemaker, one printer, a washing woman, a grocery shop, a pamphlets and stationery shop, a small dry goods shop, and an oyster house." A theater group opened with bravado in the capital in August 1800. It closed in September. The only entertainment that remained in the district were the outdoor weekly concerts by the Marine band, dancing assemblies at local taverns, and, eventually, outdoor cockfights and horse races.

Slaves were a common sight; they worked alongside the laborers in building the President's House and the Capitol. Local newspapers prominently featured ads for the sale of slaves and the recovery of runaway slaves. Typical was one placed in *The Centinel of Liberty* that read: "negro woman named KATE. . . . She is about 4 feet 11 inches high, has a large scar on one of her legs, a little above the ankle, believed to be on the right."

Among the traders and salespeople hustling a living out of the still nascent capital, the state agent for Maryland was especially busy since the capital was created in part from his state's territory. He also served as the agent for the new Department of the Navy and had various side deals in progress. Acting on behalf of Maryland, he placed an advertisement for a slave for sale in *The Centinel of Liberty*: "A NEGRO MAN FOR SALE. On Saturday, the 13th, inst. at 12 o'clock, will be offered at public sale, at my office, in George-Town, for cash, a negro man the property of the State of Maryland. WILLIAM MARBURY. Agent for the State of Maryland."

In June 1800, the nation's capital, including the home of the Supreme Court, officially became Washington, District of Columbia.

A few sloops teeming with sundry cargo docked at Lear's Wharf on the Potomac River in the newly christened District, near the site that now houses the Watergate office building. The vessels carried chairs and tables, maps and books, bedsteads, a gin case, a cradle, and other prosaic instruments of everyday life. The ships' arrival at the modest dock, built by Tobias Lear, George Washington's former personal secretary, meant that the equipment and personal possessions of the federal employees had successfully navigated the route from Philadelphia.

The new capital reflected the fragility of the country's democratic institutions. Washington was a patchy place, teeming with ramshackle dwellings, sharp-eyed land speculators, hapless investors, and political connivers. Many buildings stood spectral and unfinished, testaments to unsuccessful land schemes.

The builder of the wharf where the sloops docked perfectly symbolized the uncertainties of the nation's new capital. Indeed, although Lear had invested heavily in Washington's cherished capital city, his business ventures had failed spectacularly, and, now, only six months after Washington's death, he was mired in financial disaster.

The capital city struck many who arrived there to work in government as an abomination. Treasury Secretary Oliver Wolcott mocked its "small, miserable huts" and observed that the inhabitants "are poor, and as far as I can judge, they live like fishes, in eating each other." The architect of the Capitol described the new city as "this Gigantic Abortion." Congressman Roger Griswold of Connecticut denounced it as "melancholy and ludicrous . . . a city in ruins." Senator Gouverneur Morris of New York acidly wrote a French noblewoman, "We only need here houses, cellars, kitchens, scholarly men, amiable women and a few other such trifles to possess a perfect city."

The entire Executive Branch workforce for the nation's new capital, as it moved from Philadelphia, comprised only 131 people, mostly clerks and messengers—a total even lower than that of the 138 congressmen and senators from the sixteen states (the original thirteen plus Vermont, Tennessee, and Kentucky).

While the gin case, cradle, and other possessions were making their way to Lear's Wharf by sloop, the Executive departments were shipping official records over land by wagon and stagecoach. The journey from Philadelphia to Washington could take from three to ten days, depending on many variables—the driver, the passengers, the horses, the roads, the weather. For security from marauders on the trail to Washington, government clerks accompanied the records, which included painstakingly handwritten ledgers and reports. The boxes of government records had been packed and carefully hooped in Philadelphia by day laborers, who were tipped by their government supervisors with beer and spirits.

Some government workers, rather than face the half-built town to which they had been transferred, quit their jobs, refusing to leave the comforts of Philadelphia.

———

ALTHOUGH THE PRESIDENT'S HOUSE and the Capitol remained unfinished when the District became the capital in June 1800, at least the government had thought of them and provided for their creation and location. The District commissioners, who had the responsibility for laying out the new capital city, had nearly skipped over the Supreme Court entirely, recommending that the Court use "one or two rooms in the new Executive or War office." It was months later when the House and Senate first passed hurried resolutions allowing the Supreme Court to meet in the Capitol, with the justices assigned a cramped first-floor room, thirty feet long and thirty-five feet wide, which they also would share with local District of Columbia courts. The architect of the Capitol reported to James Madison that the small room for the

Supreme Court, Committee Room 2, was half-finished, "meanly furnished, very inconvenient."

The lack of planning for the Court was telling. It was by far the least significant of the three branches. Only one of President Washington's six initial appointees continued to serve.

The chief justice at the start of the year, Oliver Ellsworth, a senator from Connecticut, and a participant in the Constitutional Convention of 1787, had emulated Jay's example of simultaneous service as a foreign emissary. He avoided the Court by spending much of his time in 1799 and 1800 in France as President Adams's representative. He sought to negotiate a treaty with the new French government under Napoleon Bonaparte, a conciliatory initiative to the French.

Twelve years after the Court's creation, its powers were completely uncharted. The new Constitution provided only that the Court had "the judicial Power of the United States," but it failed to explicitly define that "Power." As the new capital was born in June 1800, it seemed clear that the Court's "power," whatever its scope and content, would no more rise to the level of being a peer of the other two branches than that Washington itself would rise to rival a significant European capital such as London or Paris.

Chapter TWO

JOHN ADAMS DEFEATED

T he political life of the country had been even more mired in uncertainty than the building of the new capital. Perhaps it was inevitable that the passing of George Washington, the defining and unifying figure of the Revolution, would create a wave of restlessness that would lead to profound change in the political firmament. As 1799 drew to a close, the whole country seemed to be draped in black. Pews in churches, the bows of ships in harbor, and the doors of public buildings, including the Presidential Mansion in Philadelphia, displayed black bunting to commemorate Washington's death. President Adams had even issued a proclamation recommending "to the people of the United States to wear crepe on the left arm, as mourning, for thirty days." The great man had died on December 14, 1799, at age 67 after suffering pneumonia. Practical to the last, he had asked to die peacefully at his home in Mt. Vernon, Virginia, after the blistering and bleeding remedies recommended by his physicians failed to improve his condition, and after instructing his family to be sure he was indeed dead before they buried him: "Do not let my body be put into the vault in less than three days after I am dead." Nearly two weeks later, on December 26, the country honored their first president with a memorial service in Philadelphia. Uniformed soldiers marched slowly from Congress Hall behind a riderless white horse with reversed boots in the stirrups. They marched six blocks through the city, accompanied by a slow and steady drumbeat and the chiming of church bells, to the German Lutheran Church at Fourth and Cherry streets. Musketeers fired their rifles while a trumpeter played a solemn, final anthem.

Bishop William White of Christ Church led the service. Those in attendance included President of the United States John Adams, and his wife, Abigail. Representative John Marshall, who had been co-chairman of the congressional committee handling the arrangements for the funeral, was present, but Washington's former secretary of state, Vice President Thomas Jefferson, was not—a conspicuous absence that revived murmurs about his disloyalty, despite Jefferson's claim that he had been delayed on his trip to Philadelphia. Many other dignitaries—Federalists and Republicans, cabinet officials and military leaders—filled the pews as Representative Richard Lee of Virginia eulogized President Washington as "first in war, first in peace, first in the hearts of his countrymen," words that echoed Congressman Marshall's eulogy on the floor of the House of Representatives days earlier.

The nation collectively mourned the passing of Washington, but it was not long before the leading political figures of the day began to assess how it might affect the impending presidential contest between President Adams, who was seeking reelection, and his challenger, Vice President Jefferson.

The two candidates, whose lives had been inextricably linked for the past twenty years, could not have been more different. Adams was short and stout, and at age 64 had a pasty complexion that was punctuated by missing teeth when he smiled, which was rarely. Reared in Massachusetts, Harvard-educated, and a lawyer by training, Adams was plainspoken, brusque, and often irascible. But he could also be charming, and his letters to his beloved wife Abigail reveal a tender and romantic spirit. Jefferson, on the other hand, had been raised in Virginia, attended William and Mary

College, and apprenticed in the law. He was tall and gangly, and at 57 had reddish hair that was beginning to gray. Jefferson had impeccable manners and enjoyed fine clothes, fine wines, and fine books, so much so that he was constantly in debt. He and Adams first encountered each other as delegates to the wartime Continental Congress. They worked closely together when Jefferson drafted the Declaration of Independence and Adams provided important changes. Both men had served as diplomats: Jefferson as ambassador to France and Adams as ambassador to Great Britain. Both men had served under President Washington: Adams as the vice president and Jefferson as the secretary of state.

In the nation's first contested presidential victory in 1796, Adams had barely eked out a victory over Jefferson, winning by only 3 votes in the electoral college. Under the Constitution at that time, the vice presidency went to the candidate with the second-highest number of electoral votes: Jefferson. Although Adams and Jefferson had once been colleagues who worked closely together, as president and vice president they fought vigorously. They had very different views on how the country should be governed. Adams believed in a strong, central government; Jefferson favored a confederation of states bound together by common interests such as trade.

Adams's and Jefferson's different visions were reflected in the two political parties that emerged in the 1790s—the Federalists and the Democratic-Republicans (or Republicans, as they were then called, an ironic ancestry for the party now known as the Democratic Party). The parties fought each other bitterly, with savage attacks on the opposing candidate in partisan newspapers, mocking caricatures, scorching personal denunciations, salacious gossip, and effigy burnings.

The political atmosphere became so toxic that talk of possible secession and civil war was common. Federalist Senator Uriah Tracy expressed concerns that the union would dissolve. Republican Senator John Taylor said that Virginia and North Carolina should consider "their separate existence." Word spread of plots to burn Philadelphia, the capital city, and riots by political partisans repeatedly broke out on its streets.

Shortly after Washington's funeral, Adams wrote a letter to a friend in which he remarked on Washington's greatness, and noted that "his departure is at a most unfortunate moment." Adams recognized that, as well as the schism between Federalists and Republicans, his own party was deeply divided between the extreme "High Federalists" and embattled moderates. Washington's presence had helped to keep the fissures within the party from widening. Alexander Hamilton, perhaps the most prominent Federalist politician after Adams, agreed, noting that Washington's loss "removes a control that was felt and very salutary." Neither man was aware that Gouverneur Morris, another leading Federalist, had felt the situation was so dangerous that he had written to Washington imploring him to return from retirement and run for president again. Morris openly expressed his worries that Adams was weak and unfit to lead. But before Morris's letter arrived, Washington was dead.

The election of 1796 was the first contested even partially on a party basis, but Federalists and Republicans were not organized in every state and there were no discernible party platforms. Four years later, the political landscape had changed dramatically. Vice President Jefferson, who had only reluctantly accepted his party's nomination in 1796, was now the clear head of the Republican Party and a fervent partisan fully engaged in the political process.

———

THE CANDIDATES for the presidency in 1800 understood that most of the political activity would occur at the state and local levels. In the upcoming election, the Federalists were favored to carry the New England states, as well as New Jersey and Delaware, while the Republicans were strongest in Virginia, Tennessee, Georgia, and Kentucky. What political analysts in a later age would call the "swing" states, where the election would be decided, included New York, Pennsylvania, Maryland, the Carolinas, and tiny Rhode Island.

The Electoral College system was conceived at the "Grand Convention" in 1787. After much debate, the Constitution provided that electors would be chosen from each state "in such manner" as its legislature might "direct." The only prohibition was that "[n]o person shall be appointed an elector who is a member of the legislature of the United States, or who holds any office of profit or trust under the United States." As historian Clinton Rossiter has explained, "The founders were trying to bar congressmen, postmasters and customs officials from having a hand in the choice of a President, and also bar a President in search of re-election from toadying to congressmen, bullying postmasters and bribing customs officers."

In eleven of the sixteen states, the electors were chosen by the state legislatures, while in the other five they were chosen directly by the people (or at least those who had the vote—generally white male taxpayers, sometimes with property qualifications as well). Thomas Bolyston Adams, the son of the president, wrote to his brother John Quincy Adams, then a young diplomat in Berlin, that "the trial of strength between the two Candidates for the chief magistracy of the Union is to be seen, not in the choice of electors by the people, but in the complexion and characters of the individual legislatures."

Thomas Jefferson recognized that New York, with its 12 electoral votes, could tip the balance. Jefferson wrote to his friend and fellow Virginian James Madison in early March 1800 that, if the imminent legislative "elections of N[ew] York is in favor of the Republican ticket," then the national winner for the Presidency later in the year would in all likelihood be Republican.

Jefferson needed someone to lead the Republican Party to victory in New York. Into this role stepped Aaron Burr, a 44-year-old blue-blooded lawyer and former U.S senator. Burr was cunning, persistent, and ambitious, once describing himself as "[a] grave, silent, strange sort of animal, inasmuch as we know not what to make of him."

Burr calculated that for Jefferson to win the presidency, the Virginian needed the kind of regional balance—victory in some northern state—that had thus far eluded the Republican Party. He also knew that if he could deliver New York to the Republican column, he would be seriously considered for a spot on the national ticket. Only one man stood in his way: Alexander Hamilton, who, like Burr, hoped that the state elections would propel him onto the national stage. Hamilton believed that he could ultimately claim leadership of the Federalist Party with a victory in New York. These two ambitious politicians had tangled before. Burr had defeated Phillip Schuyler, Alexander Hamilton's father-in-law, for the U.S. Senate in 1791. Three years later, Hamilton degraded Senator Burr to President Washington, who was considering the senator as a possible candidate for American minister to France. For his part, Burr helped defeat Hamilton's brother-in-law, Stephen van Rensselaer, in the New York governor's race.

With the New York legislature deciding the presidential contest, the latest contest between Burr and Hamilton would be over their ability to influence the state's legislative elections. Burr cajoled and ultimately persuaded a prominent group of New York Revolutionary War veterans—men such as former governor and war hero George Clinton—to stand as Republican candidates for the legislature. In contrast, President Adams's wife Abigail described the slate of Federalists standing for election in New York as "men of no note, whol[l]y unfit for the purpose." Burr's strategy was to turn Republicans out in droves in New York City. The polls opened on April 21 and, according to one New York congressman, Burr had at the ready "carriages, chairs and wagons" to transport Republican sympathizers to polling stations around the city. He campaigned "for 24 hours without sleeping or resting." At sunset on May 1, the polls closed.

When the votes were tallied it was evident that Burr had out-worked and outmaneuvered his archrival. The Republicans won a decisive victory. It was, as ardent Federalist Gouverneur Morris remarked, "a bad sign" that the Federalists would face serious difficulties in the presidential election. The outcome revealed deep support for the Republicans in a state that President Adams had carried in his narrow election victory over Jefferson in 1796. Even more ominously, New York's Republican legislature now would play a decisive role in the fall in determining the state's 12 electoral votes for president, the fourth-largest prize of any state.

Ten days after the New York election, Republicans held their first national party caucus in Philadelphia. For his efforts in New York, the leaders of the party unanimously agreed to support Aaron Burr for vice president. With Thomas Jefferson as their candidate for president and Aaron Burr as his running mate, Republicans believed that they had a winning ticket.

Such unity eluded the Federalists. Alexander Hamilton, sensing that Adams's prospects for reelection were now in serious doubt, refused to support him wholeheartedly, which aggravated the split in the Federalist Party. Adams responded quickly by purging his cabinet of "High Federalists"—men whom he believed were more loyal to Hamilton than to himself. First, he fired James McHenry of Maryland, the secretary of war. Adams summoned McHenry from a dinner party and told him, "You are subservient to Hamilton who ruled [President] Washington and would still rule if he could." Next he asked his secretary of state, Timothy Pickering—also a holdover from the administration of Washington—to resign. Pickering refused, so Adams dismissed him.

The cabinet shake-up sparked a national uproar. Some in the press even accused President Adams of "a political arrangement with Mr. Jefferson," implying that Adams was deliberately wrecking the Federalists' chances—an odd notion since Adams himself was the candidate. Hamilton, meanwhile, claimed that Adams "is more mad than I ever thought him and . . . as wicked as he is mad."

Adams moved quickly to mitigate the damage to his party and the disruption to his presidency. First he announced that he had nominated John Marshall, a 44-year-old congressman from Virginia, as secretary of war. But Adams had not bothered to ask Marshall, who declined the appointment. Five days later, however, Adams asked Marshall to join his cabinet in the more prestigious position of secretary of state. This time Marshall accepted. Adams then nominated Samuel Dexter as his secretary of war. Benjamin Stoddert remained at Navy and Oliver Wolcott remained at Treasury, the only two other cabinet departments. Federalist warhorse Charles Lee remained as attorney general, a part-time position.

———

On May 27, 1800, a tottering President Adams set out from Philadelphia for his first visit to the still rickety new capital in Washington. The trip provided Adams with a brief respite from the never-ending political disputes. Under clear skies and on lush terrain, the embattled president spoke to friendly crowds at Lancaster, Pennsylvania; Frederick, Maryland; and other stops along the way. As Adams arrived in Washington after a week-long journey, citizens on horseback met him at the District line and escorted him to the Union Tavern in Georgetown. The city militia and marines from Baltimore greeted him with a gunfire salute, and Adams happily addressed the assembled crowd.

The next day, Adams toured the capital. Although the city appeared raw and unfinished, the president proclaimed that he was pleased with the progress of the public buildings. He planned to move into the uncompleted "President's House" in the fall.

Adams's delegation in the capital included John Marshall, in office as secretary of state for less than a month. Adams and his coterie, including Marshall, stayed at Tunnicliff's City Hotel and worked out of their rooms in the hotel during their two-week stay. Tunnicliff's stood in the fledgling neighborhood near the new Capitol.

Adams found temporary solace in the festivities. The city's leading citizens held a dinner for him. He also visited Martha Washington, a widow for only six months, at Mt. Vernon. Attorney
General Charles Lee hosted a boisterous dinner in Adams's honor
at his home in Alexandria. Adams was so enraptured by the
warmth and hospitality of Lee's dinner that he exclaimed to Abigail, "Oh! That I could have a home!" On June 14, a little more
than two weeks after arriving in the capital, Adams departed to
join his wife for the summer at their farm in Braintree, Massachusetts. He left Secretary of State John Marshall in charge in the new
capital.

———

JOHN MARSHALL PLUNGED into his new responsibilities running
the government with characteristic good humor, while Adams
summered in New England. With little space available in the
new city, Marshall moved into the upstairs quarters of the unfinished President's House, becoming the first person ever to actually live in the residence that would later be known as the White
House. He oversaw foreign affairs, kept an eye on the departments, and administered the ongoing construction. Treasury Secretary Oliver Wolcott, who initially had been suspicious of
Marshall, was impressed with the young secretary of state's performance. "He is actually a state conservator," confided Wolcott
to Federalist leader Fisher Ames on August 10, 1800. "His value
ought to be estimated not only by the good he does, but by the
mischief he has prevented."

Marshall's best efforts, however, could not overcome the difficulties besetting the new capital. The scramble for government office
space was on, but buildings simply were not available. Only the
Treasury Department next to the President's House was ready for
occupancy. The Navy building, also near the President's House,
stood unfinished and uninhabitable. Navy Secretary William Stoddert directed his agent William Marbury, a 38-year-old operator in

the thicket of politics and business, to find a suitable temporary headquarters for the Navy. Marbury tried, but was unsuccessful. For himself, however, he managed to buy a lovely home from Mayor Uriah Forrest in Georgetown overlooking the Potomac River. The home, the site of a celebratory dinner with George Washington in 1791 after Washington selected the national capital site, still stands today on M Street in Georgetown. It would be Marbury's command post when he filed suit against the Jefferson administration in December 1801 and set in motion the chain of events leading to the Supreme Court case bearing his name.

———

As SPRING TURNED TO SUMMER, the Federalists, despite their internal turmoil, seemed to be holding on for a possible victory. Because the presidential election consisted of a series of state elections over the course of several months, the perceived momentum shifted many times. In Maryland, which was shaping up to be a pivotal state, the Federalist Party was as fractured as it was on a national level, but the state's Federalists still believed that they outnumbered Republicans. Maryland was one of three states that allowed its citizens to select presidential electors by individual district rather than on a winner-take-all basis for the state. (The Constitution, then and now, leaves that choice to the states; Maine and Nebraska currently are the only states that opt for presidential electors by district instead of winner-take-all.)

At Hamilton's urging, James McHenry, the former secretary of war, encouraged Maryland Governor Benjamin Ogle to call a special session of the General Assembly to change the system in Maryland to winner-take-all. But the governor demurred since it was his party, the Federalists, who had initially decided on the selection of electors by district.

Maryland Federalists had another plan: They would change the process by which the electors were chosen. Instead of being elected by the people, the electors would be hand-picked by the legislature. Party leaders in Maryland encouraged a number of local Federalists to run on the platform of legislative choice, calculating that if the presidential election could be removed from the people and safely housed in the Federalist-controlled legislature, Maryland's 10 electoral votes could be cast en bloc for a Federalist president. To help him organize the counties of southern Maryland, party leaders enlisted the aid of William Marbury.

Marbury was a wildly ambitious striver who had elbowed his way to wealth, influence, and notoriety. Born in 1762 near Piscataway, Maryland, he hailed from a prominent family that owned a vast tobacco plantation. But farming tobacco in the eighteenth century was a difficult business, subject to the vagaries of boycotts, weather, and economic depression. Marbury's father lost everything, including his land. Perhaps as a result of his family's misfortune, Marbury always seemed to be grasping for social, financial, and political acceptability.

Marbury affected the air of English gentry in his dress and mannerisms. He commissioned Rembrant Peale, the celebrated painter, to paint his portrait: Somewhat overweight, Marbury strikes a confident pose. He had parlayed a reputation as a savvy investor among Maryland's financial elite into an appointment in 1796 as the agent for the state of Maryland, the state's chief financial officer. As agent, he was responsible for collecting taxes, selling estates, and exchanging debt certificates for federal stock. He charged a commission on most of these transactions and accumulated substantial wealth as a result. Marbury had first met James McHenry in 1796 when, as the agent for Maryland, he had lobbied McHenry, the newly installed secretary of war. Marbury sought payment for arms and other material that the state had lent the federal government to quell the Whiskey Rebellion two years earlier. After Marbury purchased his Georgetown home from former Georgetown mayor Uriah Forrest, the two men became friends and occasional business partners.

The election campaign in Maryland was perhaps the most vigorous and contentious of those in any state in the country. People debated politics, as one observer noted, "at a horse race, a cock fight, or a Methodist quarterly meeting." The *Baltimore Gazette* reported on one summer gathering where "the different candidates for elector of president and members of assembly attended and harangued the voters." The *Gazette* described a Republican who defended Jefferson against "the charges of pusillanimity and deism," while a Federalist argued that "the path laid down by Washington had been faithfully pursued by Adams." Also in the newspaper was an allegation that William Marbury attempted to bribe a Federalist candidate to step aside because he did not favor presidential election by the legislature.

Besides Marbury, one of the fiercest campaigners in Maryland on behalf of President Adams was Samuel Chase, associate justice of the United States. Like Adams and Jefferson, Justice Chase had been a signer of the Declaration of Independence. Elected to the Maryland Assembly at age 23, the royal governor accused him of being "a busy, reckless incendiary, a ringleader of mobs, a foul-mouthed and inflaming son of discord." President Washington had considered appointing Chase his first attorney general, but opted instead to make him a member of the Supreme Court in 1796. Justice Chase never lost his partisan zeal, and at six foot one, with a broad face and reddish complexion, he was known as "Old Bacon Face" and as an intimidating and effective advocate. In one local Maryland debate, Justice Chase applauded the "firmness, uprightness and ability" of the Adams administration, crediting it with bringing "justice at home and tranquility abroad."

As each state organized itself for the fall election, the campaign between Adams and Jefferson was noisiest in the press, where there was little pretense of objectivity. While the Philadelphia *Aurora*—founded by Benjamin Franklin Bache, Benjamin Franklin's grandson, and published by William Duane since 1798—was the Republican standard-bearer, the vast majority of newspapers throughout the country supported the president. The *Washington Federalist* praised Adams as "among the surviving, steady and tried patriots." The newspaper commended Adams for making "his sole object . . . the present freedom and independence of his country and its future glory." The editor of another leading Federalist newspaper, the *Gazette of the United States*, referring to the passage of the Sedition Act in 1798, proudly declared: "It is patriotism to write in favor of the government, it is sedition to write against it."

Most Federalist newspapers, however, spent less time extolling the presidency of Adams than attacking the character of Thomas Jefferson. They denounced Jefferson as godless and immoral, and spread baseless rumors of bizarre worship ceremonies at Monticello. Allegations of an affair between Jefferson and an unnamed woman were widely circulated.

Thomas Jefferson became convinced that the best way to win the election was by using all of the different modes of press then available: newspapers, pamphlets (generally fifteen to fifty pages in length), and one-page circulars. He would later acknowledge that he personally underwrote the Republican press: "I as well as most other Republicans who were in the way of doing it, contributed what I could to the support of the republican papers and printers," including "sums of money for the *Bee*, the *Albany Register*, etc. when they were staggering under the sedition law, contributed to the fines of Callender himself, of Holt, Brown and others suffering under that law."

The Republican propagandists' refrain was similar to what it had been four years earlier, when much was made of the fact that Adams had once suggested giving titles to members of the Executive Branch. Republicans portrayed Adams as a monarchist who was determined to return the American government to a style and political system modeled on Great Britain. One leading Republican newspaper, the *Aurora*, attacked Adams as "blind, bald, crippled, toothless, querulous."

Vice President Jefferson also wrote a number of private letters, which he must have known would be made public, laying out the broad themes of his candidacy. In a letter to Elbridge Gerry, Jefferson emphasized the importance of a decentralized government and listed a number of reforms, including retiring the national debt, reducing the size of the Army, and relying on the militia in order to safeguard internal security.

Yet it was not Jefferson or the Republicans who did the most damage to the Federalist cause. It was instead someone who was renowned as a Federalist himself: none other than Alexander Hamilton. In October, just weeks before the election, Hamilton published a fifty-four-page diatribe entitled "Concerning the Public Conduct and Character of John Adams," in which he vilified the president as possessed of "great and intrinsic defects in his character." Hamilton claimed that among the president's flaws were "distempered jealousy," "extreme egotism," and an "ungovernable temper." Hamilton was furious at Adams for perceived slights, and, to the extent that he had a rational plan, he apparently hoped that he could swing the election to Adams's running mate.

Hamilton's taunts damaged the reputation of President Adams, but they tarnished Hamilton's image as well. The Republican press had traditionally tied Adams to Hamilton. Now, it cheerfully and pointedly reminded readers that Hamilton had once called for "the establishment of a permanent executive, and . . . the total suppression of the states." Republicans also criticized Adams and Hamilton for having "run up a total debt in excess of $20 million," which they characterized as "[a] piece of imbecility and imprudence."

No SINGLE ISSUE roiled the nation's political waters more during the election of 1800 than relations with France and England. The French Revolution in 1789 had generated strong passions among Americans. Led by Thomas Jefferson, who had served as ambassador to France from 1784 to 1789, the Republicans admired the French overthrow of aristocracy and detested the former colonial masters in England. In contrast, "High Federalists" like Roger

Griswold of Connecticut and Fisher Ames of Massachusetts denounced the French as wild and anarchic. They admired British civil society and order.

Almost from the beginning of his presidency, Adams had been bedeviled by problems with American relations abroad. Adams, ambassador to England in the 1780s, venerated the country. He frequently was ridiculed for what some saw as his Anglophilia and aristocratic pretensions, such as his suggestion that he ride in an emblazoned carriage as vice president, his preference for the term "His Excellency" for the president, and his admiring essay on the virtues of a monarchy. During Adams's vice presidency, the United States negotiated the Jay Treaty with Great Britain, giving Britain a most-favored-nation status in trade and inciting France to intercept American agricultural products bound for England. By December 1796, France had seized more than 300 American ships on the high seas.

In Adams's first year in office, he sent a secret delegation to Paris to negotiate with the French government for a lasting settlement of Franco-American issues. The delegation consisted of Elbridge Gerry, a longtime Adams associate in Massachusetts; Charles Cotesworth Pinckney, an easygoing Federalist from South Carolina; and John Marshall, then just a talented young lawyer from Richmond, Virginia, who had served as an aide-de-camp to General George Washington in the Revolutionary War. After their arrival, French Minister Talleyrand, who had lived in the United States during the Revolutionary War, refused to meet with them for months. Talleyrand eventually sent word, through emissaries, that bribes would be required before he would meet, a request that outraged the visiting Americans, who returned to the United States. Initially, the American public learned only that the mission had been unsuccessful, but not the reasons why. Republicans in Congress confidently suspected that the Americans had botched the mission, or deliberately undermined it. They insisted that Adams release the correspondence from the emissaries. Adams happily

complied by making the letters public; the reports of the shake-
down of the three Americans by the three unidentified emissaries
to France, dubbed "X," "Y," and "Z," inflamed the American people.
John Marshall showed nothing but contempt for the corrupting
French. Marshall emerged as the informal leader of the delegation
and was later identified in the American press. He returned to
Philadelphia a national hero and was feted, honored with a parade,
and saluted at a 120-person banquet at a fashionable Philadelphia
hotel. As reported in the Republican-sympathizing *Aurora*, one of
the speakers memorably toasted him for having defended American honor before French skullduggery: "Millions for defense, but
not one cent for tribute!" Some talked of war.

President Adams reacted to the national outrage over the XYZ
Affair by asking Congress to appropriate six and a half million dollars to build up the American military, which had withered since
the Revolution. Adams expanded the Army, established an American Navy, and commissioned several warships. But his most controversial action and one that would bring otherwise remote
foreign policy arguments deep into every American community,
was to sign into law the Alien and Sedition Acts in July 1798.

The Acts targeted those who were not American citizens. Among
their sweeping provisions, the Alien Acts authorized the president
to deport or detain any noncitizen he viewed as dangerous to the
United States. Many French and Irish immigrants promptly fled the
country.

The Sedition Act, in turn, actually made it a crime to criticize
the federal government. Constitutional historian Geoffrey Stone
has called the Sedition Act "perhaps the most grievous assault on
free speech in the history of the United States." Passed a mere
seven years after the nation adopted the First Amendment with its
broad guarantees of freedom, the Act criminalized all "false, scan-
dalous and malicious" comments about the government of the
United States.

Congress, dominated by Federalists, passed the Alien and Sedition Acts in the belief that the young republic was perched precariously on the edge of war and it was therefore a matter of national security for the government to quash dissension. Criticism of the president was tantamount to subversion. Republicans, on the other hand, looked to the Bill of Rights, passed just a decade earlier, and argued that what made America unique—and strong—was the free exchange of ideas. The different points of view were embodied in a very personal fracas between two members of the House of Representatives. Congressman Matthew Lyon of Vermont, Irish born, was a well-known Republican leader who regularly taunted the Federalists for pomposity and aristocratic airs. When Federalist Congressman Roger Griswold of Connecticut mocked Lyon for rumors of Lyon's Revolutionary War cowardice by asking about his "wooden sword," Lyon strode across the House floor in Philadelphia and spat in Griswold's face. An indignant Griswold and his fellow Federalists sought to have "Spitting Matt" expelled from the House, but the motion failed to attract the necessary two-thirds vote. Two weeks later, Griswold spied Lyon sitting alone at his desk on the House floor. Griswold calmly walked over to Lyon and brutally beat him with his hickory cane. Wounded, Lyon managed to grab a pair of fireplace tongs and swung them wildly in self defense. As the two men fought each other, House members cheered them on for several minutes before finally pulling them apart.

Just a year later, in 1798, Lyon became the first person charged under the new Sedition Act. His crime? He had sent a letter to the editor of the *Vermont Gazette* stating that President Adams's "consideration of the public welfare" was "swallowed up in a continual grasp for power, in an unbounded thirst for ridiculous pomp, foolish adulation, and selfish avarice." Lyon also was charged with quoting from a letter that said Congress should send Adams to a "mad house." For these crimes, Lyon was convicted, fined one thousand dollars, and sentenced to four months in jail (longer if he failed to pay his fine).

Like every other federal employee, Federal Marshal Jabez Fitch of Vermont had been appointed by the Federalists. Immediately after Lyon's conviction, Fitch seized him, led him on a two-day journey across the state, and put him in a cell with a "stench about equal to the Philadelphia docks in the month of August." While Lyon languished in jail, Vermont voters overwhelmingly reelected him to Congress. A national subscription drive, led by supporters in Vermont and Virginia, raised funds to pay the fine.

Armed with the sedition law, Federalists launched a wave of prosecutions against Republican critics. In less than three years, Federalists arrested twenty-five well-known Republicans under the Act, indicted fifteen, and charged several others with common-law sedition. Federal Marshal Fitch, for example, grabbed the editor of the *Vermont Gazette* at his home "at a very early hour" and required him to ride sixty miles in a cold rain. He put the editor in "a filthy prison at midnight, notwithstanding his entreaties to be permitted to dry his clothes."

Critics of the government knew that they could be arrested and charged at any time. Jefferson called it the "reign of witches."

While riding circuit, certain Supreme Court justices played a leading role in the Sedition Act prosecutions. Justice William Paterson, also born in Ireland, presided over Irish-born Matthew Lyon's trial and instructed the grand jurors to note "the seditious attempts of disaffected persons to disturb the government." Justice Samuel Chase presided over sedition trials in Maryland and Virginia, decried by critics as "Chase's Bloody Circuit." Jefferson attacked federal judges as "objects of national fear." Although defendants in Sedition Act trials sometimes raised constitutional objections, federal judges swatted them aside. Not surprisingly, nobody bothered to appeal to the Supreme Court since individual justices who had presided over circuit court prosecutions were unlikely to reverse themselves or to be overruled by their Federalist appointed brethren.

Republicans turned to states, rather than to federal courts, for constitutional protection. Jefferson and Madison secretly drafted the Virginia and Kentucky Resolutions, enactments by those states that declared the Sedition Act null and void.

———

JOHN AND ABIGAIL ADAMS moved into the "President's House" in November 1800, barely one month before the election. The president arrived first, on November 2, 1800, and spent a restless first night in the cavernous mansion, with its unfinished stairways, exposed pipes, and barren rooms. He wrote Abigail, "May none but honest and wise men ever rule under this roof," words that now are inscribed over a fireplace mantel in the White House.

Abigail arrived from Braintree on November 10. Her carriage got lost in the woods of Maryland. According to Abigail, a "black man" eventually stumbled upon them and led the wagon carrying the First Lady and her driver back to the road. Arriving in the capital, Abigail was both intrigued and repelled. The capital was "romantic, strange, full of wilderness," but Georgetown was "the very dirtyest Hole" she had ever seen.

The President's House in November 1800 was not for the faint of heart. Building equipment littered the yard. The mansion and grounds were open to public view, surrounded only by a wood-rail fence. Curious gawkers frequently wandered in and out of the house, a phenomenon that led Marshall to ask the capital's commissioners for a system of regulating the visitors. Although builders were beginning to install indoor water closets in some new houses, none had been provided for the president. The president and First Lady had to venture out in the exposed yard to a wooden privy. Abigail Adams frequently hung laundry in the East Room.

As the election of 1800 came to a close, President Adams addressed Congress for what he knew might be the last time. Arriving by carriage at the newly opened Capitol, Adams spoke before a joint session of House and Senate members in the Senate chamber. He celebrated the accomplishments of his administration and called for "simple manners, pure morals, and true religion" to "flourish forever." More significantly, he called for reform of the Judicial Branch of government, noting the urgency for "improvements which may have been suggested by experience."

Two weeks later, on December 3, as electors from each state cast their ballots for the presidency, Adams, awaiting the results in the President's House, received a postrider with a dispatch from East Chester, New York. Adams opened the letter and read that his son Charles, who for years had battled alcoholism, had died on November 30. Adams's somber mood darkened over the next few days as election results trickled in and it was clear that he had lost. His consolation was the knowledge that he was at last free to return with Abigail to their farm in Massachusetts. He wrote his son Thomas, "Be not concerned about me. I feel my shoulders relieved from the burden."

"The jig's up!" crowed the *Baltimore American*, a steadfast Republican newspaper. Although the results had not been formally announced, newspapers around the country had already begun to speculate about a Jefferson presidency. By the middle of December, however, it was clear that the unthinkable had occurred. The Republicans had defeated the Federalists but tied themselves: Thomas Jefferson and Aaron Burr had received an equal number of electoral votes. There was no definitive winner.

Republicans had also captured control of the Congress. But since the new Congress would not be seated until months after the presidential inauguration on March 4, under the Constitution the outgoing House of Representatives, still dominated by the Federalists, would decide the outcome of the election by a simply majority vote. The rival, losing party could end up choosing the president. It had been widely understood by the general public, by the press, and by the candidates themselves that Jefferson was the presidential candidate and Burr was his running mate. Indeed, Burr initially seemed entirely willing to defer to the gentleman from Virginia: "It is highly improbable that I shall have an equal number of votes with Mr. Jefferson, but if such should be the result, every man who knows me knows that I should utterly disclaim all competition."

Secretary of State Marshall wrote to the defeated vice presidential candidate Charles Pinckney in South Carolina on December 18, 1800, noting that it remained "extremely uncertain on whom the choice will fall." Marshall, who had served in the House, now had "no voice in the election, and in fact scarcely any wish concerning it." For his part, he intended to return to Richmond and to "recommence practice as a lawyer . . . [and to] never again fill any political station whatever."

Chapter
THREE

THE RISE OF THE COUSINS: A NEW CHIEF JUSTICE AND A NEW PRESIDENT

L ess than two weeks after learning of his defeat, on December 15, 1800, John Adams sat and brooded in the unfinished President's House. The Republican takeover of the presidency and Congress loomed. A new president, a Republican—either Jefferson or Burr—would take office in ten weeks; Republicans would take control of the Senate and House at the sitting of the next Congress.

Adams focused on the very next day, Tuesday, December 16, when he would submit a proposed treaty with France's new leader, Napoleon Bonaparte, to the Senate for ratification. The agreement faced skepticism in the Senate, especially from Adams's fellow anglophile Federalists, who were suspicious of any agreement with the French. Adams's envoy, Chief Justice Oliver Ellsworth, had negotiated the treaty, known as the Convention of Mortefontaine, in Paris with Napoleon's older brother, Joseph Bonaparte, as a balanced response to the Jay Treaty.

As he was considering his diminishing options in the period before he had to hand over the presidency to the Republicans,

Adams received a letter from Ellsworth in Paris announcing his resignation from the Supreme Court. Ellsworth's diplomatic mission had kept him away from the Court for more than a year. He was ill, and his doctor forbade a trans-Atlantic trip. Ellsworth would spend the winter receiving mineral treatments in England at Bath. The letter had taken two months to reach the president.

Mulling the vacancy, Adams thought of his old friend and colleague John Jay.

Adams discussed the opening that cold December day in the cavernous and unfinished President's House with the man who had become his closest adviser, John Marshall. Marshall suggested promoting Supreme Court Justice William Paterson to the now-open position of chief justice.

From humble origins, Paterson had built an illustrious career. Born in Ireland, he had been brought to Princeton, New Jersey, as an infant. He grew up working in his parents' general store serving the students and faculty at the new College of New Jersey (later renamed Princeton University) and soaking up the academic environment. After attending a preparatory school founded by Aaron Burr's father, Paterson stayed in town and attended the College of New Jersey. At the Constitutional Convention in 1787, Paterson had been the leading advocate for a Congress in which each state had an equal vote, a position that eventually led to the bicameral compromise in which the Senate would be organized on Paterson's basis of equal votes for each state. Paterson had served as governor of New Jersey before resigning to join the Supreme Court in 1793. An ardent Federalist, he was a hero to the party's extreme wing, based in part on his zealous condemnation of Matthew Lyon and the firmness with which he enforced the controversial Sedition Act.

But Adams swatted away Marshall's suggestion of Paterson. He told Marshall that appointing Paterson as chief would insult Justice William Cushing, Adams's old friend and colleague from Massachusetts. Cushing was now 68, the only original appointee of George Washington still serving on the bench, and a man who seemed increasingly ancient and frail. Four years earlier, in 1796, Cushing already had declined Washington's nomination of the chief justice post on the ground that his "infirm and declining state of health" prevented it. (He actually was confirmed by the Senate and served one week before resigning and returning to his post as associate justice; during that week as chief, he heard no cases and his only official action was attending a dinner.)

Marshall understood that selecting the more junior Paterson would mean bypassing Cushing. But Marshall also knew that Adams had a deeper, more personal objection to Paterson. Still smarting from his defeat in the election, Adams was in no mood to appoint somebody closely aligned with Hamilton and the "High Federalists."

On Thursday, December 18, 1800, Adams sent the name of John Jay to the Senate for confirmation as third chief justice of the United States. The next day he penned the letter to Governor Jay announcing that he wanted him to return to his previous job. "I have nominated you to your old station," Adams proclaimed. Clearly worried, Adams implored Jay that his appointment could be an "opportunity" from "providence" to inhibit "the increasing dissolution of morals."

Adams gave the letter to Marshall for formal transmittal, and Marshall included a cover note encouraging Jay to accept. "The President, anxious to avail the United States of your services as Chief Justice, has nominated you to the senate for that important office, now vacant by the resignation of Mr. Ellesworth. In the hope that you may be prevaild on to accept it, I feel peculiar satisfaction in transmitting to you the commission."

Marshall knew that the odds were against Jay's acceptance, and he was worried about the consequences. Marshall confided to Charles Pinckney, "Mr. Ellsworth has resignd his seat as chief justice & Mr. Jay has been nominated in his place. Should he as is most probable decline the office I fear the President will nominate the senior Judge." The "senior Judge" was Cushing.

As THE CENTENNIAL YEAR came to a close and a showdown in the Congress loomed, Washington City was abuzz with political intrigue. The city was teeming with reporters, speculators, and lawmakers who huddled in hotel lobbies and crowded the city's boarding houses awaiting the outcome of the election. The president and First Lady hosted the first New Year's Day dinner party in the President's House. At the brilliantly candle-lit dinner table, Thomas Jefferson sat next to Abigail Adams. Jefferson surveyed the rest of the table: He recognized a number of congressmen and was undoubtedly sizing up who would be in his corner when Congress chose the next president. When he confidently remarked to the First Lady that many of the dinner guests were familiar to him, she replied that she knew them all.

Abigail Adams had once liked and admired Thomas Jefferson. They had enjoyed many stimulating evenings together in Paris when both Adams and Jefferson were commissioners representing the United States. But the election of 1800 had colored her view of her former friend—she resented that Jefferson, her husband's vice president, had collaborated with journalist James Callender's slandering of the president. She would later tell her son that she pitied Jefferson's "weakness." Nevertheless, in the aftermath of the election, though still publicly uncommitted between Jefferson and Burr, the Adamses had invited Jefferson to dinner.

Vice President Jefferson continued to engage the First Lady on the subject of her dinner guests, inquiring what she thought "they mean to do" about the impending vote in the House of Representatives. Mrs. Adams must have smiled at Jefferson—whose ambition and charm had become familiar to her. She told him that she had no idea how the House would vote and that the election was a subject she did not "choose to converse upon." And then, to leaven the conversation, she repeated an axiom that when people "do not know what to do, they should take great care that they do not do they know not what." According to her diary, "At this he laughed out, and here ended the conversation."

Jefferson maintained his sense of humor, but he had good reason to be concerned about the election. If Aaron Burr initially had seemed reluctant to even be considered for the presidency, after the votes were counted, and the deadlock became official, he let it be known privately that he wanted the top job. He may have been impressed by the support of the many prominent Federalists across the country who openly preferred him to Jefferson, a man whom many considered an atheist, an elitist, and a coward. Fisher Ames of Massachusetts, for instance, thought Burr "might impart vigor to the country," while Jefferson was "absurd enough to believe his own nonsense."

Around the New Year, Jefferson received support from a most unlikely ally: Alexander Hamilton. Hamilton, who had played such an important role in the months leading up to the voting, now once again intervened. An ardent Federalist, he had been sharply critical of President Adams for being too moderate. But his disdain for Jefferson and his Republicanism paled in comparison to the abiding hatred that he had for his old adversary in New York, Aaron Burr. Fearing that members of his party, the Federalists, who controlled the Congress until a new one was seated, might tilt the election toward Burr, Hamilton launched a campaign of letters to steer the Federalists to Jefferson. In a letter to his friend Gouverneur Morris, Hamilton mused that Burr "is sanguine enough to hope everything, daring enough to attempt anything, wicked enough to scruple nothing." Hamilton wrote Oliver Wolcott, Jr., his successor as secretary of the Treasury, that Burr was "bankrupt beyond redemption, except by the plunder of his country. His public principles have no other spring or aim than his own aggrandizement. . . . He truly is the Catiline of America."

Secretary of State Marshall received a similar letter from Hamilton but he remained uncommitted. Marshall claimed to be "totally unacquainted" with Burr, yet deeply concerned by how Hamilton had depicted his character. As Marshall put it, "Such a man as you describe is more to be feared and may do more immediate if not greater mischief." Despite Hamilton's dire descriptions, Marshall concluded that he would remain neutral in the outcome of the House vote because "I cannot bring myself to aid Mr. Jefferson."

Jefferson continued to be very skeptical of the behind-the-scenes machinations of Federalist politicians. He especially didn't trust his cousin, Secretary of State Marshall, who he speculated might himself covet the presidency. In a letter to his friend James Madison, Jefferson claimed that Federalists were delighted to prolong the election deadlock and might even be scheming to give the presidency to "Mr. Jay, appointed Chief Justice, or to Marshall as Secretary of State."

IN MID-JANUARY, Governor Jay's letter to President Adams refusing the chief justice position arrived on Secretary of State's Marshall's desk. Jay separately acknowledged "the polite Letter" Marshall had sent urging him to accept. But Jay reiterated his decision. "I am very sensible of the honor done me by this appointment. [But] (independent of other Considerations) the Incompetency of my Health to the fatigues incident to the office, forms an insuperable objection to my accepting it." Foremost among "other Considerations" was Jay's deeply held conviction that the Supreme Court never would possess any meaningful authority, stature, or power.

On Monday, January 19, 1801, Marshall met with Adams to advise him of Jay's refusal. Adams listened attentively. The situation was complicated by the fact that legislation pending in Congress would reduce the size of the Supreme Court from six to five justices at the time of the next vacancy. If Adams did not move quickly, the vacancy probably would not be filled at all. Now, as Adams considered Jay's response, the defeated president pondered his options.

Marshall later recalled that the president then turned to him and asked, "Who shall I nominate now?" Marshall again suggested Justice Paterson, but Adams "said in a decided tone 'I shall not nominate him.'"

Having firmly rejected Paterson, Adams, after what seemed to Marshall like "a moment's hesitation," said, "I believe I must nominate you." Marshall recalled that he "had never even thought of it," but "was pleased as well as surprised, and bowed in silence." The next day he was nominated.

Marshall may have expected Adams to name another. But his claim that he never even thought of himself for the post seems an assertion of modesty for posterity. Marshall greatly prized his reputation as a leading lawyer and appellate advocate in the Virginia courts. Marshall could hardly have forgotten that, in 1798, Adams had offered to appoint him to the Supreme Court to succeed the late James Wilson. When he declined, Adams had instead appointed Marshall's close friend, Bushrod Washington, George Washington's nephew. Now, as secretary of state, Marshall controlled the paper flow to and from potential chief justices and was intimately involved in the selection process. The thought of filling the post himself must have occurred to him.

In any event, Marshall immediately accepted. Adams forwarded Marshall's nomination to the Senate on Tuesday, January 20, 1801. He later would call it one of the proudest moments of his presidency.

———

BORN IN 1755, the oldest of fifteen children, John Marshall was raised in a wooden cabin in the foothills of the Blue Ridge Mountains of Virginia. He had no formal childhood education, but his father taught him to read and steeped him in the classics. After the outbreak of the Revolutionary War, Marshall enlisted and soon became an aide to George Washington, serving with him during the bitter winter at Valley Forge. Marshall was athletic and well-liked; he was said to be the only man in Washington's army who could jump six feet high.

After the war, Marshall became one of the first students at the new law school at William and Mary. He filled his law notebooks with detailed notes on English cases, as well as with doodles and idle scrawls about the woman who would be his wife, Polly Ambler. After graduation Marshall quickly became a successful lawyer in Richmond, handling trials, wills, contracts, appeals, and anything else that had a fee behind it. ("A client is just come in," Marshall wrote a friend in 1789, "pray heaven he may have money.") He also became a part-time public official, serving on a state board and in the state legislature, but throughout the 1780s and most of the 1790s he made clear that law practice was his first priority.

In 1788, Marshall played a crucial role in the legendary Virginia constitutional ratification. Virginia's decision to support the new federal constitution, more than any other state's, would determine its fate: Virginia was by far the largest state, with one-fifth of the nation's population and over one-third of its commerce, and a successful nation without Virginia's participation was inconceivable. Marshall teamed with James Madison to win ratification, by only a few votes, against a galaxy of leading Virginia citizens, including Patrick Henry and George Mason. Throughout the weeks of debate, Marshall genially hosted dinners and drinks at his home and at local inns and taverns. Marshall's hospitality contributed significantly to a softening of opposition that made the narrow ratification possible. Marshall also delivered a pivotal speech, defending the proposed federal judiciary against the charge that it would lead to an imperial federal government. He had a gift for turning opponents into friends and allies. His ardent foe on ratification, Patrick Henry, was so impressed with Marshall's skill and personality that he later became Marshall's close friend and occasional law partner.

Marshall was instinctively convivial; he loved feasting, imbibing, and socializing. In his hometown of Richmond, he was a founder and charter member of the "Quoits Club," or "Barbecue Club," a club devoted to quoits, a game involving the pitching of a metal ring onto a pin several yards away, usually accompanied by raucous eating and drinking. Marshall remained a member and enthusiast of the club his entire life, spending every Saturday there from April to September. Marshall particularly enjoyed a special punch that he developed, a mix of brandy, rum, and Madeira. According to the informal club rules, which Marshall cheerfully enforced, no politics, business, or religion could be discussed. Violators were fined a case of champagne, to be consumed at the next club meeting.

In September 1798, just a few months after Marshall's return from France and the XYZ Affair that had made him a hero a home, George Washington summoned Marshall and Bushrod Washington, his nephew, to Mt. Vernon. The former president was greatly concerned about the potential threat from the rising Republicans and he implored his nephew and his protégé to run for Congress for the Federalists. After dinner that night, Marshall explained to the former president that he was reluctant to leave his flourishing law practice. The following morning, Marshall planned to flee Mt. Vernon before dawn so that he would not have to see Washington again. As Marshall approached the stable to saddle his horse in the early morning, he found Washington waiting for him. Only an inch taller than Marshall, the former president nevertheless was an imposing and often intimidating figure. Washington reminded Marshall that, against his personal desires, Washington had given up the pleasures of private life to serve his country. Marshall reluctantly agreed to run.

Virginia was a hotbed of Republicanism, with Jefferson, Madison, and Governor James Monroe setting the tone in the state. But Marshall made a key decision in his congressional campaign. He signaled that he did not agree with the Federalist position on the Alien and Sedition Acts, and that he would not have voted for them. Although a Federalist, Marshall made clear that he was not an ideologue and could make common cause with those outside his party. In the heat of the contest, Republican hero Patrick Henry delivered a strong endorsement of Marshall.

On election day, both Marshall and his opponent, John Clopton, actively solicited votes at the polling place. According to the practice of the day, Marshall stood at one end of a table with a jug of whiskey and his opponent stood at the other. Voting was not a private matter as voters publicly announced their choices at the polling place. Marshall later recalled that two ministers had arrived together: One voted for him and the other for his opponent. One of the ministers explained that the votes would cancel each other out, "and nobody could say that the clergy had influenced the election."

The election was close, but Marshall won.

Arriving in Philadelphia as a new congressman, Marshall found himself in a cauldron of enmity toward President Adams from his own party as well as from the Republicans. Two decades younger than Adams, Marshall seemed the opposite of his prickly president. Marshall was six feet two and gregarious. Supreme Court Justice Joseph Story later remarked of Marshall, "His laugh was too hearty for an intriguer." Marshall lounged comfortably in plain clothes, priding himself on his down-home manner and lack of airs. Even as a public luminary, he once happily rode alongside the driver of a crowded carriage-for-hire because there was no room for him within the carriage. Another time, while he was on the Supreme Court, he helped a citizen carry groceries for miles. The citizen, thinking Marshall a workman, tipped him. Marshall pocketed the tip and gleefully added the story to his repertoire.

Despite their differences in personality and manner, from Marshall's first days in Congress in 1799 he was one of Adams's few devoted loyalists on the House floor. He defended Adams's policies against onslaughts from the High Federalists on one side and the Republicans on the other. His easy manner and effective advocacy built friendships and alliances with both factions, but, almost alone, he vigorously supported the president. At the same time, when a motion to repeal the Sedition Act arose on the House floor, he was one of the only Federalists to vote for it.

From his first days, Marshall's speeches in the House had an impact. In the celebrated "Jonathan Robbins affair," for example, Marshall delivered an electrifying three-hour speech on the House floor defending Adams's decision to hand over "John Nash," a fugitive sailor sought by the British for desertion. Nash claimed actually to be "Jonathan Robbins," an American citizen immune from extradition. A federal judge found that Nash had not established his American identity as "Jonathan Robbins" and ordered him extradited. Despite a firestorm by Republicans against the hated British, Adams refused to intervene and refused to block the judge's action. The British promptly tried and hanged Nash, and Republicans savaged Adams and sought his censure in the House.

Marshall took the House floor and powerfully defended the president's position. Congressman Albert Gallatin, the Republican scheduled to speak after Marshall, is said to have turned to colleagues at the conclusion of Marshall's speech and advised, "Gentlemen, answer it yourself. For my part, I think it is unanswerable."

Beneath Marshall's easy airs and bonhomie, he was energetic, efficient, pithy, and luminously logical. Marshall woke early every morning, walked six miles, and began working hard before the day had begun. Lawyers and listeners from across the spectrum admired his turn of mind and his razor-sharp reasoning.

Marshall was devoted to his wife, Polly, who suffered from nervous exhaustion, anxiety, and depression from the time of his trip to France in the XYZ Affair until her death in 1831. Polly frequently was an invalid, confined to her bedroom and requiring complete quiet around her at all times. When in Richmond, Marshall doted on her and took elaborate actions to try to ensure a hushed environment.

Even with his devotion to Polly, Marshall richly appreciated the art of flirtation. He remarked once that young men now seemed excessively timid in their pursuit of women. In his stay in Paris during the XYZ Affair, Marshall lodged with the Marquise de Villette, who had been raised by Voltaire and who kept Voltaire's heart in a silver case in her sitting room. Marshall was thoroughly enthralled with the Marquise, leading to speculation that they may have had an affair, the only suspected liaison in his fifty-year marriage to Polly.

There was however one exception to Marshall's almost constant affability with friend and foe alike: his cousin Thomas Jefferson.

Jefferson was Marshall's second cousin, once removed. Jefferson's grandfather, Isham Randolph, and Marshall's great-grandfather, Thomas Randolph, were brothers.

Family feuds undoubtedly played a part in the mutual enmity between Marshall and Jefferson. Marshall's grandmother, Mary Randolph Isham Keith, had battled with the Randolph family and had been disowned by the Jefferson family. In addition, Marshall's mother-in-law, Eliza Ambler, had been Jefferson's first fiancé, and she nursed an abiding resentment toward her former lover.

Political differences also played a part in the breach. Jefferson, for example, had been critical of George Washington in the notorious "Mazzei letter," in which Jefferson ridiculed Washington as the "shorn Samson." Jefferson had written a letter providing an overview of American political life to his old friend Phillip Mazzei, an Italian who translated the letter and published it in a local Italian newspaper. The letter was then translated back into English and published in London newspapers. When those newspapers arrived in America in May 1797, the Mazzei letter shocked Washington loyalists such as Marshall. Like some other Revolutionary War veterans, Marshall also may have resented Jefferson's actions in the Revolution; as the wartime governor of Virginia, Jefferson hastily fled Richmond as the British approached, a panicked flight that led to criticism throughout his career.

Whatever the reasons, their mutual dislike was clear and unshakeable. In a letter to Madison in 1795, Jefferson privately scorned Marshall's "lax lounging manners" and his "profound hypocrisy." Jefferson eagerly passed on rumors that Marshall had enriched himself during the XYZ Affair by looking after his private matters while in Europe. Jefferson also cast doubt on Marshall's version of events with Talleyrand, writing Edmund Randolph in 1799 that the account of the XYZ Affair was merely "a dish cooked up by Marshall, where the swindlers are made to appear as the French government." Jefferson was distressed when Marshall won election to Congress, and he privately condemned Patrick Henry for his "apostasy" in supporting him.

For his part, Marshall similarly was caustic about Jefferson. As Henry Adams concluded, "[T]his excellent and amiable man clung to one rooted prejudice: he detested Thomas Jefferson." Late in life, Marshall would write that he had never believed Jefferson to be honorable. He derisively referred to Jefferson as the "great lama of the mountains," meaning that he was aloof and didn't care about anyone else.

As public figures, however, Jefferson and Marshall occasionally had to deal with each other. When Marshall returned to Philadelphia after the XYZ Affair, Vice President Jefferson twice tried to visit him at his hotel. On the second try Jefferson left a note saying that he "was so lucky as to find that he [Marshall] was out on both occasions." Catching himself, Jefferson then scrawled an "un" onto the note above the "lucky."

———

THE HIGH FEDERALISTS were furious at Adams's nomination of Marshall to be chief justice. They did not trust him, and they had hoped for the appointment of Paterson, their champion and ally. Senator Jonathan Dayton of New Jersey, Paterson's home state, erupted. He wrote Paterson that he was filled with "grief, astonishment and almost indignation," and that Marshall's nomination was "contrary to the hopes and expectations of us all." Dayton immediately demanded that Adams reverse his decision. The outraged senator privately fumed that Adams's recent appointments "have manifested such debility or derangement of intellect, that I am convinced, in common with most of our Federal members, that another four years of administration in his hands would have exposed us to destruction."

The Republicans' response, in contrast, was muted. Many viewed Marshall as far less objectionable than other Federalist possibilities.

The exception among the Republicans was James Callender, imprisoned under the Sedition Act and not yet estranged from Jefferson. Callender wrote in the *Richmond Examiner*, a Republican newspaper in Marshall's hometown, "we are to have that precious acquisition, John Marshall, as Chief Justice. . . . The very sound of this man's name is an insult upon truth and justice."

For his part, Adams was delighted with his appointment of the 45-year-old Marshall. Receiving a letter from New Jersey lawyers urging Adams to appoint himself as chief justice, Adams enthusiastically responded that he instead had nominated "a gentleman in the full vigor of middle age, in the full habits of business and whose reading in the science [of law] is fresh in his head." At a time when all was bleak to Adams, with the President's House about to be occupied by Jefferson or Burr and the Republicans poised to take over Congress, his appointment of Marshall to head the judiciary gave him great satisfaction.

Justice Paterson tried to snuff out the rebellion being waged on his behalf. He wrote Dayton warmly endorsing Marshall. Paterson stated that he felt "neither resentment nor disgust" about Marshall's appointment and believed that Marshall was "a man of genius" whose "talents have at once the luster and solidity of gold."

Support for Marshall in the Senate was harder to secure—even from Adams's own party. The Federalists had shown themselves willing to contradict the president; on January 23, 1801, just a few days after Adams nominated Marshall to be chief justice, the president suffered a humiliating defeat when the Senate rejected the Convention of Mortefontaine. Every vote against the treaty with France was cast by Adams's fellow Federalists.

Within days of Marshall's nomination, a delegation of Federalist senators met with Adams to pressure him to withdraw Marshall and nominate Paterson. But Adams was adamant. As Dayton confided to Paterson, "all voices with the exception of one only were united in favor of the conferring of this appointment upon you.

The President alone was inflexible, and declared that he would never nominate you."

Dayton and the other Federalists reluctantly decided to let Adams have his way on the chief justice nomination, figuring that if they blocked Marshall, the president's replacement probably would be "not so well qualified, and most disgusting to the Bench." Dayton advised Paterson that Marshall "was not privy to his own nomination, but had previously exerted his influence with the President on your behalf." Marshall apparently had found a way, either directly or through a back channel, to temporarily mollify his most outspoken opponent by confiding that he had supported Paterson. But even after his vote for Marshall's confirmation, Dayton remained bitter. He angrily derided Adams as "a wild freak of a man whose administration, happily for this country, is soon to terminate."

On January 27, 1801, one week after Adams's nomination of Marshall and without a hearing in the Senate (which would not occur for a Supreme Court nominee until 1925), the outgoing Senate unanimously confirmed John Marshall to be the third chief justice of the United States.

Marshall was thrilled and wrote Adams warmly accepting the appointment. "This additional and flattering mark of your good opinion has made an impression on my mind which time will not efface," Marshall advised the president. "I shall enter immediately on the duties of the office and hope never to give you occasion to regret having made this appointment."

Marshall may have been thrilled, but it was not clear that he even had a court to lead. On the same day that Adams announced his nomination of Marshall, Congress was still scrambling to find a place for the forgotten Branch to meet. The District commissioners, whose job was to plan the city and find housing for the various departments of the government, had written twice in recent months asking for recommendations on where to locate the

Court: The letters, addressed to Secretary of State John Marshall, had not been answered.

On January 20, 1801, the Speaker of the House requested to Congress that the Supreme Court be accommodated in the Capitol. A few days later, on January 23, the House and Senate finally adopted a resolution formally giving leave to "the Commissioners of the City of Washington to use one of the rooms of the Capitol for holding the present session of the Supreme Court of the United States."

Most newspapers were matter of fact about the Marshall nomination and paid it little attention. The *National Intelligencer* blandly reported, "The President of the U.S. has nominated JOHN MARSHALL, *Chief Justice* of the United States."

Newspapers focused instead on a mysterious fire that had erupted at the new Treasury Department building, next door to the President's House. "Last evening about dusk a fire was discovered in the TREASURY DEPARTMENT," announced the *National Intelligencer* on the same day as Marshall's nomination. "When discovered, one of the rooms of the Accountant was in a full blaze. The papers in this room are said to be entirely destroyed, and those in an upper and an adjacent room, to which the flames extended, are said to be considerably injured. The fire was extinguished in about an hour and a half."

Rumors spread that Federalists had set this fire, along with other fires at War Department offices in Washington and Massachusetts to hide damaging secrets from the incoming Republicans. As Republican Congressman John Fowler explained in a letter to his Kentucky constituents, the fires, "at a period when patronage and the secrets of office were about to be transferred to different hands, could not but excite the worst suspicions."

As MARSHALL PREPARED to be sworn in as chief justice, he still had duties, and worries, as secretary of state. He had agreed to

Adams's request that he continue to serve in the cabinet until the new president, whoever it would be, named a new secretary of state on March 4—a simultaneous wearing of hats in the Executive and Judicial branches that would be unthinkable today. Secretary of State Marshall's most pressing problem was the Convention of Mortefontaine with France, so recently rejected in the Senate by rebellious fellow Federalists. He maneuvered to reverse the decision by releasing a letter from Rufus King, the respected ambassador to England with great credibility among the Federalists, reporting that the British government had no objection to the treaty. Perhaps feeling that they had accomplished their goal of inflicting intramural pain on Adams, the Federalists now reversed course. On February 3, 1801, to Marshall's great relief, the Senate finally ratified the Mortefontaine treaty between the United States and Napoleon Bonaparte's new government.

The following day, on February 4, 1801, a cold and rainy Wednesday morning in the capital, William Cushing of Massachusetts, the elderly senior associate justice, administered the oath of chief justice of the United States to John Marshall. Justice Bushrod Washington of Virginia, Marshall's close friend, attended the brief ceremony, as did Justice Samuel Chase, the fiery, bombastic, partisan judge from Maryland. But otherwise, the event was sparsely attended. The other two members of the Supreme Court, Paterson of New Jersey and Alfred Moore of North Carolina, stayed home.

Marshall wore plain black robes, which set him apart from the other justices, who wore florid scarlet and ermine robes or academic gowns. It had been the custom of Virginia judges to wear such black robes. The simple black style suited Marshall. It symbolized a lack of pretense and pomp while maintaining an aura of dignity and authority.

The following week, on February 10, 1801, the Supreme Court met for the first time in a dark, cramped room in the Capitol, a room that the Supreme Court would share with the local District of Columbia courts. Chief Justice (and still Secretary of State)

John Marshall presided. Once again, only Cushing, Washington, and Chase were in attendance; Paterson and Moore remained at home. There was no court reporter; Alexander Dallas, who occupied the position in Philadelphia, had refused to move to Washington. (He would eventually be elected Pennsylvania attorney general.)

Marshall called the Court to order.

Within days, the February session was over. The Court had neither considered nor decided anything of consequence.

———

THOMAS JEFFERSON had no apparent reaction to the installation of his cousin as the third chief justice of the United States. He must have been somewhat annoyed that a man he so disliked had been elevated to such a position. But perhaps Jefferson was so preoccupied with the deadlocked election and the looming vote in the House of Representatives that he did not pay much attention.

Several days after Marshall was confirmed as chief justice, Jefferson returned to the White House to have tea and say goodbye to Abigail Adams, who was preparing to return home in advance of her husband. In a letter to her son, Abigail wrote that Jefferson had visited her "to take leave and wish a good journey. It was more than I expected." There is no other record of their visit. It seems unlikely that Jefferson ever mentioned the impending House vote as he had at the dinner party several weeks before, but it would later become clear that Jefferson hoped for John Adams's intervention on his behalf. Jefferson was genuinely fond of the First Lady, but he was also aware of the extent to which her opinion mattered with the president; he undoubtedly hoped that Mrs. Adams would implore her husband to help. Jefferson knew that if President Adams could influence just one vote in the House of Representatives, the election would be his.

On February 11, as snow blanketed the city, House members assembled in the Senate Library to try to decide between Burr and

Jefferson. The lower house's chamber in the south wing of the Capitol still lacked a roof. The delegation of each state was allowed a single vote for president; as there were sixteen states, the winner needed a simple majority of 9 votes. Although Federalists had a majority in the House, Republicans had a majority of the delegations in eight states, Federalists had a majority of the delegations in six states, and two states (Maryland and Vermont) had delegations evenly split.

On the first ballot, six states voted for Burr, all of them the Federalist-controlled states. Eight states, the Republican-controlled states, voted for Jefferson. The evenly split delegations of Maryland and Vermont cast no votes. The session droned on for twenty hours with periodic votes. Servants brought in food, spirits, and water for the members in their seats. Four fireplaces heated the large rectangular room, but many congressmen wore their long overcoats and some of the lawmakers even curled up on the floor to catch a few hours of sleep between votes. Others smoked pipes or cigars. One legislator, too ill to sit at his desk, lay on a cot in a room just off the Senate floor. At nine o'clock the next morning, with still no progress, the Speaker announced that the House would adjourn until the following day.

The next day, lawmakers returned to the Capitol but again made no progress. Another day went by and the impasse continued. Then another. Rumors began to circulate that Federalists might stall the vote until after March 4, Inauguration Day, and then appoint their own candidate as president—perhaps former Supreme Court Chief Justice John Jay, or even the new chief justice, John Marshall—just as Jefferson had long suspected. Outside the Capitol building, demonstrators chanted Jefferson's name. Several men rode a large wooden sleigh through the snowy streets waving a big banner proclaiming "Jefferson, the Friend of the People." But concern over the deadlock went beyond protests and demonstrations. In Pennsylvania, Governor Thomas McKean, who had campaigned actively on behalf of Jefferson, pledged to call out the state militia, estimated at 20,000, and to march on the capital if Federalists attempted to deny the installation of a Republican president. There was talk of civil war.

Jefferson, staying at his boardinghouse near the Capitol, conferred regularly with his Republican allies in the House; his frustration mounted as the deadlock dragged on. On February 14, he noted in his diary that General Armstrong had told him that Gouverneur Morris wondered "that Burr who is four hundred miles off (at Albany), has agents here at work with great activity, while Mr. Jefferson, who is on the spot, does nothing?" Jefferson now feared that the election might be stolen from him. As he would later recount in a letter to Benjamin Rush, "I called on Mr. Adams to have this desperate measure prevented by his negative."

President Adams received his vice president in his personal office in the President's House, but it was quickly apparent that he was in no mood to help. With only a few weeks left in his presidency, he was desperate to return to Massachusetts and to his wife who had left the city the day before. But Adams's irritability was also grounded in his belief that this was a question for the legislature to decide and that separation of powers dictated that he have no say in the outcome of the election.

After Jefferson made his case for intervention, Adams snapped at him, "Sir, the event of the election is within your own power. You have only to say you will do justice to the public creditors, maintain the navy, and not disturb those holding office, and the government will instantly be put in your hands. We know it is the wish of the people it should be so." According to Jefferson, Adams spoke "with a vehemence he had not used towards me before." Jefferson replied, "I will not come into government by capitulation." With these words, the last he would ever speak to Adams face to face, Jefferson left the President's House.

Jefferson did not give up. While there is no public record of his next moves, he seemed to signal to certain key Federalist lawmakers, either directly or through intermediaries, that he would be flexible on matters of both policy and patronage. One such lawmaker was James A. Bayard of Delaware. Delaware was tiny and had only a single member of Congress, which meant that Bayard himself was the entire state delegation. If he switched sides, Jefferson would have his majority of nine states.

Bayard had been first approached by Representative John Nicolas of Virginia, a close friend of Jefferson's. He would later recall that he had told Nicolas, "I considered it not only reasonable but necessary that offices of high discretion should be filled by men of Mr. Jefferson's choice," but Bayard wanted assurances from Jefferson of support for the public credit, the maintenance of the naval system, and security for minor office holders. These were essentially the same terms that President Adams had previously advised Jefferson to offer the Federalists. They represented a recognition of the importance of a national bank and a strong military—both central tenets of the Federalist Party—and, now that they were in the minority, grudging support for a two-party system. Bayard could not obtain a promise from Nicolas, but Samuel Smith, a congressman from Maryland, reported to Bayard that his requests "corresponded with his [Jefferson's] views and intentions and that we might confide in him accordingly." Jefferson would later dispute that he had authorized Smith to make such a representation.

On February 17, six days after their first vote, House members cast their thirty-sixth ballot. Representative Bayard of Delaware submitted a blank ballot, thereby removing his state's vote from the Burr column and putting it in the "not-voting" category. At the same time, following Bayard's lead, Federalists in the evenly split states of Maryland and Vermont now abstained, allowing their Republican counterparts to cast their states' votes for Jefferson. Federalists in the South Carolina delegation, which consisted only of Federalists and which had been supporting Burr, likewise did not vote. The logjam had been broken: Jefferson won decisively with

10 votes (Maryland and Vermont added to his original 8) to Burr's 4. Two states—Bayard's Delaware and South Carolina—abstained.

As news of the outcome spread, Republicans gathered in bars, meeting houses, and parlors to raise toasts to the new president. The *Federalist Gazette* reported somewhat sarcastically, "The bells have been ringing, guns firing, dogs barking, cats mewing, children crying, and Jacobins getting drunk."

An excited pro-Jefferson mob celebrated raucously in the streets of the capital. They marched to houses of well-known Federalists demanding a sign of acquiescence. Abigail Adams's nephew, William Cranch, obliged the mob by placing a candle in his window. The crowd moved on to Georgetown and assembled outside the prominent two-story brick home belonging to William Marbury, who was by now a well-known Federalist. They cheered President-elect Jefferson and demanded a similar sign of surrender. Marbury staunchly declined. According to the *Washington Gazette*, "[h]e refused in the most resolute manner to obey the mandate, and the mob left him imprecating vengeance."

The Republican *Aurora* proclaimed that "[t]he Revolution of 1776 is now, and for the first time, arrived at its completion." Jefferson would later refer to his election as "the revolution of 1800," for it marked the first peaceful democratic transfer of power from one political party to another in America's short time as an independent nation, and in the history of the world. But others, such as Chief Justice John Marshall, quietly worried about the direction of the country, fearing that the new president would "strengthen the state governments at the expense of . . . the Union . . . and transfer as much as possible the powers remaining with the general government to the House of Representatives."

The institutions of the young democracy had been strained, but they had not crumbled. They would soon be tested again.

Chapter
FOUR

THE MIDNIGHT JUDGES

John Adams now had exactly two weeks left as president. Adams's presidency would end on Wednesday, March 4; Jefferson would be inaugurated at noon on that day.

As Adams looked ahead to his last days in office, one task consumed him above all else—scores of last-minute presidential appointments to federal offices, appointments that would secure positions for loyal Federalists in the new Republican administration, appointments that would include those who soon would be known as the "midnight judges."

Adams's appointments came in two waves: The first filled federal offices, including judges, throughout the country, while the second filled local offices for the newly established District of Columbia.

During February 1801, his last month in office, Adams submitted a staggering total of 217 nominations to the Senate, an average of more than 7 per day, every day of that momentous month. The appointments included 93 judicial and legal offices, 53 of which were for the District of Columbia, and 106 military and naval positions. Adams was determined to make every possible federal appointment in his final days and hours in office. The

"Burden upon me in nominating Judges and Consuls and other offices . . . is and will be heavy," Adams reported to Abigail. "My time will be taken up."

Adams relied on one man most of all to help him with this burden—Secretary of State, and now the newly installed Chief Justice, John Marshall. Marshall was in the thick of the last-minute appointments. Job-seekers and their patrons flooded Marshall with letters as Adams's representative. Marshall was extraordinarily busy overseeing the logistics of the nominations—writing to nominees, preparing and submitting the actual nominations, formalizing the appointments with official commissions, having the commissions delivered to the new office holders.

The first wave of Adams's "midnight judges" was a result of the Judiciary Act of 1801. It reduced the size of the Supreme Court to five at the next vacancy, created a new system of appellate courts between the trial courts and the Supreme Court, and eliminated the controversial obligation of Supreme Court justices to ride circuit; the new appellate judges would assume this responsibility.

Most Federalists hailed the new law while Republicans overwhelmingly lambasted it. Adams only had to present his nominations for the new judgeships to the outgoing Federalist majority in the Senate and have them confirmed by March 4, the date that the new president would take office. Republicans objected that the new appellate courts not only gave the lame-duck president an opportunity to extend his influence beyond his term but also increased the role and power of the judiciary, the least democratic branch of the national government.

Reformers, principally Federalists, had sought these changes for years. President Washington's first attorney general, Edmund Randolph, had called on Congress to convert the district judges to circuit court judges, thereby allowing the Supreme Court to meet only in the capital. The justices themselves regularly had requested the changes as well, both to shed their hated circuit-riding and to avoid sitting in review of their own decisions. Supporters of the new law justified a reduction in the number of justices from six to five as a way of ensuring that the Court had no tie votes. But the theoretical possibility of a tie had never been a problem. Republicans believed the reduction was nothing more than an obvious gambit to deny the new president a Supreme Court appointment when the next vacancy occurred.

As a congressman, John Marshall had worked for federal judiciary reform, and he supported the new Judiciary Act enthusiastically. When the bill passed Congress, he praised its "separation of the Judges of the supreme from those of the circuit courts, and the establishment of the latter on a system capable of an extension commensurate with the necessities of the nation."

The bill created six new federal courts of appeals, from Vermont to Tennessee, with sixteen appellate judgeships. The number of federal judges throughout the young country thus would soar. Adams signed the Judiciary Act into law on Friday, February 13, just a few days before the House finally selected Jefferson on the thirty-fifth ballot the following Tuesday, February 17.

Partisanship framed the new law. The bill passed over unanimous Republican opposition in both the Senate and the House of Representatives: the House by a 51–43 vote on January 27, with a few Federalists joining all Republicans in opposition, and the Senate by a 16–11 straight party-line vote on February 11. As vice president and presiding officer of the Senate, Jefferson had to sign the Act and attest to its passage by the Senate. He did so with visible displeasure.

Federalists and Republicans alike saw great political significance in the Act.

Senator Gouverneur Morris of New York, a Federalist leader, confided that, although he thought the judiciary bill had merit, it would be an obvious vehicle for partisan goals. The bill would bring justice "near to men's doors," Morris proclaimed to a friend. "Depend on it that, in some parts of this Union, *justice* cannot readily be obtained in the State courts." At the same time, he acknowledged that "the leaders of the federal party may use this opportunity to provide for friends and adherents," adding that "if they were my enemies I should not condemn them for it. . . . They are about to experience a heavy gale of adverse wind. Can they be blamed for casting many anchors to hold their ship through the storm?" Federalist Senator William Bingham of Pennsylvania explained the bill's urgency: "[T]he Federal Party wish the appointments to be made under the present administration. . . . [T]he Importance of filling these Seats with federal characters must be obvious." Senator Dwight Foster of Massachusetts noted approvingly that, if the Act "now passes, Mr. Adams will have the nomination of the Judges to be appointed."

Republicans, meanwhile, were outraged. Virginia Congressman John Randolph mocked Adams for making the judiciary a "hospital for decayed politicians." The *Aurora*, the leading Republican newspaper, criticized the new legislation as "one of the most expensive and extravagant, the most insidious and unnecessary schemes that has been conceived by the Federal party." Virginia Senator George Mason complained that the Judiciary Act had been "crammed down our throats without a word or letter being suffered to be altered." Jefferson had confided to Madison that the Judiciary Act worried him greatly because of the permanence of the appointments. "I dread this above all the measures meditated," wrote the president-elect, "because appointments in the nature of freehold render it difficult to undo what is done."

Adams began filling the new federal judgeships on February 18, the day after Jefferson's selection by the House, and continued filling them for the next week, through February 24. Despite his rifts with his own party, Adams reached out to well-known Federalist colleagues and prominent figures. Adams even nominated his former secretary of the Treasury, Oliver Wolcott of Connecticut, with whom he had feuded and who had been forced to resign in December amid allegations of financial improprieties, for an appellate post on the new Second Circuit. John Marshall played a central role in this peace-making between the former allies. "I will allow myself to hope," he wrote Wolcott, "that this high & public evidence given by the President of his respect for your services & character will efface every unpleasant sensation respecting the past & smooth the way to a perfect reconciliation." Wolcott gratefully accepted.

Adams similarly sought to nominate his loyal and reliable attorney general, Charles Lee, to be chief judge of the new Fourth Circuit. Lee declined, eager to return full-time to his legal practice and perhaps leery of the fight that loomed over the new judgeships.

The most controversial judicial nomination, and the one to generate the most significant recorded opposition in the Senate, was that of Philip Barton Key, a prominent Maryland Federalist whose nephew Francis Scott Key would pen the national anthem thirteen years later. Key's nomination revived the accusations that Adams was an Anglophile determined to force a quasi-monarchical authority on the states. Key had been a Loyalist during the Revolution and actually had fought for the crown against the Revolutionaries as a captain in the Maryland Loyalists Batallion. He and his battalion were captured by the Spanish in Florida. He was imprisoned in Havana, Cuba, for a month before being paroled. Key had decamped to England after the Revolution, eventually returning to Maryland and redeeming himself as a prosperous landowner and active Federalist. He recently had lost his bid to be reelected to the state legislature, but Adams found him a place on the Fourth Circuit. Republicans in the Senate were outraged and sought to block his appointment. Even though nine Republican senators voted against him, Key was confirmed.

Adams's other appointments to the new federal judgeships were men of substance and significant professional standing. Political considerations, however, were never far from his mind. One letter of entreaty to Adams stated that he should appoint "Men of legal Abilities, Friends to Govt. & good Order & of unstained moral Character, & *Enemies to the fatal Philosophy of the Day*" [emphasis added]. Still brooding over his defeat, Adams readily agreed, with a pointed political reference: "The character of an enemy to 'the fatal philosophy of the day' has great weight with me, although it appears to have none with our nation."

Adams elevated six district court judges to appellate posts, which then created additional openings at the district court level. Adams filled the six vacancies at the district court level with three Federalist senators and one Federalist member of the House of Representatives, but he was constitutionally barred from appointing congressmen to the new appellate judgeships—a fact that had given Jefferson a modicum of solace.

At the same time, for the most part, Adams eschewed the extreme wing of the Federalist Party, which had given him so much trouble as president and had vexed him as a candidate. Not surprisingly, his Federalist appointees tended to be those with whom he had been on better terms than the extremists in his party.

Adams's Republican opponents objected to what they saw as the clear political hue of his appointments. After the president had completed his busy first week of judgeship nominations, the *National Intelligencer*, Washington's leading Republican newspaper, observed on February 25 that "in all these instances [Adams] named men opposed in political opinion to the national will, as unequivocally declared by his removal and the appointment of a successor of different sentiments." The Philadelphia *Aurora* claimed that Federalist Congressman Robert Goodloe Harper had boasted that the Judiciary Act "is as good to the party as an election," and that Federalist Harry Lee had said that the Act was "the only resource [for] which the government would have to secure strength since the standing army could not be retained."

Whatever the merits of the new judges, Federalists unquestionably viewed these appointments at least in part in political terms. One senator wrote to Marshall advocating a talented young lawyer with decidedly Federalist beliefs: "If you can conceive that political opinions often have an influence in decisions upon private rights, you will readily perceive the importance of placing in the Circuit Courts a man well attached to the federal government, by way of counterpoise [to the Republicans] . . . and a friend to the government." He got the appointment.

Jefferson and Madison were appalled by Adams's actions. On February 18, the day after his election by the House as president, and a busy day for Adams on the appointments front, Jefferson wrote Madison that "Mr. A. embarrasses us." Jefferson well knew the hazards of sending confidential messages through the U.S. mail carried by nosy Federalist postmasters, but he could not contain himself. As he told Madison, "Notwithstanding the suspected infidelity of the post, I must hazard this communication." Madison likewise expressed his dismay about the last-minute appointments to Governor James Monroe of Virginia. "The conduct of Mr. A is not such as was to have been wished or perhaps expected," sighed Madison. "Instead of smoothing the path for his successor, he plays into the hands of those who are endeavoring to strew it with as many difficulties as possible and with this view does not manifest a very squeamish regard to the Constn." Madison, in turn, asked James Monroe about whether some of the appointments could be challenged as "null."

Family connections also played a role in Adams's midnight appointments. The new U.S. district attorney in New Hampshire was the son of New Hampshire's Senator Samuel Livermore. Two of John Marshall's brothers-in-law received federal appellate judgeships—William McClung on the Sixth Circuit and Keith Taylor on the Fourth Circuit. A Third Circuit judgeship was offered to the governor of Delaware, Richard Bassett, who happened to be the father-in-law of James Bayard of Delaware, the prominent Federalist congressman who resolved the electoral deadlock for president. "2,000 dollars are better than anything Delaware can give you," Congressman Bayard exclaimed to his father-in-law, "and not an unpleasant provision for life." Bassett quickly agreed and accepted the nomination. But other nominees were less impressed by the salary. The $2,000 salary "will not support ... my family," complained Theophilus Parsons of Massachusetts in declining a First Circuit appointment. The pay "would not maintain my family," agreed Jared Ingersoll of Pennsylvania in rejecting a Third Circuit appointment.

By February 24, one week after the selection of Jefferson, Adams had made most of his appointments under the new Judiciary Act. Now, however, with very little time remaining for Adams's presidency, Congress passed still another bill giving him a bevy of new federal appointments. The Act Concerning the District of Columbia was enacted by the Senate on February 5 and the House on February 24, and became law on Friday, February 27, 1801.

The District of Columbia Act established three new appellate judges and a wide range of offices for the new District, which now would be separated into two counties—Washington County for the eastern side of the Potomac, including Georgetown, and Alexandria County for the western side of the Potomac, including Alexandria. Adams, and his trusted lieutenant, John Marshall, now had just a few days, until Wednesday, March 4, to nominate dozens of people for local District posts, get them confirmed by the Senate, and deliver commissions to them before the government changed hands and Jefferson was inaugurated.

Once again, Adams and Marshall readily turned to family for appointments. For one of the District of Columbia judgeships, Adams nominated William Cranch, his nephew. Cranch was born in Braintree, Massachusetts, not far from the farm of his aunt and uncle. He graduated from Harvard College where he was a classmate of his cousin, the future president, John Quincy Adams. After graduation, he moved to Washington, D.C., as the agent for a real estate investment firm that was making a large gamble on land prices in and around the new capital. The investments proved disastrous. Cranch lost money, but his career was rescued when his uncle, now the president, appointed him to be commissioner for public buildings for the District of Colombia—a pure patronage job.

For another District of Columbia judgeship, President Adams nominated Marshall's brother, James Marshall. The younger Marshall had been born in Virginia and served in the First Virginia Artillery during the Revolutionary War. Afterward, he followed his family to Kentucky where he entered politics, ultimately losing a race for Congress. In 1795 he married Hester Morris, one of the richest heiresses in America, and over time he became one of the largest landholders in Virginia, acquiring over 180,000 acres.

For the third post, the chief judge position, Adams nominated the only nonfamily member—former Supreme Court Justice Thomas Johnson, who had resigned from that post in 1793 because of health problems. But Johnson declined a few days later—a refusal that left a vacancy for Jefferson and that pained John Marshall deeply for his lapse as a counselor on nominations. A couple of weeks later, he confided to his brother James, "I am excessively mortified at the circumstances relative to the appointment of the Chief Judge of the district. There was a negligence in that business arising from a confidence that Mr. Johnston [*sic*] would accept, which I lament excessively."

Job-seekers and their patrons again deluged Marshall with letters, this time about the new local District of Columbia positions. A Maryland judge implored Marshall to accept his recommendation for U.S. marshal for the District of Columbia. Virginia representatives sent Marshall their recommendations for chief judge, U.S. attorney, and register of wills. With every passing day, the letters kept coming.

With the new District of Columbia Act becoming law on Friday, February 27, Adams and Marshall had only the weekend to sift through the options, make decisions, and get nominations to the Senate on Monday for confirmation and delivery of commissions on Tuesday, before Jefferson's inauguration on Wednesday, March 4.

Among the new positions were dozens of justice-of-the-peace posts. The bill allowed the president to appoint "such number of discreet persons to be justices of the peace, as the President of the United States shall from time to time think expedient, to continue in the office for five years." A justice of the peace had broad authority for peace-keeping, including resolving minor violations up to twenty dollars in value. The job was far from lucrative—rather than by a salary, the justice of the peace was compensated by a percentage of the fines that he meted out. But it was viewed as a significant political launching pad, combining legislative, executive, and judicial powers, and as a prestigious perch for community leaders. Thomas Jefferson and many other prominent politicians had served as justices of the peace.

Adams appointed many prominent Federalists to be justices of the peace. The appointees in Washington County included Secretary of the Navy Benjamin Stoddert, two former mayors of Georgetown (Uriah Forrest and John Threlkheld), and a former Maryland state representative (William Hammond Dorsey); those in Alexandria County included two former mayors of Alexandria, Robert Townshend Hooe and Dennis Ramsay. The appointments also included lesser-known figures, such as political insider William Marbury (referred to as "Marberry" in the presidential nominating papers) in Washington County and William Harper in Alexandria County.

Not all of Adams's justice-of-the-peace appointments were Federalists. In Washington County, Adams appointed Republicans to be six of the twenty-three. Five were incumbent justices of the peace, and the sixth was William Thornton, architect of the Capitol, which remained under construction. In Alexandria County, five of the nineteen were Republicans.

On Monday, March 2, after what must have been a feverish weekend for Adams and Marshall, the president submitted the nominations for forty-two justices of the peace, as well as local notaries public, registers of wills, judges of orphans courts for each county, and other positions. The Senate considered and confirmed them throughout the day on March 2 and on into the day and evening of March 3, the eve of Jefferson's inauguration. Adams worked in the President's House until well into the night on Tuesday, March 3, signing commissions and sending them on to the State Department and to Secretary of State Marshall for finalizing and transmitting.

The State Department, meanwhile, was in a state of chaos. Marshall had loaned one of his two clerks to Jefferson, at Jefferson's request, to help him prepare for the presidency. Marshall was responsible for countersigning the commissions and having them delivered. He prevailed on his brother James, himself a new judicial appointee, to deliver the commissions. James signed for a batch, found that he could not carry the dozen or so documents all at once, so he returned some and crossed them off his list. John Marshall noticed that some commissions remained undelivered, but, in the frenzy of the moment, he thought little of it. As he explained to James later, "I did not send out the commissions because I apprehended such as were for a fixd time to be completed when signd & Sealed. . . . [T]o withhold the commissions of the Justices is an act of which I entertained no suspicion. I should however have sent out the commissions which had been signed & seald but for the extreme hurry of the time & the absence of Mr. Wagner [the State Department clerk] who had been called on by the President to act as his private Secretary."

Among the commissions that went undelivered were those for William Marbury as justice of the peace in Washington County, and Robert Townsend Hooe, William Harper, and Dennis Ramsay as justices of the peace in Alexandria County. The commissions would remain on a table in the State Department for the next two days until an unlikely visitor discovered them.

PRESIDENT JEFFERSON

John Adams stepped into the carriage and looked back one last time at the President's House, illuminated from the inside by candlelight and from the outside by a quarter moon under a clear, cold sky. It was four o'clock in the morning on Inauguration Day, March 4, 1801, but Adams had decided to forgo the ceremony to gain an early start for the long ride to his home in Massachusetts. He traveled by public coach, accompanied by two loyal aides, Billy Shaw and John Briesler. As the first president to be voted out of office, Adams apparently could not bear to witness the ascension of his successor.

Three hours later, as the first light of the day streamed through his window, the president-elect awoke in his rented room at the Conrad and McMunn boardinghouse across from the Capitol. At home in Monticello, Jefferson typically ate his breakfast—bread or corn cakes with cold ham—at around eight o'clock, and he probably did so on this day. Breakfast was served in the dining room with the other boarders, who sat at a long communal table. The most coveted seat was near the fireplace, but according to his friend Margaret Bayard Smith, Jefferson had "occupied during the whole winter the lowest and coldest seat" and on inauguration day "no other seat was offered to him." After breakfast, he may have made some last-minute revisions to the third draft of the inaugural speech that he had been working on for the last two weeks, perhaps while soaking his feet in icy cold water, a ritual that he believed had medicinal value.

On the other side of the Capitol, Chief Justice John Marshall sat at the desk in his rented room at the Washington City Hotel. Marshall, who had moved out of the President's House when John and Abigail Adams moved in, had a simple room with his most notable possession: a footlocker of documents and letters that Martha Washington had given him when she learned in December that he had undertaken to write a biography of the first president. But on this day Marshall began a letter to his friend, the failed Federalist vice presidential candidate, Charles Cotesworth Pinckney. Marshall, who had already been informed of President Adams's departure, wrote: "Today the new political year commences. The new order of things begins. . . . I wish however more than I hope that the public prosperity and happiness may sustain no diminution under democratic guidance." Marshall was not optimistic: "The democrats are divided into speculative theorists and absolute terrorists. With the latter I am not disposed to classify Mr. Jefferson. . . . [If Jefferson goes with the terrorists] it is not difficult to foresee that much calamity is in store for our country—if he does not they will soon become his enemies and calumniators." At this point, Marshall paused and put down his pen. It was time for him to leave for the Capitol.

———

IN 1797, THOMAS JEFFERSON had seriously considered skipping his own swearing-in as vice president because he felt the ceremony too closely resembled the coronation of European royalty, which he viewed as anathema to American democracy. As the president-elect, he gave a great deal of thought to the kind of ceremony that he wanted for himself on March 4, 1801. He had written to Chief Justice Marshall two days earlier to ask if he would accept a temporary reappointment as secretary of state until his successor was in place. More important, in his letter to Marshall, Jefferson asked his cousin to administer the oath of office of the presidency. He also asked the chief justice whether "the oath prescribed in the Constitution be not the only one necessary to take." Congress required that all Federal officers recite a much longer oath than that required for the presidency by the Constitution. After receiving the letter, Marshall had replied on the same day: "I shall with much pleasure attend to administer the oath of office . . . and shall make a point of being punctual." Marshall also informed his cousin that State Department records "furnish no information respecting the oaths which have been heretofore taken. That prescribed in the Constitution seems to me to be the only one which is [appropriate]."

In planning the ceremony, Jefferson studied the inaugurations of George Washington and John Adams. Washington had ridden to his first ceremony in a grand carriage pulled by six white horses. Clad in his military uniform with a sword strapped to his side, he had cut a regal figure. Adams had decided on "a simple but elegant enough" carriage drawn by just two horses. Vowing to be "a republican President in earnest," he had worn a suit of gray broadcloth and a cockaded hat, and he, too, had carried a sword at his side. Jefferson decided that he would differentiate himself from his predecessors; he wanted to send a signal to the American people that his administration would live up to the democratic ideals on which the nation had been founded. Jefferson wore a plain suit with no sword and no powdered wig or hat to cover his reddish, graying hair. Instead of riding in a carriage, he had decided to walk to the Capitol.

At just before eleven o'clock, he emerged from his boardinghouse and was cheered by a number of Republican congressmen and senators who had gathered to accompany him to the Senate chamber. Leading the procession for the short walk to the Capitol was the Alexandria militia and several U.S. marshals. It was a clear and mild day in Washington. Spring was in the air as the temperature hovered in the mid-fifties.

Conrad and McMunn's was located on the south side of Capitol Hill and the parade could not have lasted more than fifteen minutes—along unpaved streets, up a hill, past a wooden fence that encircled the Capitol, and to the building's entrance from which the president-elect was then escorted to the Senate chamber. Jefferson entered the chamber to thunderous applause from the Republicans and polite clapping on the part of the Federalists. He was led to the dais, where Aaron Burr and John Marshall were already seated. The two men stood to greet him and after perfunctory handshakes, Jefferson sat between them. Burr, who had tried to snatch the presidency from him, sat at his right; and Marshall, the cousin who openly disdained him, at his left.

As the room quieted, Vice President Burr, who had been sworn in earlier that day, rose to introduce the new president to the nearly 1,000 people who filled the Senate chamber. Jefferson was not an especially accomplished public speaker and he began his address in a nervous, "almost femininely soft" voice. People in the rear of the chamber leaned forward to hear him, but his tremulous voice did not carry beyond the first few rows. While he may have lacked oratorical skills, Thomas Jefferson was a masterful writer who understood the power of language, and his address on that day was an eloquent call for national healing and reconciliation. Jefferson had arranged for copies of his address to be printed. As many inside the hall read the speech they could not hear, the new president sounded a note of hope that, notwithstanding the political divisions within the country, so bitterly apparent during the recent election, all Americans would "arrange themselves under the will of the law and unite in common efforts for the common good." Jefferson appealed to a broad nationalism when he said, "We are all republicans, we are all federalists." He was referring not to political parties per se but, rather, to the principle that undergirds the particular form of American democracy—a commitment to the union and to republican government, which Jefferson called the "world's best hope."

Jefferson went on to address many broad themes that Americans, whatever their political affiliation, would probably have agreed with. Although he had been pilloried as a Francophile during the campaign, Jefferson now declared that he sought "peace, commerce, and honest friendship with all nations—entangling alliances with none."

Jefferson then laid out what he "deem[ed] the essential principles of our Government," declaring his support for "state governments in all the rights, as the most competent administration of our domestic concerns and the surest bulwarks against antirepublican tendencies; the preservation of the General Government in its whole constitutional vigor, as the sheet anchor of our peace at home and safety abroad."

He also paid tribute to George Washington, hailing him as "entitled . . . to the first place in his country's love and destined . . . for the fairest page in the volume of faithful history."

The new president never made any specific reference to the judiciary. Instead, he only briefly mentioned his support for "trials by juries impartially selected." This is somewhat surprising given that, years earlier, he had written his friend James Madison about the Bill of Rights, noting the importance of putting "the legal check . . . into the hands of the judiciary." As he then had prophesized, the judiciary "if rendered independent and kept strictly to their own department, merits great confidence for their learning and integrity." Since that remark, however, Jefferson had seen the federal judiciary enforce the Alien and Sedition Acts and generally become identified in his mind with antidemocratic Federalists.

Rather than mention the judiciary in his inaugural address, Jefferson reached out to the "gentlemen, who are charged with the sovereign functions of legislation," in whom he would "find resources of wisdom, of virtue, and of zeal on which to rely under all difficulties." Since the House and the Senate were now controlled by Republicans, Jefferson's words were warmly received. But not everyone was impressed by the speech. Gouverneur Morris noted in his diary that it was "too long by half and so he will find himself before he is three years older." The speech had taken less than thirty minutes to deliver, but Morris, portly and impatient, may have been reacting to the fact that the room was overcrowded, hot, and uncomfortable.

Morris's complaint notwithstanding, when Jefferson concluded he was greeted with enthusiastic applause. Chief Justice Marshall then stood and held the Bible that Jefferson had designated for the occasion. After Marshall administered the presidential oath, Jefferson left the chamber and the Senate adjourned until the following day.

After the ceremony, Marshall returned to his hotel, where he finished his letter to Pinckney, adopting a far more optimistic tone than the one he'd used that morning when he had begun it. The chief justice considered Jefferson's address "in general well judged and conciliatory. It is in direct terms giving the lie to the direct party declamation which has elected him: but it is strongly characteristic of the general cast of his political theory."

———

PRESIDENT JEFFERSON did not occupy the President's House for another few weeks, but well before his inauguration he had been making plans both for his new residence and for the government that he would head. Jefferson needed a personal and professional staff. He asked Meriwether Lewis, a young army officer from Virginia and a family friend, to serve as personal aide. On advice from his friends in the foreign diplomatic corps, Jefferson hired a French chef and a French steward. Next, he made arrangements to obtain "a handsome chariot for both city and country use."

He also engaged in a great deal of correspondence—personally replying to the dozens of congratulatory letters, writing to old acquaintances in France (he entrusted the letters to fellow Virginian

John Dickinson, who was travelling to Paris), and forwarding to former President Adams a stack of letters that had arrived after his departure from Washington. Just before his term expired, Congress adopted a law giving free postal service for all mail to Adams in his new role as a private citizen—"all letters and packets to John Adams, now President of the United States, after the expiration of his term of office, shall be carried by mail, free of postage." Adams, who was both a prolific correspondent and a parsimonious yankee, welcomed the perquisite. Adams replied to Jefferson on March 24 that he was in a "state of tranquility" in Massachusetts and he wished Jefferson "a quiet and prosperous administration."

Over the course of the next several weeks, President Jefferson began to fill out his cabinet, notably appointing his close friend and confidante, fellow Virginian James Madison as secretary of state, Albert Gallatin as secretary of the treasury, and Levi Lincoln as attorney general. The appointments were well received, especially by Republicans such as Congressman John Fowler of Kentucky, who, in a letter to his constituents, described his "unspeakable satisfaction and universal confidence in the talents and integrity of the new administration."

Unlike President Adams, who felt compelled to hold over many of President Washington's cabinet members, Jefferson had the freedom to appoint an entirely new government. Despite the fact that he hailed from Federalist Massachusetts, Levi Lincoln was a loyal Republican who had served several terms in the state house of representatives and in the state senate before being elected to the U.S. Congress. Harvard-educated, he was also a fine lawyer who was involved in some of the most important legal cases in the history of the state, notably *The Commonwealth v. Nathaniel Jenison*, dealing with the claimed right to own a slave in clear opposition to the state's Bill of Rights. Lincoln successfully argued against the legality of slavery in Massachusetts. Jefferson thought highly of Lincoln and not only appointed him attorney general but asked him to assume the duties of acting secretary of state—replacing Chief Justice John Marshall—until James Madison arrived in Washington.

While he maintained a low profile as secretary of state, James Madison was President Jefferson's closest adviser during his presidency. Jefferson once remarked, "I can say conscientiously that I do not know in the world a man of purer integrity, more dispassionate, disinterested . . . nor could I in the whole scope of America or Europe point out an abler head."

Born in 1751 in Port Conway, Virginia, Madison graduated from Princeton College, completing a four-year course in just two years. Like many of his contemporaries, he studied law and subsequently entered politics, winning a seat in the Virginia House of Delegates while still in his mid–20s. Madison lost his bid for reelection when he refused to set up barrels of whiskey at polling places, insisting instead that he would win because voters preferred his views on the issues. But state leaders thought so highly of Madison that they immediately arranged for his appointment to the Governor's Council, a nonelective body with significant influence.

Five feet four inches tall and weighing only 100 pounds, he did not cut an imposing figure. Moreover, he was painfully shy. Yet Madison had a disarming quality about him that undermined his opponents, calmed his competitors, and enthralled his admirers, including, to the surprise of many, at least one charismatic member of the opposite sex. His wife, Dolley Madison, was buxom, vivacious, and smart; she was a 26-year-old widow when she met and quickly married the slight, pale congressman who was seventeen years older than her.

Madison was unfailingly polite and gentle, but also demonstrably brilliant. He had a significant hand in many of the fundamental decisions that shaped the new republic. He played an important role in drafting the Constitution, earning him the title "Father of the Constitution", and made a major contribution to its adoption by collaborating with Alexander Hamilton and John Jay to write the Federalist essays. He and Hamilton became close friends, but subsequently had a falling-out over political and policy differences when Hamilton became secretary of the treasury.

Madison served eight years in Congress and helped frame the Bill of Rights. Working with Thomas Jefferson, the two Virginians organized the Republican Party in response to the Federalists and in 1798, secretly co-authored the Kentucky and Virginia Resolutions to protest the Alien and Sedition laws. Madison and Jefferson were not only colleagues, they were close friends and enjoyed spending time together. Jefferson often loaned books to Madison.

Madison did not attend the inauguration of Thomas Jefferson: His father, who had lingered near death for several weeks, died days before the ceremony, and it was several more weeks before Madison assumed his duties as Jefferson's secretary of state. When Madison finally did return to the nation's capital, Jefferson invited him and Dolley to live in the President's House. With only Meriwether Lewis occupying the East Room of the large house, Jefferson may have been lonely: He wrote his daughter that he and Lewis were "like two mice in a church." The Madisons moved into the grand residence for several months and Dolley often acted as hostess at afternoon teas and dinners.

With the naming of Jefferson's cabinet, the "quiet revolution" was nearly complete. In his Farewell Address in 1796, President Washington had warned "in the most solemn manner against the baleful effects of the spirit of party." But political parties representing divergent political philosophies had taken root in America, and notwithstanding Washington's foreboding, the leadership of government had changed hands democratically and peacefully. Both the Legislative and Executive branches of the government were now in the control of the Republican Party. The judiciary, the weakest branch of government, remained the last bastion of Federalist power.

THE BATTLE LINES
ARE DRAWN

Although his inaugural address had sounded a note of national reconciliation and healing, President Jefferson privately contemplated an agenda to put the government onto solid Republican footing. Just three days after his eloquent speech in the Capitol, he wrote to fellow Virginian James Monroe that he viewed the Federalists as "incurable" and that he would never "turn an inch out of my way to reconcile."

Jefferson was adamant that his administration eliminate all vestiges of monarchical and aristocratic rule that had characterized the Federalists; in its place would flourish the kind of agrarian-based democracy that he had long envisioned. Alexander Hamilton had sought to centralize and augment the power of government; Jefferson, for his part, now was determined to return power to the states and their citizens. He abhorred a national debt, opposed a standing army and navy, and felt strongly that the judiciary, largely controlled by the Federalists, was in need of serious reform.

The day after his inauguration, President Jefferson decided to pay a visit to the Department of State. In the spring of 1801, the Department, with its nine employees, was located near the President's House in a rented, small, two-story, clapboard house; later that summer the Department would be relocated to the Treasury Department Building. The reason for President Jefferson's visit is nowhere recorded but perhaps he was already contemplating the Department's move.

Thomas Jefferson had served as secretary of state under President Washington from 1790 until 1793. As secretary, Jefferson had been the nation's chief diplomat although President Washington in practice set the agenda for international relations. Jefferson knew from experience that the secretary of state had many other duties besides overseeing the foreign policy of the country: running the post office, printing and disbursing government documents, supervising the mint, overseeing the patent office for inventions, and "establishing federal standards for coinage, weights and measures."

While he was in the State Department that day, President Jefferson noticed on a table a sheaf of documents with the seal of the United States. Upon closer inspection, Jefferson discovered that they were commissions for federal justices of the peace that had been signed by President Adams on the evening of March 3, his last night as president. Jefferson responded with alacrity. "I forbade their delivery," Jefferson wrote many years later to Justice William Johnson, offering a tightly reasoned, legalistic explanation: "[I]f there is any principle of law never yet contradicted, it is that delivery is one of the essentials to validity of the deed. Although signed and sealed, yet as long as it remains in the hands of the party himself, it is in fieri [incomplete], it is not a deed and can be made so only by its delivery."

Jefferson, of course, could have made sure that the commissions were delivered, but he was extremely angry with Adams, who he claimed was guilty of knowingly "crowd[ing] nominations after he knew they were not for him." Jefferson characterized the former president's actions in a letter to his friend, Revolutionary War hero and statesman John Dickinson, as "indecent conduct." And in a letter to Abigail Adams in 1804, Jefferson stated, "I can say with truth that one act of Mr. Adams' life, and only one, ever gave me a moment's personal displeasure. I did consider his last appointments to office as personally unkind. . . . It seemed but common justice to leave a successor free to act by instruments of his own choice."

After discovering the commissions and deciding to withhold them, Jefferson seemed conflicted as to what to do next. Although he objected to all of the appointments that Adams had made after losing the presidency, he differentiated between attorneys and marshals, who served at the pleasure of the president, and judges, who had lifetime appointments. He claimed that "the only shield for Republican citizens against the federalism of the courts is to have the attornies and marshals removed."

But Jefferson ultimately backed off a wholesale purge of Federalist office holders, whether they were lifetime appointments or serving at the pleasure of the president, because "[g]ood men, to whom there is not objection, but a difference of related principles, are not proper subjects of removal." In a letter to Thomas Randolph, his son-in-law, he noted that "a few removals from office will be indispensable . . . chiefly for malconduct, and mostly in the offices connected with the administration of justice."

Turning to the new appointments for the District of Colombia, Jefferson decided to limit the number of local justices-of-the-peace to thirty, instead of the forty whom Adams had proposed. And of the thirty, the president actually allowed many of the men—and they were all men—who had been chosen by his predecessor to stay in office.

After hearing of Jefferson's plans, William Cranch and James Marshall, two of the recently appointed "midnight judges," made it clear that they would not be intimidated by President Jefferson. Within months of their appointments, during the very first session of the Washington City Circuit Court, Cranch and Marshall recommended that the district attorney for Washington City file charges for sedition against the editor of the *National Intelligencer*, the most prominent Republican newspaper in the country, because the paper had published a letter attacking the judiciary for being politically motivated and biased. In demanding prosecution, Judge Marshall decried the "licentiousness of the press." Because the Sedition Act had expired, the judges urged use of "common law" principles.

Federalist judges such as Marshall and Cranch were undoubtedly aware that, only four days after taking office, President Jefferson ordered all fines under the Sedition Act refunded. A month later, he pardoned two men who had been convicted under the Act, including the firebrand publisher James T. Callender. He also excused William Duane, the editor of the *Aurora* newspaper, from his impending trial for seditious activity. Cranch and Marshall may have been testing the new Republican administration, but in the end they should not have been surprised that their recommendation was ignored.

As for the judges whom Adams had appointed on the eve of his departure, President Jefferson did not make public pronouncements on the subject, but boldly stated his views in letters to friends and colleagues. In a letter to John Dickinson, Jefferson warned that the Federalist use of the judiciary would cause "republicanism to be beaten and erased by a federalist club of judges. . . . [T]hey have multiple judges reserved to strengthen their phalanx." In a letter to Archibald Staunton, Jefferson stated unequivocally that the appointments would stand "until the law [creating the new judgeships] is repealed, which we trust will be in the next Congress." Nonetheless some Republicans were highly critical of Jefferson, believing the president was moving too timidly to assert Republican control over the judiciary: Congressman William Branch Giles of Virginia, who, ironically, had been introduced to politics a decade earlier by John Marshall, wrote Jefferson that "the revolution is corrupted so long as the judiciary is in possession of the enemy." Giles called for "the repeal of the whole judicial system, terminating the present offices and creating an entirely new system." The *New York Citizen*, a leading Republican newspaper, echoed a similar frustration with the new president: "It is rational to suppose that those who removed John Adams from office would naturally expect the removal of the lesser culprits in office. If this should not be the case, for what, in the name of God, have we been contending? Merely for the removal of John Adams that Mr. Jefferson might occupy the place which he shamefully left."

———

THE PRESIDENT'S PUSH for judicial reform was sidetracked when, a few months after taking office, he faced his first international challenge. Pasha Yusuf Karamanli, the ruler of Tripoli, one of the states of north Africa, declared war on the United States. After Barbary pirates attacked American merchant ships in the Mediterranean, President Jefferson convened his cabinet—the first time he had done so—to plot a course of action. But when Jefferson proposed a declaration of war there was immediate dissent from his attorney general, Levi Lincoln. According to Lincoln, the president unquestionably had the ability to call out the military to defend U.S. interests, but only Congress could declare war and Congress was not in session. In the end, Lincoln was outvoted by the other members of the cabinet, including Secretary of State James Madison, who had just arrived in Washington from his home at Montpelier. The issue of who in the government could declare war was temporarily set aside when President Jefferson ordered a squadron of American warships in Norfolk, Virginia, to sail to the Mediterranean.

Other international challenges loomed as well. Jefferson, who had lived in France and had generally been supportive of that nation's Revolution, was increasingly alarmed by the actions of Napoleon Bonaparte, the French leader who was exhibiting a seemingly endless appetite for expansion and power. Jefferson was particularly concerned to learn that Spain was secretly negotiating with France to cede the Louisiana Territory. Jefferson feared that Napoleon might seek to control commerce on the

Mississippi River and ultimately might have designs on the rest of the continent.

On Friday, August 7, 1801, the *National Intelligencer* reported on its front page news from the French colony of Santa Domingo that Alain Touissant had been appointed governor for life "by a convention of deputies of the blacks," and that he "regularly corresponds with Bonaparte."

The paper also reported, almost in passing, that three days earlier, the members of the Supreme Court had gathered for the August term at Conrad and McMunn's boardinghouse on Capitol Hill. The chief justice had been absent from Washington the entire spring and most of the summer; he had departed Washington two days after the inauguration for his home in Richmond, Virginia, where he had spent the last several months working on his biography of President Washington. Now back in Washington, he had arranged for all of the justices to stay together under one roof—without wives—for the session. Justice Alfred Moore of North Carolina arrived first, having sailed up the eastern seaboard to the Potomac River. Marshall had come from Richmond by horse, followed by Chase from Baltimore, Cushing from Massachusetts, and Paterson, who arrived last, from New Jersey—all by carriage.

With the justices housed under one roof, Chief Justice Marshall immediately set about cultivating an atmosphere of camaraderie and conviviality. Justice Story, who would join the Court in 1812, described how Marshall conducted business: "[W]e take our dinner together, and discuss at the table the questions which are argued before us. We are great ascetics, and even deny ourselves wine, except in wet weather." But, as Story explained, Marshall liked to ask him "'to step to the window and see if it does not look like rain ... and if I tell him that the sun is brightly shining,' Judge Marshall will reply, 'All the better, our jurisdiction extends over so large a territory that the doctrine of chances makes it certain that it must be raining somewhere.'" Story summed up Marshall as "brought up on Federalism and Madeira, and he was not a man to outgrow his early prejudices."

During the August session, the justices assembled each day in the committee room on the lower level of the Capitol. Although the Court was sparsely attended, changes were apparent to anyone who bothered to take note: The justices were meeting in a designated if small room in the Capitol, and most startling of all, the associate justices had abandoned their academic robes in favor of the black robes worn by the chief justice. This was an especially radical departure for Justice Cushing, who previously had emulated British judges by wearing colorful ermine robes and even donning a white powdered judge's wig for the first meeting of the Supreme Court in 1790.

The Court heard only one case that August: *Talbot v. Seeman*. As it turned out, *Talbot* was an important case, not only for its substance but for what it presaged about the operations of the Marshall Court. The case involved the seizure of a French merchant ship by an American frigate on the high seas. The *Constitution*, captained by Silas Talbot, captured the *Amelia*, a ship once owned by a Hamburg merchant, Hans Seeman, that in turn had been captured by the French and refitted with armaments. Since the United States was involved at that time in a low-grade naval conflict—often referred to as the "quasi-war"—with France, Captain Talbot claimed a right of salvage, or payment equal to half the value of the ship's contents, in order to turn the ship back over to its original owner, the Hamburg merchant. The case was politically explosive not only because of the ramifications for relations between France and the United States but also because of its political symbolism at home. Captain Talbot had won his claim in Federal District Court but the decision was overturned on appeal in the circuit court, where the case had been argued by old foes: Alexander Hamilton representing Captain Talbot and Aaron Burr representing the Hamburg merchant. The case had become a classic struggle between Republicans and Federalists.

John Marshall and his five colleagues sat in heavy wooden chairs for four days and listened as Congressman James Bayard, representing Talbot, and Alexander Dallas, the former reporter of decisions for the Supreme Court in Philadelphia and lawyer for the Hamburg merchant, presented oral arguments. Bayard argued that a 1799 law allowed salvage if the ship had been taken from the enemy. Dallas claimed, however, that since the Hamburg owner was a neutral, no salvage should be paid. During the proceedings, Chief Justice Marshall asked numerous questions, while the other justices sat mostly in silence.

On August 8, the chief justice announced the "opinion of the Court": The *Constitution* had the right to attack and seize the *Amelia* because it was flying a French flag and the American captain did have a right to salvage. As Marshall put it, "We cannot presume this seizure to have been unacceptable to the Hamburger because it has bettered his condition." The merchant had the whole of his ship returned to him. And then Marshall grounded the Court's decision in contract law: "To give a right to salvage, it is said there must be a contract, either express or implied." Marshall concluded that the service of recapturing the boat signified an implied contract and therefore "the recapture is entitled to salvage." In other words, since Captain Talbot had performed the service of capturing the *Amelia*, he was entitled to something.

The decision foreshadowed Marshall's brilliance at balancing both the legal and the political equities of a case. He had clearly bolstered the Federalists by recognizing that the United States was involved in a quasi-war with France. But Republicans, as the party in power, had reason to cheer the decision as well: He made it clear that only Congress had the right to declare war. This was contrary to the position that John Adams had maintained during his presidency. Marshall also slashed the amount of Talbot's recovery from one half of the value of the ship to one sixth of its value. By awarding Talbot such a meager monetary salvage award, Marshall seemed to suggest that the Federalists had won only a symbolic victory.

The decision was greeted in the press with near universal acclaim. The *Aurora* praised Marshall for having considered "at length the arguments on each side," and the *National Intelligencer* called the decision "important" and reprinted the opinion in its entirety.

The case was important for another reason: It marked the first time that the Supreme Court had delivered an opinion representing the entire court. Previously it had issued individual decisions. The practice of announcing individual decisions meant that it was often difficult to discern whether the Court was actually united on any particular issue: Justices often emphasized different facts and used different rationales, even when they agreed. Marshall styled the innovation after the format used by Judge Edmund Pendleton in the Virginia Court of Appeals. Pendleton was a revered figure in Virginia legal circles and Marshall, as a young lawyer, greatly admired him. By issuing only one opinion—read by the Chief Justice—instead of independent, separate decisions, Marshall made the Court look united, strong and decisive. This was a conscious change by Marshall who must have also understood that from this point forward, the Supreme Court would take on an identity: it would come to be known as the "Marshall Court."

MARBURY FILES SUIT

In December 1801, the new capital prepared for its first Christmas under the Jefferson administration, the first "Christmass," as the local newspapers called it, under a Republican Congress. In fact, the new Republican Congress, the nation's seventh, was only now convening nearly one year after its election. Congress had adjourned the day of Jefferson's inauguration and representatives and senators had returned to their home districts and states.

An air of giddiness swept the city. Republicans and Federalists alike delighted in the details of the "Mammoth Cheese" sent to Jefferson for the holiday by "the republican ladies of Cheshire, Massachusetts," a gift in recognition of Jefferson's commitment to the separation of church and state. It weighed in at 1,235 pounds, more than a half-ton, and measured four feet four inches in diameter, with a thickness of one foot three inches. The Cheshire ladies had sent the Mammoth Cheese to Washington by sloop, and from Smith's wharf, it was hauled through the muddy streets by wagon to the President's House.

The leaders of the new Congress streamed into town. In the Senate, John Breckinridge of Kentucky would be Jefferson's Republican leader on the floor. Kentucky had been admitted to the union as the fifteenth state in 1792, and Breckinridge conducted himself with a frontier bluntness. In the 1790s, Breckinridge had worked closely with Jefferson and Madison on the Virginia and Kentucky Resolutions rejecting the validity of the Alien and Sedition Acts, and had sponsored the Kentucky Resolution in the state legislature.

For the Federalists, now in the minority, Senator Gouverneur Morris of New York would be in the thick of the action. Morris played a key role in drafting the Constitution—Richard Brookhiser has called him the "rake who wrote the Constitution." Morris was a bon vivant, a bachelor who loved to dine, drink fine wines, and seduce women despite his portly frame and wooden leg. He had served as ambassador to France during the French Revolution and during that time had carried on an affair with Adelaide Marie Emile, the beautiful and independent Comtesse de Flahut and much younger wife of the aged Count de Flahut. After returning to the United States, he was elected senator from New York in 1800. During most of his public life, he recorded his daily observations in a diary, interspersing accounts of the weather, Senate floor debates, meals, Madeira, and, most cryptically, hunches about whether women had "a good disposition"—whether he could bed them. During his time in Washington, he was particularly enamored of Dolley Madison, the enchanting and enormously attractive wife of Secretary of State James Madison. Morris often mentioned in his diary spending time with Dolley, and once noted that "Mrs. Maddison . . . has good dispositions which from the shrivelled condition of the secretary are the less to be wondered at."

In the House, the new Republican Speaker would be Nathaniel Macon of North Carolina. In the first official action of the Seventh Congress, on December 7, 1801, the House elected Macon Speaker over the Federalist candidate, James Bayard of Delaware, by a 53–26 vote (with 2 votes for another representative). Macon was a Jeffersonian fiercely committed to limiting the size and power of the federal government. He had passionately opposed ratification of the Constitution. Bayard, the Delaware congressman who had broken the presidential election logjam in February 1801, had emerged as the leader of the shrunken band of Federalists in the House.

Even in the midst of the holiday festivities and giddiness, raw enmity between the Republicans and the Federalists was never far from the surface. The Republicans were triumphant and exultant; the Federalists, bitter and apocalyptic.

For the Republicans, the dawn of a glorious new age had arrived. The Republican *National Intelligencer* hailed "the first sittings of the first truly Republican Congress." William Duane, editor of the Philadelphia-based *Aurora*, announced that he would move to Washington during the congressional debates so that he could report "with regularity and fidelity in the approaching important session."

But, for the Federalists, the opening of the new Congress was a time of dread and foreboding. "The present session of Congress will command more attention, and excite more anxiety," the *Washington Federalist* proclaimed, "than any preceding. A new scene opens. . . . [T]he winds become adverse, the tide shifts, the moon of democracy yields a dying light, the helmsman is drunk with power and passion."

From the Federalist perspective, everything about Jefferson was wrong, even his use of language, a popular target of ridicule in the pages of the *Washington Federalist*. The newspaper mocked him for describing "four pillars of prosperity" as "thriving," an inelegant metaphor that he included in his State of the Union address. No issue, however, enraged the Federalists more than Jefferson's removal from office of selected Federalist officials and his perceived interference with Adams's midnight judicial appointments. The subject dominated political conversation. Federalists claimed that Jefferson, acting on flimsy pretexts and what the *Federalist* called "a spirit of apparent revenge," had removed or blocked honest, hardworking officials for abject partisan reasons.

Jefferson differentiated somewhat between political and judicial appointments. With nonjudicial appointments, Jefferson occasionally took the view that any appointment made after Adams had lost the election was invalid and Jefferson exercised his power of removal. One celebrated example involved the Collector of the Port in New Haven, Connecticut. Adams had appointed Elizur Goodrich on February 19, 1801, less than two weeks before leaving office. Jefferson removed Goodrich and instead appointed Samuel Bishop, a 77-year-old patriarch of a leading local Republican family, a rare species in Federalist Connecticut. Seventy-eight "merchants of New Haven" sent Jefferson an angry, widely publicized "remonstrance" complaining about Bishop's appointment.

Jefferson issued a point-by-point reply to the merchants. He rejected their criticism of Bishop's age by invoking the revered Benjamin Franklin: "[A]t a much more advanced age our Franklin was the ornament of human nature." He blasted what he saw as the partisan nature of Adams's appointments: "[D]uring the late administration, those who were not of a particular sect of politics were excluded from all office. . . . [B]y a steady pursuit of this measure, nearly the whole offices of the US were monopolized by that sect." He left no doubt that the midnight appointments, made by Adams on his way out of office, rankled. He objected to "persons appointed in the last moments of an administration, not for its own aid, but to begin a career at the same time with their successors, by whom they had never been approved, and who could scarcely expect from them a cordial cooperation." Any "displacements" necessary to reflect "the will of the nation" and "an administration of government according with the opinions of those elected" should begin with these last-minute appointments.

As far as the judicial appointments were concerned, Jefferson generally recognized that his hands were tied. But if he found any imperfection with the appointment, he stopped it. In a much publicized incident, a federal judge failed to win a seat on the bench because, in the haste of the midnight appointments, his commission had been filled out erroneously. Jefferson refused to reissue a corrected commission.

The public debate did not initially focus on the justices of the peace whose commissions had not been delivered. But their situation perfectly reflected what Federalists saw as Jefferson's interference with legitimate and duly appointed office holders. Some Federalists, bent on revenge, even began discussing the possibility of Jefferson's impeachment—a suggestion that was both laughable and impossible in light of the lopsided Republican majority in both houses, but which illustrated the depth of Federalist fury.

Throughout December 1801, Republican newspapers such as the *Aurora* and the *National Intelligencer* launched vitriolic attacks on the Federalists. In one issue of the *Aurora*, for example, Duane casually described Federalists as "idiots" on the front page. Duane also obtained letters that had been left by an editor of the *Federalist* at Stelle's Hotel in Washington. He gleefully quoted from them on the front page of the *Aurora*, an embarrassment that led the *Federalist* to publish an angry offer of a $50 reward for the recovery of the letters or information about their theft.

The members of the new Congress followed the Washington press wars closely. Of the thirty-two senators in the Seventh Congress, thirteen had subscriptions to both the *National Intelligencer* and the *Washington Federalist*, ten read only the *National Intelligencer*, and seven read only the *Washington Federalist*. Only two senators refused to have a subscription to either newspaper.

Not everything in the newspapers in December 1801 was deadly serious. Alongside the *Aurora*'s attacks on the Federalists, the paper regularly printed advertisements touting visits to a "Learned Pig" who could read and speak, add, subtract, and multiply, and tell time ("both the hours and the minutes"). The pig was "A Curiosity, in which The Public will not be Disappointed," and it could be seen for a mere twenty-five cents, half-price for children. Newspapers of all stripes in the new capital also regularly announced the publication and availability of new books, including the new two-volume *Nocturnal Visit*, and other diversions, such as horse racing challenges. New businesses and trades continued to sprout to serve the bustling new capital. "Dr. Tongue" announced the opening of his practice in "physick and particularly surgery" on Pennsylvania Avenue near the War Office; he had been "a private pupil of Dr. Rush, from whom very satisfactory information can be given of his qualifications as a physician."

As the month began, the Supreme Court also returned to Washington for its December sitting. At Marshall's urging, the justices again stayed together at Conrad and McMunn's boardinghouse on Capitol Hill, the same hotel where Jefferson had lived prior to his inauguration. Even though Stelle's Hotel was where many Federalist congressmen lived, Marshall chose an establishment that had a decidedly more Republican clientele. The boardinghouse, originally a residence, had been converted into a hotel by two experienced innkeepers from Alexandria, Virginia. It was on the south side of Capitol Hill and, according to Margaret Bayard Smith, "was on the top of the hill, the precipitous sides of which were covered with grass, shrubs and trees in their wild uncultivated state . . . and [it] commanded an extensive and beautiful view."

The Court's business was fitful. On December 7, it tried to meet but could not because it lacked a quorum—only two of the six justices were present. On December 8, the Court convened again in the bleak confines of Committee Room Two, one floor below the House of Representatives. All of the justices except Alfred Moore now were on hand. The Court convened and then abruptly adjourned at 11:00 A.M. so that the justices could hear President Jefferson's first State of the Union address.

Jefferson broke with tradition. Unlike Washington and Adams, he did not deliver it personally but instead sent the message to be read by the Clerk of the House—an action, predictably, lauded as a gesture of democracy by Republicans and derided as an insulting stunt by Federalists. (Presidents would continue to deliver the State of the Union in writing for more than a century, until Woodrow

Wilson restored the tradition of personal appearances in 1913.) Jefferson sent his State of the Union speech to the Capitol with Meriwether Lewis, his talented young aide and secretary, whom Jefferson would appoint eighteen months later to head an expedition with William Clark to explore the unknown West.

Jefferson's speech sounded familiar themes. He began with foreign affairs, on which there was a rare consensus. Jefferson noted that the most pressing immediate trouble spot was Tripoli and the Barbary States. The president gave a full accounting of his use of the Navy in Tripoli over the summer, and he sought congressional support.

Jefferson then turned to domestic affairs. He suggested that the federal government had grown too large and cumbersome, weighed down by unnecessary bureaucracy. It could be reduced, he went on, and federal taxes (on goods, because there was no federal income tax) could be cut or eliminated. This was the Republicans' sweet spot, and the Federalists' sore spot. Federalists not only objected to Jefferson's proposal to slash the federal government; they took the criticism personally as an attack on the Adams and Washington administrations. For Jefferson, however, it fit a philosophy in which "the States themselves have principal care of our persons, our property, and our reputation," and "agriculture, manufactures, commerce, and navigation" are "most thriving when left most free to individual enterprise." The fact that Federalist appointees would be removed by the Jefferson administration, with the elimination of their federal offices, was unmentioned but unmistakable.

Jefferson went on to address the Judiciary Act, which, after its passage in the last days of the Adams administration, had led to the expansion of the federal judiciary and the appointment of the midnight judges. He suggested that the Act might well be altered: "The judiciary system of the United States, and especially that portion of it recently enacted, will of course present itself to the contemplation of Congress." Jefferson pointedly noted that he had requested a report on the workload of the federal courts, and of the cases "which were depending when additional courts and judges were brought in to their aid." The message was clear—he was gathering evidence to make a case that the new judges were unnecessary.

Even more interesting than Jefferson's comments about the judiciary was a passage that he deleted from the speech shortly before he sent it to Congress. In that passage, Jefferson initially noted that he had received "[a]pplications from different persons suffering prosecution under the act usually called the Sedition act." Jefferson observed that "our country has thought proper to distribute the powers of it's government among three equal & independent authorities, constituting each a check on one or both of the others, in all attempts to impair it's constitution."

According to Jefferson, each branch's judgment of the constitutionality of its own actions must be final and unreviewable. "[T]o make each an effectual check, it must have a right in cases which arise within the line of it's proper functions, where, equally with the others, it acts in the last resort & without appeal, to decide on the validity of an act *according to it's own judgment, & uncontrouled by the opinions of any other department*" (emphasis added). Jefferson emphasized his view that each administration was not bound by the constitutional views of its predecessors. "Succeeding functionaries have the same right to judge of the conformity or nonconformity of an act with the constitution, as their predecessors who [passed] it. For if it be against that instrument it is a perpetual nullity." Jefferson concluded by declaring that he had found the Sedition Act "to be in palpable & unqualified contradiction to the constitution," and therefore "a nullity."

It was a remarkable discussion. Jefferson emphasized that each branch of the government was the final judge of the constitutionality of its own actions. Although Jefferson's views were expressed in a context in which he was finding *unconstitutional* actions that other branches might have deemed constitutional (namely the Sedition Act), his language about the unreviewability of a branch's actions were not limited to instances in which a president found action *un*constitutional. He explicitly referred to the finality of a branch's views on the *"conformity* or non-conformity" of an Act with the Constitution—thereby holding out the possibility of one branch finding its actions constitutional even if another branch found them unconstitutional. Jefferson was likely reflecting his displeasure with the Sedition Act, which he vehemently opposed on constitutional grounds; he recognized that the federal courts, and justices riding circuit, had applied it enthusiastically.

Until the last minute, Jefferson kept this momentous passage in his State of the Union address. But, shortly before sending the address to Congress on the morning of December 8, 1801, he deleted it. Jefferson noted in the margin of his draft that he had deleted it only because he feared the uses that the Federalists would make of his position: "This whole paragraph was omitted as capable of being chicaned, and furnishing something to the opposition to make a handle of. It was thought better that the message should be clear of everything which the public might be made to misunderstand."

Many Federalists reacted acidly to the speech that Jefferson did send. Hamilton decried Jefferson's comments about the judiciary as "the symptom of a pigmy mind." Fisher Ames of Massachusetts objected that the "message announces the downfall of the late revision of the Judiciary. . . . The U.S. Government is to be dismantled like an old ship." The *Washington Federalist* lambasted Jefferson's address. The "attack upon the independence of the judiciary" was "the first part of a system which, if pursued, will plunge our unhappy country into all the miseries of civil war, anarchy and despotism." (The newspaper noted that it agreed enthusiastically with one part of Jefferson's address—his call for the elimination of postage on newspapers.) Other Federalists were less hostile. John Quincy Adams, son of the defeated president, stoically noted that "the violence of party spirit has very much subsided."

With the State of the Union address delivered, the Supreme Court justices got down to business. The marquee case for the

December session was similar to the one the court had heard four months earlier in that it involved the seizure of a ship on the high seas. The *Peggy*, a French schooner, had been captured as a "prize" by American seamen in 1800 before the Mortefontaine treaty with France. The treaty provided that all property "captured and not yet definitively condemned" must be returned. The French owners accordingly sought the return of their ship and cargo: The schooner had not been "definitively" condemned, they argued, because their suit to recover the ship and cargo was pending. The case had become a cause célèbre in federal court in Connecticut. Jefferson had ordered the return of the ship and cargo to the French owners. Sitting on circuit, however, Justice Cushing had ruled that Jefferson's order was erroneous and invalid. Now the case was before the Supreme Court, and spectators wondered whether the new Marshall Court was headed for a confrontation with the new administration.

Sitting in the cramped confines of Committee Room Two, the justices heard arguments in the case for several days. (All of the justices were present except the frequently absent Alfred Moore, who was ill and never showed up for the December sitting.) Ultimately, on December 21, 1801, Marshall issued a unanimous opinion upholding Jefferson's position without ever mentioning the president. Even Cushing reversed course and joined Marshall's opinion, which interpreted the treaty and emphasized that, under the Constitution, a treaty is "the supreme law of the land." A high-stakes confrontation between Jefferson and the Federalists on the Supreme Court had been avoided—at least for the moment.

Meanwhile, however, on Wednesday, December 16, 1801, former Attorney General Charles Lee, Marshall's colleague from the Adams cabinet, appeared before the Court with a curious request. Lee represented four men who had been nominated by the president as justices of the peace in the District of Columbia and confirmed by the Senate. Dennis Ramsay, Robert Hooe, and William Harper had been appointed to be justices in Alexandria County;

and William Marbury had been appointed to be a justice in Washington County. Their presidential commissions never had been delivered, and they had not been permitted to take office.

The four plaintiffs were all prominent citizens and well-known community leaders in Alexandria. Dennis Ramsey had served as mayor of Alexandria in 1789 and had given the farewell address to George Washington as the general left Virginia to go to New York to be sworn in as the First President of the United States. At an emotional ceremony Ramsey praised Washington as "[t]he first and best of citizens" and spoke for Washington's "neighbors and friends" in applauding "the spontaneous and unanimous suffrage of three millions of free men in your election to the supreme magistracy." Ramsey had been one of six of Washington's old army friends to be selected as an honorary pallbearer at Washington's funeral while Colonel William Harper had commanded an artillery company at the funeral. Harper, the father of twenty-nine children, was an Alexandria merchant who had served as a captain in the Revolutionary War and wintered at Valley Forge. Robert Hooe was a former sheriff of Fairfax County who had made a small fortune in real estate.

The fourth was from Maryland. Since moving to Georgetown from Annapolis in 1800, William Marbury had become one of the city's leading businessmen and most prominent Federalists. In 1799 Marbury had been named to the Board of Directors of the Bank of Columbia and the following year became the naval agent for the Port of Georgetown. He was also a manager of the dancing assemblies for the social elite and the head of the Federalist Party in Georgetown. He owed his rapid rise to Benjamin Stoddert, Adams's former secretary of the Navy, whom Marbury had helped when Stoddert faced financial difficulties. After Stoddert left office in 1801, Marbury lost his position. A little more than four months after Jefferson's inauguration, on July 9 1801, Jefferson's secretary of war, Henry Dearborn, fired Marbury from his job as naval agent. Marbury was tagged with enormous cost overruns in the construction of a seventy-four-gun ship. On July 9, Dearborn wrote Marbury: "The continuance of a Navy Agent at this place being considered unnecessary you will please to deposit in this office the contract or other public papers now in your possession . . . and deliver all other public property now in your possession. You will consider your agency as discontinued upon receipt of this letter." Marbury was undoubtedly resentful. Not only had he been denied a justice-of-the-peace position, now he was being sacked by the Jefferson administration from his job as naval agent.

On behalf of his clients, Lee requested a judicial order compelling action—a writ of mandamus, in the technical parlance. Lee asked that the Supreme Court order Secretary of State James Madison to deliver the withheld commissions to the four men so that they could take office.

Lee filed affidavits from the four would-be justices of the peace. Their affidavits explained that they had been nominated by the president and confirmed by the Senate, and that pursuant to the president's instructions their commissions had been prepared, but they had never received them. The plaintiffs also announced that they recently had gone to see Madison to ask him for their commissions. Madison had told them that he was too busy to meet with them and they should see Jacob Wagner, the chief clerk of the State Department. Wagner, in turn, had told them that he didn't know what had happened to the documents—if they still even existed—and that they should check with Levi Lincoln, the attorney general, who had been acting secretary of state at the beginning of the Jefferson administration. But Lincoln also had not been helpful about the status or location of the commissions.

Next, the would-be justices had petitioned the Senate to turn over any records of the nominations in order to establish evidence of the appointments. But the Senate ignored them. Now they were telling the Court that they had been given the runaround. Only judicial action could give them their lawful positions.

The affidavits did not mention why they had waited since March to file their case or why the men had not filed suit during the Court's sitting in August.

Although Marbury and his colleagues failed to explain their timing, perhaps Jefferson's State of the Union speech the preceding week, the sitting of the new Republican Congress, and the swirling charges and countercharges about midnight appointments and Executive removals had prompted their suit to reclaim these highly valued offices. Shortly before Jefferson's State of the Union address, the *Washington Federalist* had warned Jefferson that he would be challenged on his interference with Federalist appointees and office holders. "After the political intolerance shown by you," the paper had intoned, "be not surprised, Sir, if in return you shall find your political principles brought to the standard of the constitution. . . . [B]e not surprised, if you shall find the conduct of yourself and those with whom you have become intimately connected in opposition to the past administration recalled to the public consideration and exposed in new points of view." The threat just days before Marbury and his allies filed suit may well have been based on inside knowledge in Federalist circles that a broadside against the administration would be filed imminently in the Supreme Court.

Lee presented his motion on behalf of Marbury and the other plaintiffs to the justices on Thursday, December 17. The five justices listened intently from their perch in Committee Room Two. Lee read the affidavits detailing that the men had been nominated and confirmed, with their commissions prepared and the Great Seal affixed to them. Lee also drew on his own experience as a cabinet official. He noted that, in his experience in the government, commissions were "esteemed done" when they were "delivered for entry" by the secretary of state's office, even if they sat in the office for several weeks. Nobody needed reminding that Lee's colleague as secretary of state at the time these very commissions were prepared, nine months previously, had been Chief Justice John Marshall.

When Lee finished, Marshall turned to Levi Lincoln, Lee's successor as attorney general, and asked him for the position of the defendant, Secretary of State James Madison. Lincoln replied that he had no instructions on the issue. Madison had received notice of the lawsuit the preceding day, but the secretary of state could not immediately turn his attention to the subject. Lincoln would "leave the proceedings under the discretion of the Court." The Jefferson administration was treating the *Marbury* proceedings with disdain: It was ignoring the Supreme Court.

Sitting in open court, Marshall turned to his colleagues and asked them how they would like to proceed. The hot-tempered Samuel Chase was ready to rule immediately. He said that, if there were some additional offers of proof supporting everything Lee had said, he was prepared to decide at once. The other justices were more cautious. Marshall announced that the Court would take the matter under advisement. Encouraged by Chase's comments, Lee announced that he would amend the affidavits to include a statement that the Great Seal of the United States actually had been affixed to the commissions.

The *Aurora*, which had promised to report any Supreme Court actions "of consequence," prominently covered the argument. The paper noted that the justice-of-the-peace positions had been "of the long and last batch of creations" in the Adams administration. The *Aurora* did not hide its contempt for the plaintiffs, their motion, and their lawyer. "Some conversation took place on the etiquette of sealing and recording commissions," the paper noted, "and Mr. Lee said the law spoke *big words*" (original emphasis). The paper described Marbury himself as "one of those concerned with Stoddert, Forrest, etc. [prominent Washington investors] who have made so much noise in the contracts for timber and banking affairs." The *Aurora* also reported the firestorm that the case had generated. "The tories talk of dragging the President before the court and impeaching him, and a wonderful deal of similar nothingness. But it is easy to perceive that it is all *fume* which can excite no more than a judicious irritation."

The *Washington Federalist* also featured the argument. The paper pointedly reminded its readers of Jefferson's role in blocking the commissions. "It is said that it was among the first acts of the new President to stop the issuing of all commissions from the office."

The next day, on Friday, December 18, Marshall announced the Court's preliminary decision. The Court would allow Marbury's action to proceed. Marbury and the other plaintiffs had been "credibly informed" that they had been nominated and confirmed; that their commissions had been prepared and issued, with the Great Seal of the United States affixed; that the commissions had not been delivered; and that Madison—or "Maddison," as the Supreme Court order consistently misspelled his name—had refused to deliver the commissions or give a "satisfactory" explanation. The Court ordered Madison to "show cause," if "any he hath," why the Court should not issue the writ of mandamus ordering him to deliver the commissions. Madison—and Jefferson—would have to justify their actions in blocking the confirmed justices of the peace from assuming their posts. Finishing with a flourish, Marshall announced that arguments in the case would be heard the fourth day of the next term, in June 1802.

For many Republicans, the Court's order was an act of shocking audacity. The Supreme Court would force Jefferson and Madison to justify their actions about who would hold office! Senator John Breckinridge sounded the alarm to Virginia Governor James Monroe, a close Jefferson ally, on Christmas Eve: "The consequences of invading the Executive in this manner are deemed here a high-handed exertion of Judiciary power." Breckinridge added that nothing of practical importance would come of the case, but that its symbolic stakes would be enormous: "[T]he intention of the gentleman is to stigmatize the Executive, and give the opposition matter for abuse and vilification. . . . They may think that this will exalt the Judiciary character, but I believe that they are mistaken." For Breckinridge, there would be no further hesitation about whether a frontal Republican assault on the judiciary was warranted. The battle over the midnight judges would be fully joined.

The *Aurora* tersely reported the Court's decision. It also printed a letter attacking the order as "a high-handed exertion of Judiciary power," without identifying the author. The paper noted that the Supreme Court's order had been considered "a bold stroke against the Executive authority of the government" and that "it is supposed [the commissions] were disposed of with the other wastepaper and rubbish of the office."

Always watchful, Jefferson reacted with veiled apprehension. The day after the Supreme Court's order, on Saturday, December 19, 1801, Jefferson wrote to John Dickinson that "[t]he Federalists have retired into the judiciary as a stronghold, and from that battery all the works of republicanism are to be beaten down and erased." And, the following day, Sunday, December 20, Jefferson advised Dr. Benjamin Rush that, although he was pleased about his progress with the new Congress, he feared trouble on the question of the judiciary and removals. "Our winter campaign has opened with more good humor than I expected. By sending a message, instead of making a speech at the opening of the session, I have prevented the bloody conflict to which the making of an answer would have committed them. . . . Hitherto there has been no disagreeable altercations." But at the same time, with an eye on the horizon, Jefferson noted that the "lopping off" of midnight judges and the "suppression of useless offices" would lead to serious problems.

The Federalists, meanwhile, did not immediately react to the Court's preliminary order in *Marbury*. The *Washington Federalist* reported the Supreme Court's action on its front page, but without any additional comment. The newspaper continued to be focused instead on the possible repeal of the Judiciary Act, which had been passed just ten months earlier. In the same issue in which it reported the *Marbury* order, the paper printed a column attacking repeal as "part of the systematic plan for the total subversion of the constitution itself," a "complete destruction of the independence of an integral part of the government," and the introduction of "a system of corruption into the sanctuary of Justice."

The Federalists' warm social relations with the Federalist-appointed justices and judges continued. Senator Gouverneur Morris arrived in Washington on Friday, December 18, the day that Marshall issued the show-cause order in *Marbury*. The next night, he paid an evening call on Justice Paterson and happily noted that he saw "there the Bench"—Paterson's judicial brethren—along with Congressman James Bayard of Delaware. Morris did not mention whether they discussed the Court's order issued the day before.

The momentous year of 1801, which had opened with an unresolved presidential election and which eventually had witnessed the nation's first democratic transition to an opposing party, was drawing to a close. President Jefferson had settled into the President's House. In the war with Barbary, the *U.S.S. Enterprise* had seized the ship *Tripoli*. As relations with France became more strained, President Jefferson named Robert Livingston as the new American envoy. Domestically, Jefferson was quietly planning an expedition to explore the American West.

In Washington, a contract finally had been signed in June to build a chamber for the House of Representatives. President Jefferson had been presented with three options and had chosen the least expensive, "an elliptical room measuring 94 feet long and 70 feet wide with sixteen arches and fourteen windows." The structure had been completed by November, but the construction had been rushed and the workmanship was visibly shoddy in places.

As Bayard, Morris, and the justices merrily celebrated the approaching holiday, the battle lines for the coming year were forming. With John Marshall's order to James Madison suggesting that the Supreme Court was inclined to overrule Jefferson's actions on the justices of the peace, and with the Republicans determined to launch an assault on Adams's midnight judges, the capital braced for a new round of political warfare.

THE FIRESTORM

Senator William Plumer arrived promptly at the President's House and banged·the large door knocker. After several minutes, the door opened and Plumer was surprised to see before him the president of the United States "dressed, or rather undressed, with an old brown coat, red waistcoat, old corduroy small clothes, much soiled, woolen hose and slippers without heels." For Plumer, a flinty, Federalist lawmaker from New Hampshire, Jefferson demeaned the presidency.

President Jefferson had undoubtedly arisen early that morning, as was his custom, and had dressed himself for comfort and warmth in the still unfinished, cold and drafty executive mansion. Although by early 1802 the white paint had finally dried on the Aquia sandstone walls, the presidential mansion was still under construction: Jefferson was having proper bathrooms with working toilets installed on the upper floor of the house to replace the outside privy. And he had consulted closely with the architect Benjamin Henry Latrobe to expand the first floor of the building outward, creating two colonnades that were designated to conceal stables and storage facilities.

Jefferson's relaxed appearance on the day Senator Plumer visited was not unusual; he often dressed casually. While his wardrobe may have seemed less than presidential to some, he brought enormous energy to his job as chief executive. He later described the "steady and uniform course" that characterized his days in the President's House. By his own estimate, he worked "10 to 12 and 13 hours a day" at his desk with "4 hours for riding, dining and a little unbending." Notwithstanding his prodigious work ethic, Jefferson's first year as president had been somewhat unremarkable. He had assumed a low profile, shunning public appearances filled with pomp and ceremony.

Jefferson, a former ambassador, had long valued quiet diplomacy as an effective tool in the art of statecraft. As president, he emphasized personal relations with his cabinet, influential members of Congress, and foreign dignitaries and leaders. He was constantly meeting with the capital's power brokers, penning notes to them, or entertaining them at the President's House. He later explained: "I cultivate personal intercourse with the members of the legislature that we may know one another and have opportunities of little explanations of circumstance which, not understood, might produce jealousies and suspicions injurious to the public interest." Margaret Bayard Smith, the wife of the owner and publisher of the *National Intelligencer*, Samuel Harrison Smith, and a first cousin of Congressman James Bayard of Delaware, was a frequent guest at the White House. She described how "Jefferson has company every day. But his table is seldom laid for more than twelve." After sitting next to him one evening, she was impressed "by his easy, candid and gentle manners." Yet, all of the President's intelligence and charm could not forestall the crisis over the judiciary that erupted in 1802.

Jefferson, an intuitive politician, deftly operated the levers of power: "[N]o piece of legislation was passed without his approval, and nothing he opposed became law." It helped that Jefferson's Republican Party controlled both houses of Congress, which had convened the previous December. The Senate comprised eighteen Republicans and fourteen Federalists, and the House had sixty-nine Republicans and thirty-six Federalists. But while Republicans were clearly in control, there were divisions within the party. The same could be said of the Federalists, who had not yet healed the wounds between the "High Federalists" who followed Alexander Hamilton and the more moderate ones who had supported President Adams.

President Jefferson never wanted to mire Congress or his presidency in a debate over the judiciary. Although he vehemently objected to Adams's midnight appointments and was mindful of the fact that when he took office there was not one Republican in the entire federal judiciary, he had shown no firm commitment to undertake wholesale judicial reform. But when William Marbury filed suit, the president became alarmed that a constitutional crisis was looming. With the Federalists still in control of the judiciary, Jefferson feared that both his and Congress's power would be circumscribed. He felt it was critical to act preemptively and establish Congress's constitutional right to legislate the establishment and abolition of inferior courts.

On January 6, 1802, Senator John Breckinridge of Kentucky, perhaps President Jefferson's closest ally in the Senate, introduced a motion calling for repeal of the Judiciary Act of 1801. The Repeal bill, also known as the President's measure, was seconded by Stevens Thomas Mason of Virginia, the Senate majority leader and another close friend and fervent supporter of the president. Mason, who had been one of a handful of young aides to General Washington during the Yorktown campaign, hailed from one of the most prominent families in America. Mason argued that the Judiciary Act of 1801 had been political retribution. The bill had been introduced in early 1800 but was acted upon only when it became clear that Federalists had lost both the presidency and the Congress: As Mason saw it, a desperate Federalist Party conceived of the judiciary as the last, best hope for establishing a beachhead against surging Republicanism.

The debate in the Senate chamber was not open to the public, but, for the first time, the senators voted to allow a shorthand writer onto the floor to record the events each day. Based on that record, the nation's newspapers covered the debate extensively, often publishing lengthy excerpts from the senators' remarks. The *National Intelligencer* set the tone for the impending debate when it editorialized: "Questions respecting the judicial power of the United States, which are about to engage our public councils and already engage the public mind, are of the first degree of importance."

Before extended debate on the motion began, the Senate president rose to read a letter from Thomas Tingley and "the vicars of Washington Parish on behalf of themselves and other members." The letter was a request for "space in the Capitol of the room now occupied by the Court." Tingley, who had served in the British Navy but was now an American citizen, inquired if it might be possible to use the room for Sunday services "during the inclemency of weather." At the time, there were only two small churches near the Capitol, described by Margaret Bayard Smith as "a very small and mean frame" Catholic chapel on F Street, and an Episcopal church at the foot of Capitol Hill that had once been a tobacco shed and had been "fitted up as a church in the plainest and rudest manner." It was the latter which Tingley, Smith, and President Jefferson all attended. Hearing no objection, the Senate granted the request.

From January 8 until January 19, the Senate debated the Judiciary Repeal motion. Senator Breckinridge was the principal spokesman for the Republicans. In framing his argument, Breckinridge echoed the early drafts of President Jefferson's State of the Union message in which the president asserted that both the Congress and the president had authority equal to that of the Supreme Court to declare an Act of Congress unconstitutional—the sedition law being the most obvious example. With the case of *Marbury v. Madison* pending before the Supreme Court, the political ground had shifted and arguments that Jefferson had dropped because he feared they were too divisive became the focus of the national debate. Citing Article III of the Constitution, which gave

Congress the power to establish rules and procedures for all tiers of the federal court system, Breckinridge argued that if the pending Repeal bill was unconstitutional, then so had been the Judiciary Act of 1801 because it had changed the court system by abolishing circuit-riding.

Over half of the Senate's members offered opinions during the debate, with some members speaking on more than one occasion. The Republican strategy for repeal of the Judiciary Act hinged on three principal arguments: First, Republicans adopted Breckinridge's talking points on the authority of Congress to shape the courts. Next, they argued that the courts needed no increase in the number of judges since the number of cases in the docket had been decreasing. Lastly, Republicans claimed that it was more desirable to have Supreme Court justices riding circuit court instead of simply huddling together in Washington two times a year where they were isolated from the American people; the justices should be more in touch with local law and custom.

Federalists, of course, had a very different view. Their leader on the floor of the Senate was Senator Gouverneur Morris of New York, who began by arguing that new judges, who had been granted life tenure, could not now be removed at will by the elimination of their position in the name of reorganization. Federalists argued that if Congress could remove a judge every time it disagreed with a decision, then the independence of the judiciary would be compromised. Countering Republican arguments on the virtues of circuit-riding, one Federalist senator proclaimed he was "not convinced that the best way to study law was to ride rapidly from one end of the country to the other." And since most cases were adjudicated on the basis of English—and the growing body of American—common law, there was no compelling need to be acquainted with local customs. Federalist congressman John Rutledge, Jr., of South Carolina believed that Federalists could make it so uncomfortable for Republican moderates that "twill be difficult for them to preserve union among themselves." In an early example of political spin, Rutledge suggested making it a fight between "the Virginia Party and the friends of the Constitution."

Throughout the debate, the case of *Marbury v. Madison* was never far from the surface. Slated for argument during the Court's June term, the central question in the case, a showing of cause as to why a writ of mandamus should not be issued to Madison (and by implication to Jefferson), became a flashpoint in the larger debate over reform of the judiciary. Federalists insisted on the power of the Supreme Court to overturn an unlawful action taken by the Executive Branch while Republicans shot back that unelected judges—accountable to no one—should not wield unfettered power. They claimed that the most effective check against the legislature was not the judiciary, as Federalists liked to argue, but rather the American people, who elected the legislators. Senator Mason likened the judiciary to the despots of Europe for their attack on James Madison in *Marbury v. Madison*. It was an echo of the earlier criticism of Adams: that Federalists were monarchists at heart and not democrats.

The most vociferous Republicans wanted a showdown with the Supreme Court to settle the question of the Court's power once and for all. "High Federalists" wanted the same thing and suggested that if the assault on the judiciary succeeded, there would be talk of secession and perhaps even the possibility of armed resistance. Meanwhile, Chief Justice John Marshall was ensconced in his house in Richmond, a two-and-a-half-story federal-style manse in one of the state capital's most prestigious neighborhoods. Marshall was likely following the congressional debate in the newspapers, but he had decided, at least for the time being, to remain silent.

———

THE NOTION THAT the Supreme Court could invalidate an act of Congress was far from novel. *The Federalist Papers*, in the famous essay number 78, written by Alexander Hamilton as "Publius," envi-

sioned exactly that role for the Supreme Court. "No legislative act
. . . contrary to the Constitution, can be valid," Hamilton wrote.
"The interpretation of the laws is the proper and peculiar province
of the courts. A constitution is, in fact, and must be regarded by the
judges, as a fundamental law. It therefore belongs to them to ascer-
tain its meaning." John Marshall, in fact, had expressed that very
view in 1788 at Virginia's convention to ratify the federal Constitution. "If [Congress] were to make a law not warranted by any of the
powers enumerated," proclaimed Marshall in advocating ratification, "it would be considered by the Judges as an infringement of
the Constitution which they are to guard. They would not consider
such a law as coming under their jurisdiction. They would declare it
void." Several state courts had invalidated statutes as unconstitutional, and lower federal courts, including Supreme Court Justices
riding circuit, had suggested that federal courts likewise had that
power.

But that view had not been universally shared, and some fiercely
rejected it as the Jefferson administration gained control. Republicans now saw the federal judiciary as a refuge of Federalist hold-
outs determined to thwart them, and they saw federal judges as a
symbol of centralized, antidemocratic federal power.

Moreover, the Supreme Court, a weak, feeble body until that
point, never had struck down an act of Congress. Nor had any
other national court in the world struck down an act of a coordi-
nate branch.

AT THE PRESIDENT'S HOUSE in Washington, Thomas Jefferson
grew increasingly concerned about the rancorous tone of the debate
in Congress over the Repeal legislation. Yet Jefferson, who backed
the bill, also suspected that some members of the Republican majority might be softening in their support for the Repeal bill. Even
more worrying to the president, two Republican senators were absent: John Armstrong of New York had abruptly resigned and had

not yet been replaced, while Stephen Bradley of Vermont was at home tending to his ailing wife. Their absences had been balanced by the absence of two Federalist lawmakers, Aaron Ogden of New Jersey and James Ross of Pennsylvania, who had not yet arrived, though they were due imminently. Jefferson continued to adopt an outwardly bipartisan tone and affable manner, but Gouveneur Morris sensed his anguish. Dolley Madison had taken Morris for afternoon tea to the President's House, where the corpulent senator from New York found "the President [to be] very civil but with evident masks of constraint." Two weeks later, on January 21, Morris dined with President Jefferson and remarked on his "constrained manner of reception," showing "enmity . . . and fear."

Worried that the two Federalist senators would arrive before their Republican counterparts and that a few conflicted Republican senators might be on the verge of changing their votes, on January 19 Senator Breckinridge sought to cut off debate by offering a motion to appoint a special committee to produce a bill repealing the Judiciary Act of 1801. The special committee, controlled by Republicans, quickly drafted a bill that, under parliamentary rules, required three readings and approval by the full Senate. The bill to repeal the Judiciary Act of 1801 passed the U.S. Senate on the first two readings with Vice President Aaron Burr, who presided over the Senate, siding with the Republicans to break a tie. But then, on the third reading, Burr voted to refer the bill back to the committee. Burr ostensibly changed his mind in hope of diminishing the fierce partisanship that had characterized debate over the Repeal bill. He wanted to allow Federalists one more opportunity to examine the legislation closely before voting on it. Burr's change of heart also reflected his personal ambivalence: He did not doubt that Congress had the power to alter the judicial system, but he questioned "if it might be constitutionally moral." Burr, like some moderate Republicans and most Federalists, apparently feared that Congress might be establishing a dangerous political precedent if it allowed the Supreme Court to be changed based on how the political winds were blowing.

But Burr was undoubtedly motivated by politics as well. Although the president made it a point to dine with his vice president on a regular basis, Burr was not part of Jefferson's circle of close advisers. He was effectively excluded from all major policy discussions and his recommendations for patronage positions were ignored. Two weeks earlier, Gouverneur Morris had noted in his diary that "Mr. Burr is disposed to go with us [the Federalists] on the judiciary—cannot however openly break with his party." Some Republicans questioned the sincerity of Burr's actions, believing this was simply another turn in the road for the politically calculating vice president. Less than three weeks later, on Washington's birthday, Burr was the only Republican to appear at a Federalist gathering to honor the first president. Burr claimed that he had arrived not knowing the nature of the gathering, but many concluded that he had switched party allegiance.

Even the conniving Burr could not entirely stop the Repeal bill from moving forward. Two days later, after the bill had been sent back to the committee, Republican Senator Stephen Bradley of Vermont returned to Washington, D.C. He had missed the debate as well as the early votes, but nevertheless remained steadfastly in the Republican column. When the bill came to yet another vote on February 13, it was Bradley, and not Burr, who broke the tie. The measure passed 16 to 15. It was the clearest indication yet that the Republican-dominated Congress viewed the Federalist-dominated judiciary with disdain. Roger Griswold complained that Republicans wanted nothing less than "to destroy the independence of the judiciary." Griswold predicted that Republican aggression would lead to "a scene . . . similar to the most violent under the French Revolution."

The Repeal bill was now pending in the House of Representatives. As in the Senate, the case of *Marbury v. Madison* was just below the surface of the debate over reform of the judiciary. The *Aurora* reprinted the remarks of Representative William Branch Giles, a Republican from Virginia who described the underlying issues in *Marbury* as "a mandatory process . . . leading to . . . executive conflict." Giles worried about an unbridled and overly powerful judiciary: "Does this, in the judges, seem unambitious?" Giles asked sarcastically. Giles had resigned from Congress in 1798 to take a seat in the Virginia General Assembly, but had returned to Congress two years later and now strongly championed repeal of the Judiciary Act. Giles was not an eloquent orator, but he was smart, dogged, and irascible. Gouverneur Morris, hearing of Giles's speech, recorded in his diary that it was reportedly "artful," but "easily to be refuted."

As the House debated, a handful of Republicans worked behind the scenes to determine whether a compromise measure could be drafted. Congressman Bayard noted that some Republican moderates "cursed" the Repeal bill and "had it been possible for them to recede, they would have joyfully relinquished the project." Gouverneur Morris noted in his diary that one Republican had written to his family, claiming that "if the question of the Repeal were taken by Ballot, they would certainly lose it but by calling for the Yeas and Neas they could hold every man to the point." The president was livid. Having now confirmed his suspicion that some within his own party were seeking to weaken the Repeal measure, he privately denounced them as "wayward freaks."

Notwithstanding the defection of a handful of Republican congressmen, the House of Representatives repealed the Judiciary Act by a vote of 54 to 32 on the third of March. Five days later, President Jefferson signed the bill into law. The Act eliminated the sixteen judgeships that had been created by President Adams and transferred cases back to the circuit courts, where the Supreme Court justices were now expected to preside. The *Washington Federalist* proclaimed, "The fatal bill is passed. Our Constitution is no more." And the like-minded *New York Post* bemoaned "the death wound of our glorious Constitution." For Federalist pundits, the concept of checks and balances, so central to the Constitution, had been dealt a mortal blow. This was somewhat ironic given that, from the earliest days of the Constitution, Federalists had by and large favored a powerful Executive Branch—until the election of Thomas Jefferson.

Although they had won a resounding victory, Republicans feared that the Repeal legislation might be challenged in the courts and ultimately overturned by the Federalist-leaning Supreme Court. In order to prevent such a possible outcome, Senate Republicans introduced another bill, the Judiciary Act of 1802.

This second piece of legislation reorganized the judiciary into six circuits. Each justice was paired with a district court judge to create a circuit court that would convene two times a year. Chief Justice Marshall, for instance, would be expected to ride circuit in his home state of Virginia, as well as neighboring North Carolina. In a letter to Justice Paterson, who had solicited his assistance in fundraising to help rebuild Nassau Hall at Princeton University, which had been destroyed in a fire, Chief Justice Marshall briefly commented on the proposed reorganization: "You have I doubt not seen the arrangement of our future duties as mark[ed] out in the bill lately reported to the senate. They are less burdensome than heretofore, or than I expected."

But the real impact of the bill was that it drastically changed the Supreme Court schedule and on this point, Chief Justice Marshall was not so sanguine. The Judiciary Act of 1801 had replaced the February and August terms with June and December terms. Those terms were now cancelled by the new act, which restored the February and August terms and provided that the Supreme Court would not meet again until February 1803. The practical effect would be to shut down the Supreme Court for a full fourteen months. Not coincidentally, the Supreme Court could not meet in the meantime either to decide a challenge to the repeal of the Judiciary Act of 1801 or to hear the case of *Marbury v. Madison*.

The second bill concerning circuit-riding and the Supreme Court schedule (suspending the Supreme Court sessions until the following year) passed the Senate on April 8 and was referred to the House of Representatives where Congressman Bayard, now showing his Federalist colors, immediately signaled his desire to test the constitutionality of the Repeal Act. He introduced an amendment to postpone the bill until July 1, 1802—thereby ensuring that the Court would convene for the June term. On the House floor, Bayard put the question directly to his colleagues: "Are the gentlemen afraid of the judges? Are they afraid they will pronounce the repealing law void?" He accused Republicans of political chicanery as they attempted "to prevent the court from expressing their opinion upon the validity of the act lately passed . . . until the act has gone into full execution, and the excitement of the public mind abated."

Bayard's amendment failed. Two weeks later, on April 23, the House approved the Judiciary Act of 1802 and six days later the bill became law and the Supreme Court was effectively shut down. The February session had come and gone, and now there would be no session in June, or in August, or in December. Besides delaying a Court hearing of *Marbury v. Madison*, the Republican Congress had effectively prevented the Court from issuing a timely response to the Repeal Act. The Judicial Branch of the U.S. government seemed more powerless than at any time in its short history.

In April, Representative James Bayard and Chief Justice Marshall met in an Alexandria tavern to eat, drink, and discuss political strategy around the future of the judiciary. Marshall had traveled to Alexandria from his home in Richmond to spend the week archiving his papers from his days as secretary of state. In all likelihood, he and Bayard met at Gadsby's Tavern on the southwest corner of Royal Street in Alexandria. This was perhaps the most famous tavern in the city, where many of Washington-area's social, business, and political elite liked to mix. The tavern was within a few blocks of the homes of Charles Lee and Marbury's co-plaintiffs Dennis

Ramsey and Robert Hooe, who undoubtedly went to Gadsby's often. On his last birthday, George Washington danced with his wife Martha in the tavern's ballroom. Gadsby's owner, John Wise, rented lodgings to James Marshall, the chief justice's brother.

Marshall and Bayard had been close friends since they served together in the House of Representatives. Bayard, Delaware's only representative in Congress, had been elected in 1796 on the state's Federalist ticket. He was married to Ann Bassett, whose father, Richard Bassett, was one of the midnight judges appointed by President Adams. Marshall had been provided a copy of the Repeal legislation by former Treasury Secretary Oliver Wolcott—himself a midnight judge.

Like Marshall, Bayard was independent minded. While in Congress, he had been a strong supporter of the Alien and Sedition Acts of 1798 and had originally backed John Adams for president in 1800. Even though Bayard's vote broke the deadlock in the House of Representatives, allowing Thomas Jefferson's ultimate victory, President Adams bore him no malice. Though a lame-duck president, Adams nominated him to be ambassador to France. Bayard was confirmed by the Senate but ultimately decided not to serve, apparently fearing either that Jefferson would recall him immediately or that he would be allowed to serve, in which case it might be wrongly viewed as a quid pro quo for his role in the presidential election.

During their meeting in the cozy and boisterous Alexandria tavern, Marshall confided to Bayard that he questioned the constitutionality of the Repeal Act and had hoped the Court might have the opportunity to hear a challenge to the Act. He strongly believed that the Constitution required distinct appointments for Supreme Court justices and for circuit court justices. And he was angry that the Court had been shut down. Yet, he explained to Bayard, Congress had put the Court in a quandary: If the justices capitulated and agreed to ride circuit, then they would be conceding the constitutionality of the Repeal Act, but, if they didn't, then they would be defying President Jefferson and the Republican majority in Congress, and such defiance might prove foolhardy. He agreed to contact the other justices to gauge their reactions.

Representative Bayard reported Marshall's views to a number of leading Federalist leaders, including his father-in-law, Richard Bassett, as well as Alexander Hamilton and Gouverneur Morris. Bassett was adamant that the Court must take a stand: He published a lengthy pamphlet titled "The Solemn Protest of the Honorable Judge Bassett," in which he called for the Court to refuse to perform its circuit court duties and to declare the Repeal Act unconstitutional. Alexander Hamilton suggested to Bayard that the Repeal Act be tested in the Supreme Court "as soon as possible." But since the Court had been shut down, Hamilton's suggestion was simply not feasible. Morris, who had breakfasted with the chief justice only days earlier, expressed mild disdain for Marshall's apparent equivocation in his diary: "I am neither surprised nor disappointed for it accords with my idea of the judge." Morris vowed that the Federalists would continue the fight: "The business must not stop here." When he was not spending time with Dolley Madison, Morris plotted with other "High Federalists" such as Senators Griswold and Ogden to force the Supreme Court to deal with the issue of judicial review.

On April 19, 1802, Chief Justice Marshall wrote to the other justices to ask whether they should comply with the new statute by riding circuit. As a former politician, Marshall understood that the court would need to be united if it directly confronted either President Jefferson or the Republican-controlled Congress: "This is a subject not to be lightly resolved on. The consequences of refusing to carry the law into effect may be very serious." Marshall admonished the justices that "the conviction of duty ought to be very strong before the measure is resolved on." However, he promised to be "bound by [their] opinion."

Justices Paterson, Cushing, and Washington responded separately to the chief justice, and were largely in agreement with one another: Since the original justices had performed circuit-riding duties, it must be constitutional. Justice Washington declared that the question should be "considered settled and should not again be moved." Justice Cushing wrote that "to be consistent . . . we must abide by the old practice." And Justice Paterson opined that the "practice has fixed construction, which is too late to disturb." The only justice who held a different viewpoint was "Old Bacon Face," Samuel Chase of Maryland. Chase argued that the Repeal Act was unconstitutional because the circuit courts already had appointed judges. Chase claimed that if Supreme Court justices acted as circuit court judges, they would "destroy the independence of the judiciary." Chase also argued that the circuit courts were courts of original jurisdiction and the founding fathers had envisioned the Supreme Court as an appellate court: "[T]he Citizen would be deprived of the benefit of a hearing in the inferior Tribunals and obliged to resort, in the Commencement of his suit, to the Supreme Court." He wanted his brethren to assemble in August and prepare a resolution for the president, calling for the reinstatement of the midnight judges with back pay and no circuit-riding by the justices. While Chase was adamant in his view that circuit-riding represented an unconstitutional expansion of the Court's original jurisdiction, he also agreed to abide by the wishes of the other justices, should they "differ from me in opinion." Marshall, like Chase, seemed to believe the Repeal Act was unconstitutional, but he was willing to abide by the wishes of the majority of the Court who felt they must acquiesce to circuit-riding in order to preserve the Court as an institution.

Both the repeal of the Judiciary Act of 1801 and the enactment of the Judiciary Act of 1802 were significant victories for the Jefferson administration, but at least one prominent Republican, James Monroe, was worried. Monroe, a close friend and confidante of Jefferson's, wrote to the president expressing his concern over canceling the Supreme Court term. Monroe feared that postponement "may be considered as an unconstitutional oppression of the

Judiciary by the Legislature. . . . Suppose Judges were to meet according to the former law, notwithstanding the postponement, denouncing the whole proceedings as unconstitutional. I am of the opinion that this postponement would give new colour to their pretensions, new pretensions to their party and a better prospect of success." This, of course, is exactly what Justice Chase had proposed to Chief Justice Marshall.

Having had enough of congressional bickering and backbiting over the Supreme Court and the judiciary, President Jefferson turned his attention to other issues. Eighteen months earlier, on October 1, 1800, Spain had ceded all of the Louisiana territory to France. The treaty between the two European powers, however, had been kept secret, and it was not until the spring of 1802 that the U.S. government was able to confirm the transfer. President Jefferson appreciated the extraordinary value of the region—with its port and access to the continent's interior—to the future security and economic growth of the United States. Jefferson, who had at one time been sharply criticized for his affinity for all things French, was deeply disturbed, and suspicious of the French intentions. On April 18, 1802, he wrote to Robert Livingston, the American ambassador in France, that "[t]here is on the globe one single spot, the possessor of which is our natural and habitual enemy. It is New Orleans. . . . It is impossible that France and the United States can continue long friends, when they meet in so irritable a position." Secretary of State Madison had earlier warned Livingston that in New Orleans "[e]very man . . . regards the free use of that river [the Mississippi] as a natural and indefeasible right."

Around this time, President Jefferson also took on an unusual project that had both personal and political dimensions. Jefferson knew that Chief Justice Marshall was writing a history of George Washington, and it irked him. Not only had Marshall emerged as a favorite of the First President, but now with full access to Washington's papers, he was writing what amounted to an account of the first years of the Republic. Jefferson was wary of what Marshall might say and so he plotted with Secretary of State Madison to find someone to write a countervailing history. They settled on Joel Barlow, a Yale-educated poet, turned diplomat, then living in Paris. On May 3, 1802, Jefferson wrote to Barlow inviting him to "write the history of the United States, from the close of the war downwards," promising that he and Secretary Madison were "rich ourselves in materials, and can open all the public archives to you." Jefferson explained to Barlow that it was important that Barlow return to America and get started immediately because: "John Marshall is writing the Life of Gen. Washington from his papers. It is intended to come out just in time to influence the next presidential election. It is written, therefore, principally with the view of electioneering purposes." President Washington had often consulted Chief Justice John Jay on any number of issues, but Jefferson viewed Chief Justice Marshall, his estranged cousin, as nothing short of a political rival.

In August 1802, President Jefferson left Washington for a two-month vacation at Monticello. As summer turned to fall, an old political rumor received new attention and focus. The *Gazette of the United States*, a Federalist newspaper, published allegations of President Jefferson's extramarital affairs, alleging that, when he was 25 years old, he had "offered love to a handsome lady, wife of his neighbor John Walker." But the most shocking allegations came from the scandalmonger James T. Callender, who had played such a prominent role in the election of 1800. Callender had moved from Philadelphia to Richmond, where he published the *Recorder*. Callender, a strident anti-Federalist, was a heavy drinker and a fierce partisan, and he had been thrown in jail during the Adams administration under the Sedition Act. After the election, he was freed by Jefferson and he wrote the new president asking to be appointed Postmaster General. When Jefferson demurred, Callender turned against him and in the fall of 1802 alleged that "[i]t is a well known fact that [Jefferson] keeps, and for many years past has kept, as his concubine, his own slave . . . by which the woman and our president had such children. . . . [T]he African woman is said to officiate as housekeeper at Monticello."

———

I𝚃 𝚠𝚊𝚜 𝚊𝚕𝚜𝚘 in the fall of 1802 that, for the first time in almost two years, the justices of the Supreme Court began riding circuit once again. Almost from the beginning, there was controversy. On September 18, in Hartford, Justice Bushrod Washington and Richard Lew, the circuit court judge, arrived to hold court. Federalist Senator Roger Griswold filed a motion on behalf of clients whom he was representing, challenging the authority of the court to even hear the case. Griswold argued that the original suit had been brought in 1801, when the old Judiciary Act had been in effect, and, since the commissions of the judges had not been constitutionally vacated, the original court still existed. The Court rejected the challenge. Federalists filed a similar motion a few weeks later in Boston, where Justice Cushing and John Davis, a circuit court judge, presided. They quickly dismissed the motion. Then, on December 2, the Fifth Circuit Court convened in Richmond with Chief Justice Marshall presiding. In the case of *Stuart v. Laird*, Charles Lee, the former attorney general and lawyer for the defendants, argued against the legitimacy of the court; Lee questioned the authority of Congress to impose circuit court duties on justices of the Supreme Court. Chief Justice Marshall dismissed the claim and found for the plaintiffs.

Marshall, who had worked hard to remove the Court from the cauldron of party politics, found the situation bleak and depressing. On November 12, 1802, he wrote to his old friend Charles Pinckney, "There is so much in the political world to wound honest men who have honorable feelings that I am disgusted with it & begin to see things & indeed human nature through a much more gloomy medium than I once thought possible."

TRIAL IN
THE SUPREME COURT

O
n New Year's Day, 1803, Thomas Jefferson stood for hours in the octagon room of the President's House and greeted a never-ending stream of visitors. It was the "levee," the president's New Year's open house, a tradition begun by George Washington in Philadelphia, continued by John Adams, and now embraced by Jefferson.

The levee was open to everybody. It seemed that all of Washington showed up—congressmen and senators, Republicans and Federalists, Executive Department heads and foreign diplomats, scores of locals, including, as the *National Intelligencer* noted, "a large number of ladies." The crowd was eager to see Thomas Jefferson's two adult daughters, Mary Jefferson Randolph and Maria Jefferson Eppes. Mary and Maria were nearing the end of their first visit to the nation's capital. They had enjoyed a seven-week stay in the President's House, and they planned to set off on their four-day journey home to southern Virginia on January 5. They had come without their husbands, both of whom were occupied with business and both of whom soon would be elected to Congress.

The city was intensely curious about the president's daughters. They were Jefferson's only surviving children (or, more accurately, in light of subsequent DNA tests on his slaves' descendants, they were Jefferson's only acknowledged surviving children). The daughters had enjoyed their stay. But Mary noted her worry about their father's "unsafe and solitary" existence sleeping alone on the top floor of the President's House.

The New Year's levee was a colorful affair. The French ambassador liked to arrive "decked in gold lace." The Tunisian ambassador favored silk slippers, a turban, and a scarlet jacket "embroidered with precious stones." Native Americans sported blankets, deerskin moccasins, and feathers in their hair. Visitors snacked on the remnants of the half-ton "Mammoth Cheese," delivered a year earlier from the ladies of Cheshire, Massachusetts, and still looming large and uneaten.

Accompanying Jefferson in the President's House was his frequent dinner companion and secretary, 26-year-old Captain Meriwether Lewis. Unbeknownst to the New Year's guests, Lewis was already immersed in a secret project. He and Jefferson had been planning an audacious trip. Lewis would lead an expedition to explore the vast unknown continent. A few weeks later, on January 18, Jefferson would send a secret, encrypted letter to Congress requesting an appropriation of $2,500 for the journey. Later that year, the trip would be announced, Lewis would recruit a team, including William Clark as his trusted colleague, and Lewis and Clark would set out on their legendary expedition. Now, on New Year's Day, 1803, amid the gaiety of the levee, Lewis began a period of intensive study for his dangerous and unprecedented adventure.

John Marshall, meanwhile, was not in Washington on New Year's Day. He was in Raleigh, North Carolina. Marshall was riding circuit, the hated duty re-imposed on Supreme Court justices by the Republicans' repeal of the Judiciary Act. With his characteristic good spirits, Marshall embraced the circuit-riding with amused enthusiasm. Marshall seemed always to have an "expression of great good humor and hilarity," noted William Wirt in a popular essay published in 1803, and "an irradiating spirit" in his eyes.

Marshall had arrived in Raleigh, a city of 700 residents, shortly after Christmas. The 165-mile trip from Richmond had taken three days. Marshall found lodging in the boardinghouse of Henry H. Cooke. It was a flimsy, simple building that delighted Marshall and became his home in Raleigh during circuit-riding for the next thirty-four years.

Marshall buoyantly wrote his wife Polly of his comic travails. He discovered that he had lost fifteen silver dollars from his waist pocket—a considerable sum at the time. When he asked Peter, his slave and valet, to unpack his clothes, Peter discovered that Marshall had no breeches. Instead, he had only modern trousers, which apparently were not suitable for a presiding judge. Marshall tried to get a new pair of breeches made, but he found all the tailors in Raleigh too busy. They apparently were not impressed that the request was coming from the chief justice of the United States. "I thought I should be a sans culotte only one day," Marshall wrote Polly in describing his "calamities," but "I have the extreme mortification to pass the whole term without that important article of dress."

Back in Washington, as January progressed, senators and representatives prepared for Congress to reconvene. Emotions between the Republicans and Federalists remained high. The *Intelligencer* highlighted a new feature on its front page, "Federal Misrepresentations," deriding what it called Federalist deceptions. Federalist newspapers, in turn, mocked Jefferson's appointment of James Monroe as an emissary to make peace with France and Spain. The *Washington Federalist* described Monroe as "ambassador to Spain, to France, to Bwatavia, and to God knows where else . . . the *dernier* hope of our friends on the western side of the Allegany." In response to the criticisms of Monroe, the *Aurora* caustically noted that "[t]here never was a party whose means of support were more despicable than those of the federalists."

The *Aurora* also speculated that Alexander Hamilton, the editor of the arch-Federalist *New York Evening Post* and bête noire of the Republicans, was conspiring with Vice President Burr against Jefferson. "It must be that general Hamilton connives at this *for party purposes.* . . . Hence we conjecture that there is an understanding between colonel Burr and general Hamilton and the ground of this conjecture is a cordial *union* of action."

The name of Federalist Congressman John Rutledge, Jr., of South Carolina was on everybody's lips. He was the son of John Rutledge, one of the original Supreme Court justices appointed by George Washington in 1790. Justice Rutledge had resigned to become chief judge of South Carolina in 1793, and then had tried to commit suicide in 1795 after the Senate refused to confirm him as the nation's second chief justice. A few days before New Year's Day, 1803, John Rutledge, Jr., publicly assaulted Republican Senator Christopher Ellery of Rhode Island, clubbing Ellery with his cane and pulling his nose and ears. Ellery had offended Rutledge by suggesting that the congressman was the secret author of letters defaming Jefferson.

The capital buzzed about the incident. Gouverneur Morris noted it in his diary. The *Aurora's* William Duane eagerly launched a high-profile campaign to prove that Rutledge had, in fact, authored the letters.

As always, Gouverneur Morris seemed to be in the middle of everything. Although Republican newspapers regularly tweaked him as a despised leader of the Federalists, Morris dined with Jefferson on a snowy evening in early January. Jefferson seemed "terribly out of spirits." An expert on extramarital intrigue, Morris speculated that Jefferson's mood might be due to "a knowledge of the Publication shortly to be made of his Letter to Mrs. Walker," Jefferson's decades-old attempt to seduce his friend's wife that Callender then was highlighting. Morris happily noted that he "pass[ed] the evening with Mrs. Maddison." He did not mention that her husband, the secretary of state, was the defendant in a pending case of enormous significance.

Throughout January 1803, Washingtonians also focused on personal concerns. Papers were filled with advertisements for remedies for numerous ailments. The *Intelligencer* featured "Hamilton's Elixir," a "sovereign remedy for colds, obstinate coughs . . . and approaching consumptions." The *Aurora* touted a "fresh supply" of "THE PATENT INDIAN VEGETABLE SPECIFIC," prepared by "Dr. Leroux," for those "unfortunately" afflicted with "VENEREAL DISEASE"; the Patent Indian Vegetable Specific would be effective in "expelling the venereal poison." "HAMILTON'S WORM DESTROYING LOZENGES," in turn, would combat the "tape worm," the "large round worm," the "small maw worm," and the "short, fleet white worm." Among "the symptoms attending worms are disagreeable breath, especially in the morning, bad and corrupted gums—itching in the nose . . . convulsions and epileptic fits and sometimes privations of speech. Starting, and grinding of the teeth." An "Approved Remedy" for the complaints of the eye not only would cure "the most inveterate complaints" of the eye but was "likewise a sovereign remedy for the toothache and preserves the teeth white, and prevents the scurvy in the gum. It will cure the St. Anthony's fire, and frozen limbs. It is excellent in cases of running sores, ulcers, and other wounds even where a mortification has commenced. Dr. Wellington, minister of the Gospel, has written a large volume on the efficacy of this remedy, and the wonderful cures performed thereby."

Washingtonians already were discovering the limits of their self-government, less than three years after the establishment of the national capital. "The situation of the District is this," explained the *Intelligencer* on January 14, 1803. "Her inhabitants are deprived of all political rights, other than those which are derived from Congress, and which may by Congress be taken away at any moment. Those political rights, which they do possess, are insufficient for their welfare. . . . The district is denied all political rights. There is a pride in the genuine American mind that disdains political degradation, and that cherishes the possession of equal rights." The article advocated a constitutional amendment guaranteeing full political rights to Washington, or, in the alternative, retrocession to Maryland or Virginia.

A new session of the Supreme Court loomed in February: the first meeting of the Court since December 1801; the first meeting since the Court issued the order to show cause in *Marbury v. Madison*; and the first meeting since Congress repealed the Judiciary Act of 1801 and cancelled the Court's term in 1802.

Two politically charged cases sat on the Court's docket, waiting for argument and decision in February. In *Marbury*, the Court would be asked to rule on whether the actions of Thomas Jefferson and James Madison in blocking the midnight appointments violated the law. In *Stuart v. Laird*, on appeal from the circuit court in Virginia, the Court would be asked to declare the Republicans' repeal of the Federalist Judiciary Act unconstitutional. If the Court found the repealing act unconstitutional, it would be the first time that the Supreme Court struck down an act of Congress as violating the Constitution.

Underscoring the political cast of the cases, Charles Lee, former attorney general under Washington and Adams (and former cabinet colleague of Marshall), represented the plaintiffs in both cases.

As the Supreme Court's term approached, Republicans vehemently denounced the idea that the Supreme Court had the power to declare a statute unconstitutional. An article in the *Intelligencer* titled "The Democrat" denounced "the monstrous pretensions set up by the partisans of the late administration, in favor of the Judiciary department." The article mocked a "judiciary" that would act as "the judges of the constitution itself." Moreover, the anonymous writer sharply criticized the notion "that under this authority, they have a right to declare a law enacted by the legislature null and void; and consequently, that they may revive and give full validity to laws, and recreate officers, not only without the consent of the people, but in direct opposition to their express will, as declared by their representatives."

"The Democrat" flatly rejected the claim that the Supreme Court could find a law unconstitutional. "However preposterous this opinion may be, it is readily admitted to be by no means new; neither wisdom nor folly are the offspring of yesterday." Then the article reached back to English common law: "This doctrine of judiciary control over the legislature, which judge Blackstone emphatically declares to be subversive of all government, became wholly exposed as absurd and irrational."

The article claimed that no court ever had invalidated a law as unconstitutional. "It is, in fact, an idea so replete with anarchy and confusion, and so inconsistent with the very existence of all government, law, and order . . . that the whim, the caprice, and misfortunes of mankind have, I believe, never yet produced but one example where the theory was reduced to practice." The fact that a few state courts already had ruled state laws unconstitutional was not mentioned.

At the end of January 1803, with the start of the Supreme Court term approaching, two incendiary petitions arrived in Congress. One petition came from twelve ousted midnight judges who sat on the Courts of Appeals that were eliminated by the repeal of the Judiciary Act, demanding payment of their salaries. The ousted judges argued that, even if Congress could reorganize the court system and eliminate their courts, they were entitled to continue receiving their salaries under the Constitution's guarantee of life tenure to federal judges (unless the judges were impeached and removed). Another petition arrived from would-be justices of the peace. William Marbury and his fellow plaintiffs asked the Senate to provide proof that the Senate had confirmed them. Both petitions sparked angry debate in Congress. The debates featured Republican denunciations of the Federalist-controlled judiciary and sweeping Republican statements that the Supreme Court lacked any power to declare a law unconstitutional.

The first to arrive was the petition for salaries by twelve midnight judges, including former Treasury Secretary Oliver Wolcott and Philip Barton Key. Introduced in the House on Thursday, January 27, 1803, the petition immediately plunged Congress into recriminations over the much-debated repeal of the Judiciary Act almost a year earlier, with debate proceeding rancorously along party lines. Leading Republicans challenged the authority of the Supreme Court to declare a law unconstitutional. "If the Supreme Court shall arrogate this power to themselves, and declare our law to be unconstitutional," threatened Republican Representative Joseph Nicholson of Maryland, "it will then behoove us to act. Our duty is defined." Republican firebrand John Randolph of Virginia similarly maintained that, because the issue presented "a broad Constitutional question," it must "be settled, in the House," not in the Supreme Court.

Both the House and the Senate rejected the ousted judges' petition on straight party-line votes, with all Republicans against and all Federalists in favor.

Meanwhile, on Friday, January 28, 1803, the day after the ousted judges' petition was rejected in the House, the Marbury petition arrived in the Senate. The petition, on behalf of William Marbury, Robert Hooe, and Dennis Ramsay, asked the secretary of the Senate for a certificate confirming that they had been nominated by the president and confirmed by the Senate to be justices of the peace in the District of Columbia. (The fourth plaintiff, William Harper, seems to have dropped out of the matter without explanation.) The unspoken but obvious context was that the trial on their claims in the Supreme Court was imminent. With the president and the State Department refusing to cooperate, Marbury, Hooe, and Ramsay needed proof of basic facts. As was the custom, the

Senate had considered the nominations in executive session, and there was no public record of the confirmations.

As with the ousted judges' petition, the justice-of-the-peace petition split the senators on party lines. If the ousted judges' petition summoned the specter of the Court declaring legislation unconstitutional (in *Stuart v. Laird*), the justice-of-the-peace petition summoned the specter of the Court finding Executive actions illegal (in *Marbury v. Madison*). Republican Senator Jackson of Georgia responded with fury. He excoriated *Marbury* as "an attack upon the Executive Department of Government," and, as a result, he was "prepared to oppose it, as often, and in whatever shape it might present itself." Breckinridge joined in the attack. Granting Marbury's petition would pave the way for "assailing the Executive Department of the Government," Breckinridge declared, and he stood opposed to such assistance. "The Senate ought not to aid the Judiciary in the invasion of the rights of the Executive."

Reflecting the Republicans' contempt for Marbury, the *Aurora* mocked the Georgetown businessman as "the person *used* by the *tories* to blow up the bubble," meaning that Marbury was acting as a tool for the Federalists in an attempt to embarrass the new administration. For its part, the *Intelligencer* ridiculed the Supreme Court. In reporting on Marbury's petition, the paper sarcastically described the Court, widely viewed as powerless, as "that *paramount* tribunal!" The Court's order to show cause, in December 1801, still stung. "The Supreme Court ought to have refused any instrumentality into this meditated, and, we may add, party invasion of Executive functions. But they so far sustained it as to allow a rule to show cause why a Mandamus should not issue. . . . It would seem, from the recent attempts to disturb the harmony of the legislature, that as much effect is calculated upon from the *ghost* of judicial power, as from the *reality* of it." The Senate rejected Marbury's petition on a 15–13 vote, with every Republican standing firm against Marbury and all but one Federalist supporting him and his colleagues. (A few Republican senators were absent and missed the vote.)

The hostility between the Republicans and the judiciary threatened to escalate. Talk of impeachment was rampant. On February 4, 1803, Jefferson transmitted to the House information about judicial misconduct by Judge John Pickering, a federal judge in New Hampshire appointed by George Washington in 1795, near the end of his second term. Pickering apparently had gone insane. His court was a debacle and a laughingstock, with Pickering presiding while intoxicated and irrational. Pickering raved and cursed on the bench, and ruled before hearing witnesses. Although Jefferson was not explicit about what action should be taken with Pickering, his implication was clear—Pickering should be impeached and removed, the first impeachment ever of a federal judge (or of any federal official). Although Pickering's unsuitability was evident, many senators and congressmen saw the proposed Pickering impeachment as the first shot in a possible fusillade of impeachments. Whispers about impeaching Marshall and other Supreme Court justices were widespread. The *Federalist* darkly joked that Republicans would blame federal judges for James Monroe's stagecoach getting stuck in the mud, and would then "immediately impeach" the judges and seize the "fortunate opportunity to rid our country of that aristocratic junto."

Jefferson confided to Federalist Senator William Plumer of New Hampshire that he longed for an easier option to remove judges. Impeachment was a "bungling way." The president should be able to unseat federal judges with the approval of Congress, Jefferson maintained, just as many governors could remove state judges with the approval of state legislatures.

On Monday, February 7, 1803, nearly two years after Jefferson assumed the presidency, the Supreme Court's long-awaited term was finally scheduled to begin. As had happened so often in the past in its brief history, the Supreme Court responded to the historic moment with a whimper. The Court lacked a quorum and could not meet. Only Justice Paterson was present. The others, including Chief Justice Marshall, had been delayed in their return to Washington.

On Thursday, February 10, 1803, the Court finally had a quorum. Chief Justice Marshall, Justice William Paterson, Justice Samuel Chase, and Justice Bushrod Washington were in attendance. Justice William Cushing had to miss the February term, and Justice Alfred Moore would not arrive from North Carolina for another week. In Committee Room Two on the ground floor of the Senate, Chief Justice Marshall called the case of *Marbury v. Madison*. Finally, it was time for Marbury's trial.

Former Attorney General Charles Lee stood to represent the remaining plaintiffs—William Marbury, Robert Hooe, and Dennis Ramsay. Since leaving government, Lee had earned a reputation as one of the most skilled lawyers in Virginia. He hailed from one of the leading families in Virginia; he was the third of eleven children and the older brother of General "Light Horse Harry" Lee, a hero of the Revolutionary War, who was famous for his daring raids on the enemy for food and supplies that he then ferried to starving American soldiers. Lee graduated from the College of New Jersey and studied law under Jared Ingersoll in Philadelphia before returning to Virginia. In 1795 President Washington appointed Lee attorney general. Lee lived in Alexandria, Virginia, and was a close friend of Chief Justice John Marshall. Their careers had paralleled one another: They had both served in the Virginia Assembly and in the cabinet of President Adams.

As he stood before the Court, Lee faced a simple but vexing problem. This was a trial, and he had to put in evidence establishing that his clients had been duly appointed. He had to show the existence of formal commissions appointing them to office, after nomination by the president and confirmation by the Senate, and he had to show that the commissions had not been delivered. He then could make his legal argument that the nondelivery of the commissions did not destroy the plaintiffs' right to the office, that the Executive Branch had acted illegally in blocking their ascension, and that the Supreme Court should require Secretary of State Madison to follow the law and give them their positions.

———·———

LEE'S SUCCESSOR, Attorney General Levi Lincoln, sat in the committee room with a watchful eye. The defendant in the case, Secretary of State James Madison, was nowhere to be found. As throughout the litigation, he was keeping as much distance as possible between himself and the lawsuit challenging the lawfulness of his actions.

Two State Department clerks, chief clerk Jacob Wagner and his assistant Daniel Brent, sat uncomfortably in the makeshift court. They had been summoned as witnesses, under threat of $333 fines for not complying with the subpoenas they had received. But they preferred to be in their warrens at the State Department, controlling the paper flow of the nation's documents. They certainly did not relish appearing before their former boss, former Secretary of State John Marshall, and testifying about actions that had occurred while Marshall still was secretary.

In the initial proceedings in 1801, Lee already had submitted affidavits from the plaintiffs setting forth their understanding of the facts, including the nomination, confirmation, and nondelivery of the commissions. But James Madison and his aides at the State Department had refused to provide Lee with proof, and the Senate likewise had refused to give them proof. Because Lee requested mandamus—the special order compelling executive action—on behalf of the plaintiffs, moreover, the Supreme Court itself, rather than a jury, would hear the evidence and make the factual determinations.

Lee announced that his first witnesses would be the State Department clerks, Wagner and Brent. No lawyer represented the Executive Branch. Levi Lincoln was in the room as an observer and a potential witness, but the government continued to refuse to dignify the litigation by officially appearing in it or having a lawyer represent the government in the proceedings.

Wagner and Brent objected to testifying. They claimed that they did not have to testify about their work as Executive Branch employees, that it was privileged. "They objected to being sworn," the Court reporter noted, "alleging that they were clerks in the department of state and not bound to disclose any facts relating to the business or transactions in the office." It was the first invocation in an American court of "executive privilege."

Lee rose to combat the claim. He argued to the Court, headed by former Secretary of State Marshall, that the secretary of state "exercises his functions in two distinct capacities; as a public ministerial officer of the United States, and as agent of the President. In the first his duty is to the United States or its citizens; in the other his duty is to the President." The State Department clerks, Lee continued, could be compelled to testify about the Department's public "ministerial" responsibilities, such as records regarding commissions and appointments, even though they could not be compelled to testify about confidential advice to the president.

Marshall swiftly rejected the blanket claim and agreed with Lee. He ordered them to be sworn in as witnesses. They had to testify. They could object to any individual question, Marshall instructed, and the Court would decide whether they needed to answer the particular question.

Wagner now took his oath. Wagner was a Federalist and had been inclined to quit soon after the Republicans came into office. But Madison prevailed on him to stay, and John Marshall had persuaded him to do so. As Wagner related to Timothy Pickering, the secretary of state who had originally appointed him, Wagner had planned to "rid [himself] from a situation subject to vicissitudes," but Marshall convinced him to stay "on public grounds." Perhaps the earliest career employee of the federal government, Wagner reported that he "easily fled into a consent to remain on honorable terms" and promised Madison that he would proceed with a "neutrality of conduct."

Wagner testified that he was working as personal secretary to Jefferson on the critical days of the change in administration (a temporary assignment arranged by Marshall, although Wagner politely did not point out that fact). Lee asked him what he knew about the justice-of-the-peace commissions for Marbury, Hooe, and Ramsay. Wagner explained that, "at this distance of time," he could not recall whether he had seen the three commissions at issue. He further explained that Marbury and Ramsay had gone to see Madison about the plaintiffs' commissions, that Madison referred them to Wagner, and that Wagner "took them into another room, and mentioned to them, that two of the commissions had been signed, but the other had not."

Lee now saw an opening, not only to establish the facts of his case but to pry into the Jefferson administration. Lee asked Wagner who had given him that information.

Wagner refused to answer. An experienced government employee, he knew that naming his superiors could lead to trouble.

Marshall upheld Wagner's refusal to answer. The question was "not pertinent to this cause," he ruled. Marshall was allowing the case to push ahead, but he was steering it carefully to avoid showdowns whenever possible.

Lee now called Brent to the stand. Brent testified that he did not "remember certainly the names of any of the persons in the commissions of justice of the peace signed by Mr. Adams." He "believed," and was "almost certain, that Mr. Marbury's and Col. Hooe's commissions were made out, and that Mr. Ramsay's was not; that he made out the list of names by which the clerk who filled up the commissions was guided." Ramsay's name apparently had been omitted "by mistake," but, to the best of his knowledge, the list contained the names of Marbury and Hooe. With a young clerk's eye for detail, Brent recounted that, after the commissions for justice of the peace were made out, he carried them to Adams for signature. Once Adams signed them, he "carried them back to the secretary's office"—John Marshall's office—"where the seal of the United States was affixed to them." He believed that "none of those commissions of justices were ever sent out, or delivered to the persons for whom they were intended; he did not know what became of them, nor did he know that they are now in the office of the secretary of state."

Brent had helped Lee considerably in establishing that, at least with Marbury and Hooe, their commissions had been duly signed and formalized.

It was time for Lee to raise the stakes. He called Attorney General Levi Lincoln to the stand. Lincoln, of course, had served as acting secretary of state on March 4, 1801, when John Marshall finally resigned as secretary of state. Lincoln continued as the acting secretary of state until James Madison took the reins on May 2, 1801.

Lincoln rose to address the Court in the dank committee room. He refused to testify, he told the justices. He respected "the jurisdiction of this court." But he also was "bound to maintain the rights of the executive." He was "acting as secretary of state when this transaction happened." Accordingly, it was his opinion that he was "not bound, and ought not to answer, as to any facts which came officially to his knowledge while acting as secretary of state." Lincoln pointedly noted that his opinion was "supported by others whom he highly respected." Whom did he mean? Madison, the defendant? President Jefferson? Lincoln did not explain. He simply requested that, if he was required to testify, he could receive the questions in writing and have a chance to decide whether he would answer them.

Lee promptly read Lincoln his questions and handed them to him. Lincoln now repeated his objection to disclosing "his official transactions while acting as secretary of state." But Lincoln raised another objection as well. He "ought not to be compelled to answer any thing which might tend to [in]criminate" himself. This was potentially a bombshell. It was perhaps the first and only time that a sitting cabinet official invoked the Fifth Amendment before the Supreme Court. What was Lincoln worried about? Had he actually destroyed the commissions, which were government property? Did he know of their destruction by somebody else? Or was Lincoln merely speaking of hypotheticals, giving theoretical reasons why he should not be compelled to testify and testing the bounds of his situation? He did not elaborate.

Lee rose to reply. He reiterated the successful argument he had made with Wagner and Brent. The "duties of a secretary state" are "two-fold"—a "public ministerial officer" and an "agent of the President." As a public ministerial officer, a secretary or former secretary could be compelled to testify. Lee agreed that Lincoln was not "bound to disclose any thing which might tend to criminate himself"—and undoubtedly delighted in repeating Lincoln's concern about self-incrimination.

Lincoln stood again. He protested that it was "going a great way to say that every secretary of state should at all times be liable to be called upon to appear as a witness in a court of justice, and testify to facts which came to his knowledge officially." Lincoln emphasized that he felt "delicately situated" between his "duty to this court" and the duty "owed to an executive department." He again implored the Court to at least give him "time to consider of the subject."

Marshall and the other justices considered Lincoln's argument. Once again, Marshall was firm but measured. The *Intelligencer* summarized Marshall's reasoning: "[I]f Mr. Lincoln wished time to consider what answers he should make, they would give him time; but they had no doubt he had to answer." Marshall went on to shred the substance of Lincoln's objections and to emphasize that any particular issues could be accommodated. "There was nothing confidential required to be disclosed. If there had been he was not obliged to answer it; and if he thought that any thing was communicated to him in confidence he was not bound to disclose it." Lincoln also was not "obliged to state any thing which might tend to criminate himself." Marshall now turned to the core of the matter. "[T]he fact whether such commissions had been in the office or not, could not be a confidential fact; it is a fact which all the world have a right to know." And, of course, if Lincoln thought any particular question improper, "he might state his objections." Justices Chase and Washington agreed that Lincoln must testify.

Lincoln asked if he could have until the next morning to respond to the questions. He had to appear before a congressional committee examining claims by Georgia against the United States, and he also wished to consider the questions. Marshall agreed.

Lincoln returned the next day. Marshall, Chase, and Washington were back on the bench, now again joined by Justice Paterson. Lincoln began by saying that he had an objection to only one question —"[W]hat had been done with the commissions?" Lincoln asserted that he had "no hesitation" in stating that he "did not know that they ever came to the possession of Mr. Madison," and he did not know whether "they were in the office when Mr. Madison took possession of it." But he did not want to "disclose what had been done with the commissions."

The participants in Committee Room Two waited for the Court's answer. Would Lincoln be ordered to say what had happened to the commissions? Had they been destroyed? Perhaps by the president? Lincoln did not state the ground for his objection, moreover. Could this have been the basis for the concern about self-incrimination? And if he was ordered to testify, would he comply?

Again, Marshall sought to avoid a skirmish while moving ahead with the case. Marshall announced that Lincoln was not bound to say what had become of the commissions. "[I]f they never came to the possession of Mr. Madison, it was immaterial to the present cause, what had been done with them by others."

With that question resolved, Lincoln quickly provided his other answers. He had seen commissions for "justices of the peace of the district of Columbia, signed by Mr. Adams, and sealed with the seal of the United States." When he "went into the office," there were "several commissions for justices of the peace of the district made out," but he "did not know that any one of the commissions was ever sent to the person for whom it was made out, and did not believe that any one had been sent." He testified that he viewed Jefferson's later "general commission" appointing justices of the peace as "superseding the particular commissions," and the individuals on the general commission list had been notified.

Lincoln's testimony was over. The *Washington Federalist* ridiculed his performance. This "great man," the paper mocked, "was asked a simple question, but could not answer it till they gave it to him in writing, and he went off and spent a whole day and night . . . with closed doors; and then he made out to remember that he had forgot all about it."

Lee now had one more piece of evidence he wanted to submit before turning to his legal arguments. It was an affidavit by James Marshall, now a judge on the District of Columbia court. The irony of the moment must have been apparent to all, most especially to Judge Marshall's brother, the chief justice, but perhaps to Justice Bushrod Washington as well. Justice Washington had previously provided an affidavit in litigation on behalf of James Marshall. The justice had sworn to the authenticity of the signature of George Washington, his uncle, in a land dispute. The *Marbury* case had been pending, but Washington had not known that he would be asked to one day sit in judgment on evidence provided by James Marshall.

Lee read the affidavit to the Court. It stated that "on the 4th of March 1801, having been informed by some person from Alexandria that there was reason to apprehend riotous proceedings in that town on that night, he was induced to return immediately home, and to call at the office of the secretary of state for the justices of the peace." Apparently, justices of the peace were needed to control the "riotous proceedings." Grabbing twelve commissions, he quickly found that he could not "conveniently carry the whole," "returned several of them," and "struck a pen through the names of those" on a receipt that he had left in the secretary of state's office. He believed that the commissions for Hooe and Harper were among the commissions he had returned.

Charles Lee now addressed the Court. He submitted that he had proved "the existence of the commissions," and he wished to make his legal arguments in support of the mandamus. Lee explained that his argument would address three central issues. First, "whether the supreme court can award the writ of mandamus in any case." Second, "whether it will lie to a secretary of state in any case whatever." And, third, "whether in the present case the court may award a mandamus to James Madison, secretary of state."

Lee now warmed to his task. First, the Court clearly had the power to issue a writ of mandamus. In its very first session, Congress had given the Supreme Court the power to issue "writs of mandamus . . . to . . . persons holding office, under the authority of the United States." Madison was a "person holding office under the authority of the United States."

Second, Lee argued, the secretary of state could be ordered to comply with the law, through a writ of mandamus, when the secretary acted in his public ministerial role, but not in his role as agent to the president. Lee now was on a winning streak with his argument that the secretary of state had dual functions, and he pressed it aggressively. Fully aware that Republicans had irately attacked the case as an assault on the president, Lee sought to deflect the criticism by saying that the president himself was not subject to mandamus. "I declare it to be my opinion," said the former attorney general, "grounded on a comprehensive view of the subject, that the President is not amenable to any court of judicature for the exercise of his high functions, but is responsible only in the mode pointed out in the constitution"—impeachment by the House and conviction by the Senate.

This nod to the president's authority, however, was the velvet glove sheathing the iron fist. When the secretary of state acts as a public ministerial officer, he must follow the law. Lee hit this point hard: "It is true he is a high officer, but he is not above the law. It is not consistent with the policy of our political institutions, or the manner of the citizens of the United States, that any ministerial office having public duties to perform, should be above the compulsion of law in the exercise of those duties." And Lee now talked harshly about the consequences of breaking the law, even for high officials like the Secretary of State. "As a ministerial officer he is compellable to do his duty, and if he refuses, is liable to indictment. A prosecution of this kind might be the means of punishing the officer, but a specific civil remedy to the injured party can only be obtained by a writ of mandamus."

Lee had raised the specter of criminal prosecution. A mandamus seemed tame by comparison.

Justice Paterson leaned forward and asked Lee whether he understood it "to be the duty of the secretary to deliver a commission, unless ordered to do so by the President." Lee replied that, once the president has signed a commission and given it to the secretary to be sealed, it becomes the secretary's "duty to seal, record, and deliver it on demand. In such a case the appointment becomes complete by the signing and sealing; and the Secretary does wrong if he withholds the commission."

Lee now turned to his final point—that, in this case, a writ of mandamus should be issued against Secretary of State James Madison requiring him to comply with the law and give commissions to the plaintiffs.

Lee acknowledged that the office of justice of the peace appeared insignificant. "This cause may seem trivial at first view," he argued, "but it is important in principle." He emphasized that his clients were not concerned with the meager "emoluments" or lowly "dignity of the office." Rather, "[t]hey conceive themselves to be duly appointed justices of the peace, and they believe it to be their duty to maintain the rights of their office, and not to suffer them to be violated by the hand of power." Lee argued that the justices "exercise part of the judicial power of the United States," and that "[t]hey ought therefore to be independent." The plaintiffs, he concluded, had established their right to the office to which they had been appointed: "If the applicant makes out a proper case, the courts are bound to grant it. They can refuse justice to no man."

Lee sat down. It had been a powerful presentation by a skilled advocate. Nobody rose to oppose him. On behalf of the United States, Lincoln tersely stated that he had "received no instructions to appear." He refused to join the issue. Marshall and the other justices seemed uncomfortable at the absence of the usual adversarial proceeding. Marshall scanned the small room and stated that the Court would "attend to the observations of any person who was disposed to offer his sentiments." Nobody replied.

The case was submitted, and now the justices would have to decide.

Chapter
TEN

DELIBERATION

"Old Bacon Face" had the gout, and it was excruciating. Justice Samuel Chase had been stricken days after the *Marbury* argument.

The justices had retreated to Stelle's Hotel, the popular establishment opened by Pontius Delare Stelle in the fall of 1800 to cater to the new capital. Like Conrad and McMunn's, where the justices previously had stayed, Stelle's stood directly across from the Capitol, on the east side (where the Library of Congress now stands), making it easy and convenient for congressmen and senators. Rooms at Stelle's were lovely—outfitted with a fireplace, "white windsor chairs," "red copperplate curtains," and "a large, handsome parlour"—and Pontius Stelle presided in the hotel lobby as a genial host.

By Tuesday, February 15, 1803, just a few days after the argument in *Marbury*, Chase could not manage to hobble the short distance to the Capitol. Chief Justice John Marshall, Justice William Paterson, and Justice Bushrod Washington showed up in the Court's dingy committee room. But, with Justice William Cushing ailing in Massachusetts and Justice Alfred Moore also suffering from illness, the Court could not conduct any business. The official minutes of

the Supreme Court for the day simply note, "From the indisposition of three of the Justices, a quorum could not be formed."

The next day, Wednesday, February 16, 1803, Chase again could
not leave the hotel and make it to the Capitol. But Marshall had a
sudden insight. If Chase could not come to the Court, the Court
could come to Chase. As the Supreme Court minutes for Wednesday, February 16, 1803, concisely explain: "The indisposition of the
Justices continuing, the Court adjourned from the Capitol to
Stelle's Hotel, as being more convenient when the Court opened."
The itinerant Court was now presiding in the parlor of a hotel.
The accommodations at Stelle's were far more luxurious than the
dreary committee room in the Capitol.

On Thursday, February 17, the Court heard four oral arguments
in its new perch at Stelle's. That very night, in the same room where
the Supreme Court had heard arguments that day, the Washington
Dancing Assembly hosted a widely advertised ball in the hotel's
spacious parlor, one of the highlights of the social season. Also in
residence at Stelle's with the justices was one "Doctor Fendall," who
had moved into the hotel earlier that year and who offered, from his
room at the inn, a wide range of dental services and a special "Den-
trifice" to make "the breath sweet and agreeable."

The *Marbury* case loomed unresolved. Many observers had an-
ticipated an immediate decision, as was common with the Supreme
Court at the time, and they speculated on the reason for the delay.
Just three days after the conclusion of the testimony and the oral arguments in *Marbury*, on Monday, February 14, 1803, the *Aurora*
noted, "The supreme court was expected to have taken up the mandamus business this day. However, the indisposition of judges
Moore and Cushing, is said to have caused it to be postponed for
this day." Throughout the week of February 14, as the Court considered and disposed of other cases, it issued no word on *Marbury*.

While "the mandamus business" sat with the Court, political
warfare between the Republicans and the Federalists continued
apace. Federalists attacked Jefferson for being too weak in his re-

sponse to Spain's shutting down of the port of New Orleans. Federalist Senator James Ross of Pennsylvania introduced legislation requiring Jefferson to summon 50,000 state militia and seize New Orleans. Senate debate on the issue, with fierce charges and countercharges, dominated the Senate for several days.

As the end of the Seventh Congress approached in March, familiar faces would be leaving both the Senate and the House of Representatives. The Republican press crowed over the imminent departure of their favorite target, Senator Gouverneur Morris. Morris had not run for reelection. The Federalist collapse in New York had been so complete that there was not even a Federalist candidate to succeed him; the New York Legislature's choice had been between two Republicans. The *National Intelligencer* could not restrain its exultation: "We congratulate the republicans and friends of representative government of New York, that the period is near at hand when they will have a *real* representative in the Senate in the room of Gouverneur Morris, who has, for several years past, instead of representing, opposed almost invariably the will of his constituents."

Meanwhile, Congressman James Bayard of Delaware was defeated for reelection by Caesar A. Rodney, a nephew of a signer of the Declaration of Independence and a Jefferson favorite who had been heavily backed by the national Republicans. Rodney bested Bayard by a mere 15 votes, but it was enough to send Bayard home to Delaware.

Massachusetts, however, bucked the trend. It selected a new Federalist senator to succeed the incumbent, and he had a familiar name. "The election of John Q. Adams as Senator has been confirmed in the Senate of Massachusetts," reported the *Intelligencer* on February 21, 1803, "by 19 votes out of 26." Only two years before, on the day of Jefferson's inauguration, John Adams had skulked out of the new capital before dawn; now his son would be returning triumphantly to serve as an opposition senator.

George Washington's Birthday, February 22, had emerged as the consensus date to celebrate the life of America's first president.

On Tuesday, February 22, 1803, eleven days after the close of the arguments in *Marbury* and with the case still pending, leading Federalist congressmen and senators gathered to honor the revered patriarch. Chief Justice John Marshall merrily joined the celebrants at Stelle's. So did Justice William Paterson, and so did Justice Bushrod Washington, the president's nephew.

As was customary, the celebration began with prepared toasts, seventeen in all. The first toast was to "THE DAY"—Washington's Birthday—a day "to us dear, to posterity sacred." Another toast undoubtedly caught the ear of the three Supreme Court justices in attendance: to "An independent Judiciary—the safeguard of civil liberty." Nobody mentioned the Republican view that the judiciary was the last bastion of Federalist power. And on it went, with toasts to "The honor of our country—her most precious treasure," to "The Heroes of The Revolution—Enshrined in the hearts of their countrymen," and to "Washington's policy—Measures founded on experience, not on theory."

Now it was time for spontaneous toasts by individuals. Congressman Bayard rose first, and, with a shimmering vision of an American geographical empire, toasted "The natural boundaries of the United States, the Ocean, the Gulph, the Mississippi and the lakes." And then it was Senator James Ross, in the midst of his fight to force Jefferson to take a tougher stand on New Orleans, with a pointed reference to his ongoing congressional battles—to "Better security than parchment for our rights on the Mississippi."

Supreme Court Justice Paterson lifted his glass. Showing his penchant for the cliché, Paterson toasted "Pure views, honorable means, and noble ends."

John Marshall now commanded attention as he began a toast. Though few knew it, the *Marbury* decision, which Marshall had been preparing out of public view, would be announced in less than forty-eight hours, on Thursday morning, February 24. Of the revelers in the room at Stelle's that night, only Marshall, Paterson, and Washington knew the outcome. Addressing the crowd in the luminous hotel, Marshall carefully offered a toast to "Those few real patriots who love the people well enough to tell them the truth." Marshall, Paterson, and Washington must have eyed one another meaningfully, and smiled.

The next day, February 23, the Court met again in Stelle's. All of the justices except Cushing now were present; Justice Moore had recovered enough to sit with the Court. The Court disposed of several cases and heard arguments in three more. One case featured Philip Barton Key representing the defendant. Key had been one of the midnight judges who lost his job when the Jeffersonian Congress repealed the Judiciary Act.

The third case that morning was *Stuart v. Laird.* This case presented the constitutionality of the repeal legislation that had taken Key and other midnight judges off of the bench by eliminating the "midnight courts" and forcing the justices to ride circuit again. Arguments would begin on Wednesday, February 23, and continue into the following day.

Charles Lee rose for Hugh Stuart. Lee attacked the constitutionality of the repeal legislation. John Laird had sued Stuart in early 1801 on a contract claim. Laird won in the new midnight court. In 1802, Laird sought an order enforcing his victory. But the midnight court had been eliminated by the repeal legislation The case was returned to the re-established circuit court in Richmond, with John Marshall presiding as part of his return to circuit-riding duties. Seeing an opening, Lee, on behalf of Stuart, had argued that the re-established circuit court was unconstitutional because the legislation restoring it—the repeal of the Judiciary Act—was unconstitutional. Marshall had rejected Lee's challenge to the constitutionality of his court on the ground that Lee's plea was "insufficient," and he found for Laird.

Lee now renewed his constitutional assault in the Supreme Court. He maintained that the repeal legislation was unconstitutional for two reasons, and therefore, since Marshall had been riding circuit, his court had no jurisdiction. First, Lee told the justices, the repeal law unconstitutionally eliminated the positions of the sixteen new federal appellate judges pursuant to the law. The Constitution guaranteed them life tenure, Lee claimed. "This provision of the constitution was intended to place the judges beyond the reach of executive power, of which the people are always jealous, but also to shield them from the attack of that party spirit which always predominates in popular assemblies." Lee pointedly invoked speeches given by John Marshall and James Madison (the defendant in Lee's other pending constitutional case) during the Virginia ratification debates.

Second, Lee continued, the repeal legislation was unconstitutional because requiring the Supreme Court justices to ride circuit was unconstitutional. "[T]he laws are also unconstitutional," Lee explained, "because they impose new duties upon the judges of the Supreme Court, and thereby infringe their independence; and because they are a legislative instead of an executive appointment of judges of certain courts." Lee now directed his remarks to his close friend Chief Justice John Marshall, who had presided on the circuit court. "The act of 29th April, 1802, appoints 'the present Chief Justice of the Supreme Court,' a judge of the court thereby established. He might as well have been appointed a judge of the circuit court of . . . the Mississippi territory." And Lee raised the prospect that a judge who sat on circuit court could not impartially review his own opinion—in this context, an unmistakable reference to Marshall. "A party in this court has a right to have his case heard by six judges," Lee elaborated. "He has a right to an unbiased court whether the whole six sit or not. A judge, having tried the case in the court below, and given judgment, must be in some measure committed; he feels an anxiety that his judgment should be affirmed."

Lee's opposing counsel responded that the Constitution gave Congress broad powers to shape the federal judiciary and that the practice of justices riding circuit was permissible, long-standing, and accepted. Lee's parting shot in rebuttal was sharp and concise:

"[T]he act of 1802 strikes off sixteen judges at a stroke, drives them from their offices, and assigns their duties to others. An error was committed in 1789. That act was unconstitutional, but the act of 1801 [creating the midnight judges] restored the system to its constitutional limits."

Marshall must have secretly chuckled at the sight of his old friend before the Court again. Lee appeared as a lawyer in several Supreme Court cases during that February sitting, in addition to *Marbury*. Supreme Court litigation at the time was incestuous, featuring not only the same lawyers in case after case but, frequently, the same litigants. Robert Hooe, one of Marbury's co-plaintiffs, had two other cases heard by the Supreme Court that sitting, both of which concerned his commercial interests.

Despite the earlier anticipation about how the Supreme Court would resolve a challenge to the constitutionality of the repeal legislation, there was no public comment or attention to the arguments in *Stuart v. Laird*. The pending "mandamus case"—*Marbury v. Madison*—now was the center of attention for those awaiting a confrontation between the Supreme Court and Jefferson and his allies.

On the morning of Thursday, February 24, 1803, at 10 A.M., Chief Justice John Marshall called the Supreme Court to order in the lobby of Stelle's Hotel. Once again, the senior associate justice, William Cushing, was missing, but the other four justices—William Paterson, Samuel Chase, Bushrod Washington, and Alfred Moore—were in attendance with Marshall. The chief justice announced that the Court would render its judgment in the case of *Marbury v. Madison*. All in attendance wondered what the Court would say about this frontal challenge to Jefferson and Madison and their adamant refusal to allow the "midnight" justices of the peace to take their offices.

DECISION

Chief Justice John Marshall looked around the parlor at Stelle's. It was the perfect meeting of man and moment.

Now 47 years old and chief justice slightly more than two years, Marshall, the first justice to have served in all three branches of government, sought an opportunity to enhance the role of the Court and elevate it to the status of co-equal branch. He inherited an institution that was little more than a laughingstock, with no dignity or stature. That was why John Jay had scorned the Court and rejected Adams's offer that he return as chief justice. Marshall had taken the first steps to forge a strong institution—having the Court issue strong opinions, arranging for the justices to live together, leading them to wear simple black robes—but he was looking for the chance to take a major leap. Marshall astutely appreciated, however, that the Court could not rise if it was viewed merely as an appendage to a political party. Nothing could be surer to bring the Court into further disrepute.

Marshall also cared deeply about the Supreme Court's authority as a matter of principle. Even before joining the Court, Marshall had long championed an independent judiciary with the power to rule on the constitutionality of statutes. He had made a powerful speech on this subject fifteen years earlier in 1788, at a pivotal moment in the Virginia convention, to ratify the U.S. Constitution, and he had impressed even giants who disagreed with him, such as Patrick Henry.

Marshall also had strong beliefs about the need to build all of the national institutions of the young country. As a soldier in the Continental Army during the Revolutionary War, Marshall later reflected, "I was confirmed in the habit of considering America as my country, and Congress as my government."

Marshall, meanwhile, was an exceptionally canny and able politician. He had a gift for bringing people along and making them feel at ease, and an instinct for finding the center and common ground. He had succeeded as a Federalist candidate in overwhelmingly Republican Virginia by signaling that he was not an extremist. In Congress, he had hewed, in almost solitary fashion, to John Adams's efforts to steer a middle course, and he had won friends and allies among both High Federalists and Jeffersonian Republicans. The sole exception was his cousin Thomas Jefferson.

Now, in *Marbury v. Madison*, like a perfect storm, all of these elements of Marshall's character—the institution-builder, the proponent of a independent judiciary that could judge the constitutionality of laws, the nationalist, the politician, and even the anti-Jeffersonian—came together in one remarkable moment. Somewhere along the way—perhaps during the fourteen months while the case was pending—Marshall had divined a way to strike down a law as unconstitutional, elevate the Court's prestige while appearing self-denying, criticize what he saw as lawlessness by Jefferson and Madison, and avoid politicization by including disparate rulings that would, at the same time, please and displease both political factions.

Nobody outside of the Supreme Court saw it coming. The fact that Marshall now viewed the case as a paramount effort and a supreme opportunity is clear from the length and complexity of the opinion he crafted. The nature of the decision made it stand out dramatically from the Court's other opinions, which tended to be terse and peremptory. Marshall now saw the *Marbury* case as a very big deal for the Supreme Court, and he was determined to present it that way.

———

MARSHALL BEGAN READING the opinion in a genial tone. Few in the room recognized that he was about to launch one of the longest opinions in the Supreme Court's brief history. It would go on for almost 9,400 words and 164 paragraphs. William Cranch, 33 years old and John Adams's nephew (his mother and Abigail Adams were sisters), had been appointed Supreme Court reporter in addition to his duties as a judge on the District of Columbia Court of Appeals (another midnight appointment by his uncle, President John Adams). Cranch furiously took notes in shorthand as Marshall spoke.

Marshall started by reminding his listeners that "[a]t the last term"—more than fourteen months earlier, before Congress had cancelled the Court's meetings for all of 1802—"a rule was granted in this case, requiring the secretary of state [James Madison] to show cause why a mandamus should not issue, directing him to deliver to William Marbury his commission as a justice of the peace of the county of Washington, in the district of Columbia." Perhaps for the sake of clarity or drama, Marshall never mentioned Marbury's co-plaintiffs, Robert Townsend Hooe, William Harper, and Dennis Ramsay. As Marshall described it, the Supreme Court case was about one man taking on the secretary of state in his implementation of the president's orders.

Marshall noted that "the present motion is for a mandamus," and he highlighted the charged nature of the proceeding. "The peculiar delicacy of this case," he emphasized, "the novelty of some of its circumstances, and the real difficulty attending the points which occur in it, require a complete exposition of the principles, on which the opinion of the court is to be founded." When Marshall referred to "[t]he peculiar delicacy" of the case, everybody in the room at Stelle's knew what he meant. The lowly Supreme Court, notoriously anemic and laughable, was being asked to override the popular president and his highly respected secretary of state. Marshall was setting the stage for an utterly compelling piece of political and judicial theater.

In a statement that must have pricked Jeffersonian loyalists in the parlor at Stelle's, Marshall now gave a verbal nod to Marbury's attorney, his friend and former cabinet colleague Charles Lee. He observed that the "principles have been, on the side of the applicant, very ably argued at the bar." Going further, he now indicated that the Court agreed with Lee's arguments—a potentially stunning development. "In rendering the opinion of the court," he explained, "there will be some departure in form, though not in substance, from the points stated in that argument." Might the Court actually repudiate Jefferson and Madison, as Lee had argued?

Marshall now turned to the body of the opinion. The Court would answer three questions. First, "Has the applicant a right to the commission he demands?" Second, "[I]f he has a right, and that right has been violated, do the laws of his country afford him a remedy?" Third, "If they do afford him a remedy, is it a mandamus issuing from this court?" The crowd in Stelle's knew that, if the Court answered yes to all three questions, a full-scale confrontation between the Supreme Court and the Jeffersonians would erupt.

Marshall took up the first question: Does William Marbury have a right to his commission to be justice of the peace? Marshall began by asking whether Marbury had been duly appointed. "For if he has been appointed, the law continues him in office for five years, and he is entitled to the possession of those evidences of office, which, being completed, became his property." For Marshall's audience, the reference to Marbury's "property" was freighted with significance. At a time when courts in general, and the Supreme Court in particular, decided few federal issues of major consequence, many people viewed the courts' principal role as the protection of property against unlawful infringement, particularly in the context of commercial disputes. By casting Marbury's claim as a defense of property, Marshall was putting it in the most sympathetic light.

Marshall emphasized that, after Marbury had been nominated by President Adams and confirmed by the Senate, Adams had signed the commission and the Great Seal of the United States had been affixed to it. For Marshall and the Court, once the commission was completed, Marbury had a legal right to the office. "The last act to be done by the President, is the signature of the commission. He has then acted on the advice and consent of the senate to his own nomination. The time for deliberations has then passed. He has decided. His judgment, on the advice and consent of the senate concurring with his nomination, has been made, and the officer is appointed."

To make sure nobody missed the point, Marshall reiterated that the Executive Branch no longer controlled the appointment after the signing of the commission and could not obstruct it. "Some point of time must be taken when the power of the executive over an officer, not removable at his will, must cease. That point of time must be when the last act, required from the person possessing the power, has been performed. The last act is the signature of the commission."

Jefferson's order not to deliver Marbury's commission—and Madison's obedience to Jefferson's order—thus broke the law. The secretary of state's obligation to deliver the duly authorized commission was a ministerial, nondiscretionary legal duty, not something the president could control.

Marshall then subtly jabbed the administration for its nonparticipation in the case and emphasized that the Court itself had tried to think of contrary arguments that could overcome this conclusion. "After searching anxiously for the principles on which a contrary opinion may be supported, none have been found which appear of sufficient force to maintain the opposite doctrine. Such as the imagination of the court could suggest have been very deliberately examined, and after allowing them all the weight which it appears possible to give them, they do not shake the opinion which has been formed." The Court had been forced to rely on its "imagination" for contrary arguments, rather than on the arguments of government counsel, who had refused to participate.

Marshall reiterated the Court's conclusion that, on the first question—whether Marbury had a legal right to the commission withheld by Jefferson and Madison—the Court found squarely for Marbury. "Mr. Marbury, then, since his commission was signed by the President, and sealed by the secretary of state, was appointed; and as the law creating the office, gave the officer a right to hold for five years, independent of the executive, the appointment was not revocable; but vested in the officer legal rights, which are protected by the laws of his country. To withhold his commission, therefore, is an act deemed by the court not warranted by law, but violative of a vested legal right." Marbury's legal rights had been violated.

One down, two to go. Marshall turned to the second question. If Marbury "has a right, and that right has been violated"—as the Court had just determined—"do the laws of his country afford him a remedy?" Marshall began by putting the topic on a broad and lofty plane. "The very essence of civil liberty certainly consists in the right of every individual to claim the protection of the laws, whenever he receives an injury." Few could doubt where Marshall was going to wind up when the stakes were "the very essence of civil liberty." "The government of the United States has been emphatically termed a government of laws, and not of men," and "[i]t will certainly cease to deserve this high appellation, if the laws furnish no remedy for a vested legal right." Marshall undoubtedly knew that John Adams, his patron, had originated the phrase "a government of laws and not of men" in support of the Massachusetts Constitution, but Marshall never acknowledged Adams by

name in the *Marbury* decision. Even the king of England, emphasized Marshall, "never fails to comply with the judgment of his
court"—an ironic statement by the Supreme Court of a nation
that had achieved its independence from the king almost exactly
twenty years earlier.

Having established the broad general proposition that the government must comply with the law, Marshall now emphasized that
certain Executive decisions were inherently political and beyond
the scope of the Court. "By the constitution of the United States,
the President is invested with certain important political powers,
in the exercise of which he is to use his own discretion, and is accountable only to his country in his political character, and to his
own conscience." When an Executive Branch official aids the president in the president's political decision, moreover, the actions of
that Executive Branch official likewise are off-limits to the courts.
In that capacity, "[h]e is the mere organ by whom that will is communicated. The acts of that officer, as an officer, can never be examinable by the courts."

At the same time, however, when Congress gives an Executive
Branch officer specific responsibilities, and when the rights of individuals are dependent on his actions, then he is subject to the
courts and to the requirement that he follow the law. "[W]here a
specific duty is assigned by law, and individual rights depend upon
the performance of that duty, it seems equally clear that the individual who considers himself injured, has a right to resort to the
laws of his country for a remedy."

Which side of the line did Jefferson's actions and Madison's actions fall on? Were they political decisions, and thus beyond the
scope of the courts? Or did they involve specific duties, which
courts could direct?

Marshall now took aim at the Executive Branch and at the
president in particular. The decision to nominate, and the decision
to appoint, were "political powers, to be exercised by the President
according to his own discretion." But once an individual was

nominated, confirmed, and duly appointed, the duty to get him the signed commission was a nondiscretionary action, which could not be blocked and which could be ordered by a court. "[C]onsequently if the officer is by law not removable at the will of the President"—and, based on the law giving him a five-year term, the Court did not believe that Marbury was removable at the will of the President—"the rights he has acquired are protected by the law, and are not resumeable by the President. They cannot be extinguished by executive authority."

Hence, based on his appointment by President Adams, Marbury had "a legal right to the office for the space of five years. . . . [H]aving a legal title to the office, he has a consequent right to the commission; a refusal to deliver which, is a plain violation of that right, for which the laws of his country afford him a remedy."

It was a thunderclap. The Supreme Court now squarely had found for Marbury on the question of whether the judiciary could issue a writ of mandamus to compel Madison to deliver the commission despite Jefferson's explicit order to the contrary. The Court seemed on the brink of a momentous confrontation. This would be what many had predicted—the all-out war between the judiciary, filled with Federalist appointees from the Adams and Washington administrations, and the surging Jefferson administration, which refused to let itself be crippled by what it saw as Adams's illegitimate last-minute appointments.

Marshall and the Court had resolved two of the three questions in Marbury's favor. If it did so with the third—whether Marbury was entitled to a mandamus order from the Supreme Court—the war would explode.

———

MARSHALL DIVIDED the pivotal third and final question into two sub-questions. The first was "the nature of the writ applied for"— the nature of mandamus—and the second was "the power of this court" to issue the writ.

On the first, Marshall again took the opportunity to acknowledge and rebut the charge that the Court was intruding too far into the Executive Branch. "The intimate political relationship," Marshall explained, "between the president of the United States and the heads of departments, necessarily renders any legal investigation of the acts of one of those high officers peculiarly irksome, as well as delicate; and excites some hesitation with respect to the propriety of entering into such investigation." Marshall noted that it was not surprising—not "wonderful," as he put it with the archaic use of that word—"that in such a case as this, the assertion, by an individual, of his legal claims in a court of justice; to which claims it is the duty of that court to attend; should at first be considered by some, as an attempt to intrude into the cabinet and to intermeddle with the prerogatives of the executive." That had been the exact claim by Jeffersonians in Congress and the press—that the Court was attempting to intrude into the cabinet and interfere with Executive prerogatives.

Having stated the objection that the Court was being unduly intrusive, Marshall now rejected it in sweeping terms. "It is scarcely necessary for the court to disclaim all pretensions to such a jurisdiction. An extravagance, so absurd and excessive, could not have been entertained for a moment. The province of the court is, solely, to decide on the rights of individuals, not to enquire how the executive, or executive officers, perform duties in which they have a discretion." His court would have nothing to do with political matters, he assured the room at Stelle's: "Questions in their nature political, or which are, by the constitution and laws, submitted to the executive, can never be made in this court."

But the situation here was not political, Marshall insisted. Marbury's rights had been violated by the Executive Branch, and the remedy required only the delivery of a piece of paper. "It has already been stated that the applicant [Marbury] has, to that commission, a vested legal right, of which the executive cannot deprive him. He has been appointed to an office, from which he is not removeable at the will of the executive; and being so appointed, he has a right to the commission which the secretary has received from the president for his use. . . . [I]t is placed in [the secretary of state's] hands for the person entitled to it; and cannot be more lawfully withheld by him, than by any other person."

Showing careful attention to all legal niceties, Marshall explored whether another legal remedy—"detinue," which gave a litigant a right to a physical object—was the proper means for Marbury to obtain his commission. But he rejected the possibility. In detinue, the judgment is "for the thing itself, or its value"; here, the object was not the value of the commission but the position itself. "He will obtain the office by obtaining the commission, or a record of it."

For Marshall, the case was overwhelming. "This, then, is a plain case for a mandamus, either to deliver the commission, or a copy of it from the record; and it only remains to be inquired, Whether it can issue from this court." One hundred seventeen paragraphs into the opinion, everything had gone Marbury's way. The Court repeatedly had found that he had a legal right to his office, that he had a right to a remedy, and that a mandamus was the appropriate remedy. It only remained for the Court to say that it could issue the mandamus to order the Jefferson administration to comply with the law.

MARSHALL KNEW that such a decision would prompt a national crisis. In the thirteen days since the argument had been first made, Marshall saw an opportunity not only to avoid a potentially catastrophic confrontation between the constitutionally defined branches of government but to establish an enduring important principle. To achieve this, bizarrely, the Supreme Court had to rule against itself. Although nobody had advocated this position, Marshall and the other justices concluded that the Supreme Court could strike down the act of Congress that gave it authority to hear mandamus actions as a trial court. In Marshall's view, the Constitution created the Supreme Court as an appellate court. In only a few clearly specified exceptions could the Court act as a trial court. The Supreme Court could lose the battle in the *Marbury* case by denying its own jurisdiction and saying that it could not rule for Marbury because it lacked the power to do so as a trial court, but win a much more significant war. It could record its view of the perceived lawlessness of the actions by Jefferson and Madison even if it lacked the power to enforce a remedy, and more important for the long term, it would establish for the first time that the Supreme Court had the power to declare an act of Congress unconstitutional.

Whether this strategy was the product of Marshall's conscious deliberations, whether it reflected his instinctive ability to transform a vexing problem into a supreme opportunity, or whether the results simply evolved from his view of the different issues in the case cannot be known with certainty. Nor can it be known whether the strategy originated with Marshall or derived from discussions among the justices in their rooms at Stelle's or in the hotel lobby.

What is certain is that, from the time Marbury filed the request for a mandamus in December 1801, through the firestorm of 1802 and the cancellation of the Supreme Court's sessions for that year, and on into the Senate consideration and rejection of Marbury's petition in January 1803, and the resumption of the case in February 1803, no record exists of anybody raising an objection to the Supreme Court's jurisdiction, even in the midst of fierce criticism of the Court for unwarranted meddling in the Executive Branch. Everyone in Washington, it seemed, reacted to the case, and the discussion spilled over into congressional debates, but nobody had focused on the question of the Supreme Court's jurisdiction. Although Supreme Court justices asked occasional questions during the *Marbury* proceedings, there is no record anywhere of such a question or comment on the matter of the Court's jurisdiction. Marbury's lawyer, Charles Lee, had included an explanation of the Court's jurisdiction in his argument, saying that the Court could properly exercise either original jurisdiction in the mandamus action (because Congress had properly authorized it) or appellate jurisdiction (because it was an appeal from actions of the Executive), but there had been no indication that the Supreme Court or any commenter on the stormy case was troubled by the point. Given the amount of hostile Republican press attention, it is notable that no Republican raised the counterargument to the Court's jurisdiction.

It must have been a dramatic surprise to those in the parlor of Stelle's when Marshall's opinion, after building relentlessly to a climax that seemed to pit the Court against the president, suddenly veered in another direction entirely. Marshall noted that the Judiciary Act of 1789 (written in large part by Framers of the Constitution) gave the Supreme Court the power to "issue writs of mandamus to . . . persons holding office, under the authority of the United States" as a trial court, with no requirement of first seeking relief from a lower court. Marshall then considered the Constitution. As Marshall explained, the Constitution provides that "the Supreme Court shall have original jurisdiction in all cases affecting ambassadors, other public ministers and consuls, and those in which a state shall be a party. *In all other cases, the supreme court shall have appellate jurisdiction*" (emphasis added). Marshall rejected the possibility that the Constitution's list of "original jurisdiction" cases could be enlarged by Congress. "[T]he plain import of the words seems to be that, in one class of cases its jurisdiction is original, and not appellate; in the other, it is appellate, and not original." If that were not the case, if the Supreme Court's original and appellate jurisdiction were entirely up to Congress to shape and mold, then the Constitution's use of the sentence "In all other cases, the supreme court shall have appellate jurisdiction" would be "entirely without meaning." Marshall likewise summarily rejected the possibility that the Supreme Court's jurisdiction in this case could be viewed as "appellate," even though the case did not come to the

Supreme Court from another court. "It is the essential criterion of appellate jurisdiction," explained Marshall, "that it revises and corrects the proceedings in a cause already instituted, and does not create that cause." As a result, the law giving the Supreme Court jurisdiction to hear original mandamus actions conflicted with Article III of the Constitution, which severely limited the Court's original jurisdiction.

Now came the decisive moment that would make *Marbury v. Madison* one of the most important cases in legal history and enshrine *Marbury* forever as the symbol of the American rule of law. What should happen when the Supreme Court finds a conflict between an act of Congress and the Constitution?

Marshall warmed to the subject. "The question, whether an act, repugnant to the constitution, can become the law of the land, is a question deeply interesting to the United States, but, happily, not of an intricacy proportioned to its interest." The Constitution is the will of "the people" and embodies "the whole American fabric." "This original and supreme will organizes the government, and assigns, to different departments, their respective powers. . . . The powers of the legislature are defined, and limited; and that those limits may not be mistaken, or forgotten, the constitution is written. . . . The distinction between a government with limited and unlimited powers, is abolished, if those limits do not confine the persons on whom they are imposed, and if acts prohibited and acts allowed, are of equal obligation."

Marshall framed the alternatives. Either "the constitution controls any legislative act repugnant to it" or "the legislature may alter the constitution by an ordinary act." "Between these alternatives," he continued, "there is no middle ground. The constitution is either a superior, paramount law, unchangeable by ordinary means, or it is on a level with ordinary legislative acts, and like other acts, is alterable when the legislature shall please to alter it."

Marshall now made two fundamental points that would ring through history. First, in a conflict between the Constitution and an act of Congress, the Constitution must prevail. "Certainly all those who have framed written constitutions contemplate them as forming the fundamental and paramount law of the nation, and consequently the theory of every such government must be, that an act of the legislature, repugnant to the constitution, is void. This theory is essentially attached to a written constitution, and is consequently to be considered by this court, as one of the fundamental principles of our society."

Second, and just as important, the judiciary would be the final arbiter of that conflict between a law and the Constitution. This conclusion was not necessarily self-evident. In Great Britain, for example, the acts of Parliament were "the supreme law of the land," in the words of one commentator, and were "unreviewable for constitutionality even by the judiciary." The Constitution, moreover, creates Congress and the president, and explicitly requires both to swear an oath to the Constitution. Why could not congressmen and the president be the arbiters of constitutionality, as some in Congress and the press had urged?

Marshall swept aside such objections and, in an act that finally established the Court as a co-equal branch with the other two branches, he claimed the mantle of constitutional adjudication for the courts. "It is emphatically the province and duty of the judicial department to say what the law is," Marshall declared. "Those who apply the rule to particular cases, must of necessity expound and interpret that rule. If two laws conflict with each other, the courts must decide on the operation of each."

Marshall concluded in bold, crisp terms. In deciding cases regarding the constitutionality of legislation, the judiciary must be the entity that makes the determination of constitutionality. The Constitution is "a rule for the government of courts, as well as of the legislature. . . . [A] law repugnant to the constitution is void; and . . . courts, as well as other departments, are bound by that instrument."

Accordingly, William Marbury must lose his case. He could not proceed with his lawsuit for an order directing Secretary of State James Madison to give him his commission as justice of the peace, even though he had been nominated by the president and confirmed by the Senate almost exactly two years earlier. In the final words of the opinion, "the rule must be discharged." Case dismissed. The law giving the Supreme Court jurisdiction was unconstitutional.

It was a stunning result. The Supreme Court had excoriated Jefferson and Madison for violating the law by withholding Marbury's commission. It was the most severe criticism of the president and the Executive Branch that had ever appeared in a Supreme Court opinion. But, at the same time, the Court had avoided the possibility of a direct confrontation with the president, which it surely would have lost. Jefferson and Madison might well have decided to defy a Supreme Court order requiring them to deliver the commission and seat Marbury as justice of the peace.

Most important for the development of the Supreme Court as an institution, and for the development of the American rule of law, the Supreme Court had invalidated an act of Congress as unconstitutional for the first time. By striking down a law enlarging the Supreme Court's jurisdiction, moreover, it had exercised this new power in a context that actually limited the Supreme Court's authority. The Court's action thus appeared self-denying even while it established the preeminence of the Court in constitutional adjudication.

The partisan newspapers were not quite sure how to react to the judgment. Jefferson and Madison had been castigated for their actions—but they had technically won, or at least not lost, the case. Marbury had been vindicated on his claim—but he had lost. The Supreme Court had found an act of Congress unconstitutional—but it had done so by limiting its own power. Marshall had engineered a judgment that seemed to suggest that to win was to lose, and to be weak was to be strong.

Many newspapers, including the *Washington Federalist* and the *National Intelligencer*, reprinted the lengthy opinion in full when Supreme Court Reporter William Cranch distributed it to them in March, spreading it over two or three issues of the newspaper. Some papers across the political spectrum praised *Marbury v. Madison* for its judicious approach. The *Federalist* hailed the decision as "attracting the attention and admiration of our readers"; all should take "an honest pride" in an opinion "animated with so laudable a zeal for the rights and liberties of the citizen." The *Marbury* decision, moreover, belied the "unwarranted insinuations" that the justices had "instigated & supported" the mandamus action as a "hostile attack upon the Executive, to gratify party spirit, and to encrease their own powers. . . . [The opinion] will remain as a monument to the wisdom, impartiality, and independence of the Supreme Court, long after the names of the petty revilers shall have sunk into oblivion." At the same time, the Republican *Aurora*, the *Federalist*'s vehement opponent on most issues, singled out Chief Justice Marshall for special praise for the *Marbury* decision: "The weight of your authority . . . calmed the tumult of faction, and you stood, as you must continue to stand, a star of the first magnitude." For these papers, both Federalist and Republican, the Supreme Court seemed to be acting as a true *court*, not simply as another political player, as many had expected.

Other newspapers were far more critical in reacting to the decision, alternately castigating Jefferson or Marshall, depending on their predilections. Alexander Hamilton's *New York Evening Post*, for example, gleefully ran an editorial titled "Constitution Violated by the President" and ridiculed Jefferson as "that meek and humble man who has no desire for power! . . . [T]he first act of his Administration is to stretch his powers beyond their limits." Some Republican writers, in turn, chastised Marshall for expressing a view on the merits of Jefferson's actions even while disclaiming jurisdiction to decide the case. In a widely reprinted article in the Virginia *Argus*, "Littleton" mocked his fellow Virginian, the chief justice: "[F]or one short moment, you should descend from the altitude of reserve to rescue your fame from the hungry jaws of obloquy, by disowning the child of which you are the chief putative parent." Littleton scorned *Marbury* as "a hideous monster; its conceptions in giant size . . . its head in the rear, its tail in front, its legs mounted on high to support the burthen, its bowels in the exterior and its hide in the interior." Beyond the rhetoric, Littleton's objection was that the Supreme Court had "decide[d] upon the merits of a cause without jurisdiction to entertain it." A correspondent in the Republican *Independent Chronicle* in Massachusetts likewise criticized the Court for giving "a formal opinion upon the merits of the question which was not officially before them." Significantly, neither of these Republican critics objected to the Court's assertion of power to invalidate the act of Congress. Instead, they argued that, precisely because the Court stuck down the law giving it jurisdiction to hear the case, it should not have opined on the merits at all.

Some interested observers, in the press and in Congress, did criticize the Supreme Court for asserting the power to invalidate a statute. A North Carolina Republican leader angrily asked a congressman from his state, "Whence originates the error in supposing that the Judges possess this new and gigantic power?" In the *Washington Federalist*, a writer calling himself "An Unlearned Layman" strongly opposed the Supreme Court's "claim to this most dangerous power" and emphasized "the danger and inconsistency of such a power residing in the judges." Along the same lines, John Quincy Adams reported that Republican Congressman William Branch Giles of Virginia had confided that he "treated with utmost contempt the idea of an *independent* judiciary [and] said there was not one word about such independence in the Constitution [original emphasis]."

There is no record that the losing (but vindicated) plaintiff, William Marbury, ever commented on the decision. Nor is there a record of comment by the winning (but criticized) defendant,

James Madison. But an extensive record does exist of severe and repeated attacks by President Thomas Jefferson, the defendant in all but name. Jefferson did not immediately react. The following year, however, in correspondence with Abigail Adams, Jefferson emphasized that "the opinion which gives to the judges the right to decide what laws are constitutional, and what not, not only for themselves, in their own sphere of action, but for the legislature & executive also, in their spheres, would make the judiciary a despotic branch." He had viewed the Sedition Act as unconstitutional even though courts had upheld it, he explained, and he thus had pardoned those convicted under the Act. Jefferson's smoldering hostility to the *Marbury* case (and to his cousin John Marshall) soon erupted far more dramatically. In 1807, during the trial of Aaron Burr for treason, presided over by Marshall on circuit, Jefferson sternly forbade the U.S. attorney George Hay from citing the *Marbury* decision, even though it was a Supreme Court precedent. Jefferson fulminated that he had "long wished for a proper occasion to have the gratuitous opinion in *Marbury v. Madison* brought before the public and denounced as not law." Jefferson attacked the opinion on all grounds. The "judges in the outset disclaimed all cognisance of the case; altho' they then went on to say what would have been their opinion, had they had cognisance of it." The Supreme Court was wrong about the commissions in any event— "to a commission, a deed, a bond, *delivery* is essential" (original emphasis). And the Court's view of constitutional power was equally flawed: "[T]he Constitution intended that the three great branches of the government should be co-ordinate & independant of each other. [A]s to acts therefore which are to be done by either, it has given no controul to another branch."

On it went through the years for Jefferson, with the *Marbury* case as a bête noire in his letters: Each branch has an "equal right to decide for itself what is the meaning of the Constitution in the cases submitted to its action"; "I deemed delivery essential to complete a deed, . . . and I withheld delivery of the commissions"; the federal courts "cannot issue a mandamus to the President or legislature, or to any of their officers"; if any one branch were to be the "exclusive expounder of the sense of the Constitution," it should be the legislature, not the judiciary; "this case of Marbury and Madison is continually cited to bench & bar, as if it were settled law, without any animadversion on its being merely an obiter dissertation of the Chief Justice"; "the practice of Judge Marshall in traveling out of his case to prescribe what the law would be in a moot case not before the Court" was "very irregular and very censurable."

For Jefferson, unlike many of his contemporaries, *Marbury* was an object of intense scorn—wrong on the validity of a commission that had not been delivered, wrong on whether mandamus could be ordered against the Executive Branch, wrong in giving a decision in a case in which it lacked jurisdiction, and, above all, wrong on the supreme role of the Court in determining constitutionality.

Within days of the *Marbury* decision, the Supreme Court had to resolve the challenge to the constitutionality of the legislation repealing the Judiciary Act. On March 2, 1803, the last day of its February 1803 term, less than a week after the *Marbury* decision, the Supreme Court met to issue its opinion in *Stuart v. Laird* and a few other pending cases. Marshall now recused himself from the case in light of his prior involvement. As William Cranch noted in his official report, "Mr. Chief Justice Marshall having tried the cause in the court below, declined giving an opinion." With Cushing still ill, Paterson was the next most senior justice, and he announced the four-paragraph opinion on behalf of the Court. In the brief opinion, the Court rejected the challenge to the repeal legislation. First, "Congress must have constitutional authority to establish from time to time such inferior tribunals as they may think proper, and to transfer a cause from one such tribunal to another." And, as to the objection to justices riding circuit, the Court brushed it aside because justices had been riding circuit since the birth of the nation: "To this objection, which is of recent date, it is sufficient to observe, that practice and acquiescence under it for a period of several years, commencing with the organization of the judicial system, afford an irresistible answer, and have indeed fixed the construction. . . . Of course, the question is at rest, and ought not now to be disturbed."

In *Stuart v. Laird*, the Supreme Court achieved a second remarkable feat. A Supreme Court consisting entirely of Federalist appointees had upheld a Republican-passed law, which was despised by Federalists and which was passed to target the Federalist-appointed midnight judges. Just as *Marbury* had established that the Court had the power to declare acts of Congress unconstitutional, so too *Stuart v. Laird* was a powerful and important statement that the Court would not use that power for naked political ends.

It is notable that Marshall refused to participate in the Supreme Court's decision in *Stuart v. Laird* because he had participated in the circuit court case. Should Marshall also have recused himself in *Marbury* because of his extensive involvement in the underlying facts? As secretary of state, he had been responsible for the commissions. It was his failure of delivery that led to the case—and, adding another level of personal involvement, it was his brother James who had been given the task of actually carrying the commissions to their intended recipients. Standards of recusal at the time generally focused on a personal financial interest rather than on other kinds of interest, including personal involvement in the underlying facts. Nevertheless, Marshall's simultaneous recusal in *Stuart v. Laird* is suggestive. That case also did not involve his personal financial interest. The apparent participation of other justices in cases in which they had sat on circuit emphasizes that, beyond the realm of personal financial interest, principles of recusal were malleable and discretionary. In any event, Marshall clearly wanted to participate in *Marbury*.

Through a remarkable decision in *Marbury v. Madison*, Marshall had established the Supreme Court's authority to strike down a law as unconstitutional. In that decision and *Stuart v. Laird*, the Supreme Court had gone a long way toward establishing that, contrary to its critics' caricature, it would not be embroiled in factional politics. At the time, however, the cauldron of toxic political brews seemed to be overflowing. In a letter to Oliver Wolcott on the last day of the February term, the same day that the Court issued *Stuart v. Laird*, Marshall exclaimed to his former cabinet colleague that an accusation of financial mismanagement at Wolcott's Treasury Department during the Adams administration was "among the most disreputable acts of the present administration." Marshall, usually cheerful and effervescent, was gloomy. "We have fallen upon evil times," he wrote from his room at Stelle's, and "I do not clearly perceive a prospect of better."

In the heat of the moment, as the Supreme Court's term drew to a close, Marshall could not fully appreciate that, in *Marbury v. Madison* days earlier, he had crafted one of the defining landmarks of legal history.

THE MEANING OF *MARBURY*

More than a century and a half after the *Marbury* decision, on a bright September morning in 1958, the Supreme Court gathered for a special term in its glimmering marble home on First and East Capitol Streets in Washington, near the exact spot where Stelle's Hotel once had stood.

Chief Justice Earl Warren called the Court to order. His eight colleagues that day were an illustrious group. In order of seniority, first came President Franklin D. Roosevelt's three appointments—Hugo Black, former Alabama senator and now a fierce constitutional guardian; Austrian-born Felix Frankfurter, a former Harvard law professor who had written extensively on the Marshall Court; and William O. Douglas, the wunderkind who headed the Securities and Exchange Commission before Roosevelt tapped him for the high Court at the age of 40. Then came the two Truman appointees—Harold Burton, a former Republican senator from Ohio; and Tom Clark, Truman's former attorney general. And, finally, the three Eisenhower appointees in addition to Warren himself—John Marshall Harlan, the courtly and brainy grandson of a nineteenth-century justice, named after both his grandfather and the chief justice appointed by John Adams in his final weeks in office; William

Brennan, a jovial Irishman who had served on the Court for less than two years; and Charles Whittaker, the rookie justice and a former corporate lawyer.

The Court faced an issue of exceeding importance. In 1954, in *Brown v. Board of Education*, one of its most momentous decisions, the Court had ruled that segregated public schools violate the Constitution. Like some other southern towns and states, Little Rock, Arkansas, brazenly defied the Court's command. Governor Orville Faubus summoned the Arkansas National Guard to block black students' entry to Little Rock's Central High School, and angry white mobs circled the school, shouting menacingly at the "Little Rock Nine." Although President Eisenhower sent the Army to escort the black students, the state legislature and the governor continued their defiance. A state constitutional amendment required the state to oppose "the Unconstitutional desegregation decisions of May 17, 1954, and May 31, 1955, of the United States Supreme Court," and massive resistance continued. Now the case was in the Supreme Court posing a fundamental question: Could the state and local authorities defy the Supreme Court's interpretation of the Constitution?

The Court heard arguments from both sides. Eighteen days later, on September 29, 1958, the Court announced its opinion. The Court took the extraordinary step of having each justice individually sign the unanimous opinion.

The Supreme Court dramatically vindicated its constitutional authority. "In 1803," the Court explained, "Chief Justice Marshall, speaking for a unanimous Court, referring to the Constitution as 'the fundamental and paramount law of the nation,' declared in the notable case of *Marbury v. Madison* . . . that 'It is emphatically the province and duty of the judicial department to say what the law is.' This decision declared the basic principle that the federal judiciary is supreme in the exposition of the law of the Constitution, and that principle has ever since been respected by this Court and the Country as a permanent and indispensable feature of our con-

stitutional system. It follows that the interpretation of the Four-
teenth Amendment enunciated by this Court in the *Brown* case is
the supreme law of the land. . . . Every state legislator and executive and judicial officer is solemnly committed by oath taken pursuant to Art. VI, cl. 3 'to support this Constitution.'. . . No state
legislator or executive or judicial officer can war against the Constitution without violating his undertaking to support it." With
Marbury as inspiration in one of its greatest moments, the
Supreme Court required that its interpretation of the Constitution
be sustained.

Marbury similarly has played a pivotal role at other important
times in the nation's history. In 1974, at the height of the Watergate
scandal, the nation faced a constitutional crisis. U.S. District Judge
John Sirica had ordered President Richard Nixon to comply with a
special prosecutor's subpoena and turn over tapes and documents
regarding the president's conversations with his aides. Nixon refused. He declared that, under his interpretation of the Constitution, the president had an absolute executive privilege, and that
courts could not order the president to comply with the subpoena
in violation of his reading of the Constitution.

In this perilous time, *Marbury* emerged as the Court's guiding
star. On July 24, 1974, Chief Justice Warren Burger wrote for a
unanimous Court that it is the role of the Supreme Court, not the
president, to resolve contested questions of constitutionality. "In
the performance of assigned constitutional duties," declared the
unanimous Court in *United States v. Nixon*, "each branch of the
Government must initially interpret the Constitution, and the interpretation of its powers by any branch is due great respect from
the others. . . . Many decisions of this Court . . . have unequivocally reaffirmed the holding of *Marbury v. Madison* that '[i]t is emphatically the province and duty of the judicial department to say
what the law is.'. . . Our system of government 'requires that federal courts on occasion interpret the Constitution in a manner at
variance with the construction given the document by another

branch.'. . . We therefore reaffirm that it is the province and duty of this Court 'to say what the law is' with respect to the claim of privilege presented in this case." Fortified by *Marbury*, the Court rejected the president's position and ordered him to comply with the subpoena, setting in motion a train of events that would result in the president's resignation two weeks later.

Former Chief Justice William Rehnquist hailed *Marbury* as "the most famous case ever decided by the United States Supreme Court." As Rehnquist explained, *Marbury*'s principle "that a federal court has the authority under the Constitution to declare an act of Congress unconstitutional" has been "the linchpin of our constitutional law ever since *Marbury v. Madison* was handed down." Former Justice Sandra Day O'Connor likewise has emphasized the breathtaking significance of *Marbury* for our rule of law: "[B]ecause *Marbury* established the courts, and especially the Supreme Court, as the final arbiters of the constitutionality of all acts of government, it is possible for an aggrieved individual to win a victory in the Supreme Court that neither Congress nor the executive branch can take away."

The continuing importance of the *Marbury* case can be glimpsed in a May 2008 interview with Justice John Paul Stevens, one of the longest-serving justices in the history of the Supreme Court. As Stevens leans forward in his chair in his chambers, which contain memorabilia ranging from his scorecard at the 1932 World Series (which he attended at age 12 and where he viewed Babe Ruth's famed "called shot") to biographies of John Marshall, he exuberantly explains that *Marbury* is "the whole basis for constitutional law" in the American system. He confides that he cites and quotes *Marbury* "at every opportunity" because of its role in the foundation for American jurisprudence. And, indeed, in the 2007–2008 Supreme Court term, Stevens cited *Marbury* in cases ranging from the availability of habeas corpus at Guantánamo prison to the meaning of the Second Amendment.

With a glint in his eye, Steven also notes that *Marbury* has an important personal meaning for him. Stevens spent his first few months in law school, at Northwestern Law School in 1945, intensively studying *Marbury* from every conceivable angle in a constitutional law class taught by the man who would be his mentor, Professor Nathaniel Nathanson. Like thousands of law students before him and after him, Stevens recalls *Marbury* as "the most memorable case of my law school experience," and "a point of entry" for "one issue after another." Smiling broadly, Stevens pulls out his law school notes from the months-long discussion of *Marbury* in his first year of law school and reads aloud from them with delight. Summing up *Marbury*'s role in our system, Stevens observes that every justice, regardless of disagreement on issues, shares the view, crystallized by *Marbury*, that "the Constitution trumps statutes."

In the two centuries since it was announced, *Marbury* has been cited in more than 200 Supreme Court cases. *Marbury*'s cardinal importance—the decision that the Supreme Court may hold an act of Congress unconstitutional—establishes the Supreme Court as a co-equal branch of government, a proposition that, before *Marbury*, would have been viewed as not only implausible but laughable.

This is not to say that the Court's authority always is used wisely, or with universal consensus. Notably, the Supreme Court under John Marshall never invalidated another act of Congress (although it did invalidate several state laws in a series of historic decisions). The next Supreme Court decision to set aside an act of Congress as unconstitutional was the notorious *Dred Scott* opinion written by Chief Justice Roger Taney in 1857, which struck down the Missouri Compromise and precipitated the Civil War (and which did not cite *Marbury*). As the scope and range of federal legislation accelerated in the late nineteenth and early twentieth centuries, so too did the Supreme Court's use of its power.

Many Supreme Court decisions early in the twentieth century striking down social and economic legislation were controversial and unpopular.

The point is not whether everybody agrees with the Supreme Court's use of its power in every case. Rather, the abiding significance of the *Marbury* case is that it stands for a system in which independent courts have the last word on the Constitution, and on the requirements of law. As the late Chief Justice Rehnquist also explained, "the establishment of the Supreme Court of the United States as a constitutional court with the authority to enforce the provisions of the Constitution—including its guarantees of individual liberty—is the most significant single contribution the United States has made to the art of government." *Marbury*, and what it symbolizes for the role of the judiciary in the American system, is the cornerstone of that contribution.

Marbury's impact has not been limited to the United States. It has been a beacon for judges, lawyers, and legal reformers around the world, especially at a time when emerging democracies are trying to give teeth to the protection of fledgling rights and freedoms. As prominent constitutional scholar and University of Virginia Law Professor A.E. Dick Howard testified to a Senate committee considering the spread of the rule of law, "In the modern world . . . constitutions increasingly look to judicial review as a key means to enforce constitutional norms. John Marshall's insights in the legal case *Marbury v. Madison* have become a familiar part of constitutionalism around the world. One may suggest that no American contribution to constitutionalism has been more pervasive or important than this one."

The traditional English model—in which Parliament, not the courts, has the final word on the validity of legislation—has given way to the American model, in which courts protect liberty and ensure the rule of law by having an independent judiciary as the final arbiter of legality. Many countries have embraced limited modifications of the American system—specialized constitutional courts, rather than courts of general jurisdiction deciding constitutional questions; judicial power to decide abstract questions about the constitutionality of laws, rather than a requirement that a constitutional question be litigated in a concrete case between adversaries. But the core principle, crystallized by *Marbury*, that independent courts have the ultimate power to decide legality has been the inspiration for countries around the world.

Chief Justice John Roberts likes to tell the story of a Russian judge attending a conference in Europe. When the Russian judge said that he would like to emulate the American judicial system, a European judge sneered, "Why did you come all the way here if you just want a can of Coke?" The Russian judge replied, "Actually, I do not like Coke. I like my wine French, my beer German, my vodka Russian, and my judicial institutions American." The judiciary's authority to invalidate or not apply a statute that it finds in violation of the Constitution—the authority established by *Marbury v. Madison*—is a fundamental characteristic of the American system of justice.

Despite its lofty place in American jurisprudence—or perhaps because of it—*Marbury* has not escaped controversy, particularly in academic circles.* These controversies, however, do not undermine,

---

*Five major lines of criticism have been leveled against *Marbury* and its role in American life. They can be categorized as criticisms related to craftsmanship, manipulation, capitulation, exaggeration, and distortion. In the *craftsmanship* objection, *Marbury* is attacked for allegedly misstating historic precedents about the Supreme Court's original jurisdiction, for opining on the merits even while finding that the Court lacked jurisdiction, and for being overly rigid in its pronouncements. In the *manipulation* objection, Marshall is criticized for purportedly twisting Marbury's case for a political goal—to grab power for the Supreme Court, or to blast Jefferson, or both. In the *capitulation* critique, meanwhile, the *Marbury* opinion, taken together with *Stuart v. Laird*, is said to reflect Marshall's abject surrender to the Jeffersonians by permitting them to seize control of the judiciary. In the *exaggeration* criticism, it is claimed that the *Marbury* decision is given far too much credit for establishing judicial review—a critique that highlights earlier precedents at the state and federal levels before *Marbury* as well as apparent public acceptance of this authority. And, finally, in the *distortion* attack, critics claim that *Marbury* has been unjustly transformed into a rationale for judicial activism of the left and of the right; they maintain that *Marbury* itself reflected a limited judicial role in refusing to apply unconstitutional statutes thrust upon the courts, not the "judicial supremacy" embodied in cases like *Cooper v. Aaron*.

and should not obscure, the larger role of *Marbury* in American life. In the genius of the American system of checks and balances, *Marbury* stands for the principle of an independent judiciary, which has responsibility for the resolution of constitutional questions concretely presented in the crucible of litigation. In the distinctive American system, the president and Congress, as well as the states, must heed the Supreme Court's determination of constitutional issues. The judiciary is the ultimate authority on constitutionality.

This role, again, does not mean that everyone will agree with the Court's constitutional decisions, whether the decisions set aside social welfare legislation in the early twentieth century or set aside abortion prohibitions in the current era. It does mean, however, that everybody respects a system in which the Supreme Court fairly resolves these contested constitutional issues. As former Solicitor General of the United States Ted Olson has explained, in *Marbury*, "Marshall embedded judicial review into the fabric of American life so deeply that it could never be removed. . . . It is emphatically the province of the judiciary to decide what the law is. The decision empowered the judiciary to act forever as a check against the President and the Congress."

In the Supreme Court justices' private dining room, two paintings hang prominently on the wall, conspicuously visible to anybody in the room. One is of William Marbury, the defiant Federalist who demanded his justice-of-the-peace position. The other is of James Madison, the absent defendant in Marbury's case, the "father of the Constitution," the fourth president of the United States. No other paired paintings of adversarial litigants grace the walls of the Supreme Court's current home, the marble palace across from the Capitol. The portraits in the Court's private dining room are a continual reminder of the case that first established the Supreme Court as a co-equal branch, and as a vital and distinctive participant in American life and government.

They are a constant reminder of the distinctive American contribution to the Rule of Law—an independent judiciary that can and does have the last word on the Constitution, and that is an essential bulwark of the checks and balances that preserve liberty and freedom.

EPILOGUE

THE EARLY YEARS of the nineteenth century had seen the rise of national political parties, the westward expansion of the country and the establishment of the most important tenet of constitutional law—the Supreme Court's right of judicial review. Washington had been a small town—one where the powerful, no matter their political affiliation, seemingly knew each other well. Because there was no cultural or social life to speak of, politics was the lifeblood of the city. Even the Supreme Court, an institution of little prestige during its early years, became an attraction, with dozens of people filling the Court's small chamber to hear decisions read.

Over the next two decades, the capital city grew in both size and stature. Many of the same people who had come to Washington to help build a new city and a new government—and who had played a role in the seminal case of *Marbury v. Madison*—continued to dominate local business and politics.

President Thomas Jefferson never relented in his view that the judiciary should be subservient to the will of the people, and though he was powerless to remove federalist judges from the bench, he supported a high-profile impeachment action. The year after the *Marbury* case, he applauded a House of Representatives investigation of Justice Samuel Chase, "Old Bacon Face," for alleged bias on the bench, including his role as trial judge in the prosecution of James Callender (who had drowned eight months earlier) under the Sedition Act.

Chase was impeached by the House of Representatives in 1804 on eight articles. The vote split along party lines and there is no doubt that some congressmen, such as William Branch Giles, voted to impeach in order to send a message to the Court in the aftermath of the *Marbury* decision. Giles, the Republican from Virginia, told John Quincy Adams, son of the former president, that if "the judges of the Supreme Court should dare—as they had done—to declare an act of Congress unconstitutional, or to send a mandamus to the Secretary of State—as they had done—it was the undoubted right of the House of Representatives to impeach them, and of the Senate to remove them, for giving such opinions, however honest or sincere they may have been in entertaining them."

The trial to remove Chase from office took place in the Senate, with Vice President Aaron Burr presiding. Only months earlier, Burr had killed Alexander Hamilton in a duel. Jefferson had subsequently dropped Burr from the national ticket and Burr ran unsuccessfully for governor of New York. A common quip at the time, while Burr presided at Chase's impeachment trial, was that, despite "the practice in Courts of Justice to arraign the murderer before the Judge . . . now we behold the Judge arraigned before the murderer." Yet Burr gained the respect of senators from both parties for the fair and lawyerly manner in which he conducted the trial. One senator said that Burr presided with the "impartiality of an angel and the rigor of a devil."

The trial lasted for nearly the entire month of February 1805. Senators called Chief Justice Marshall to testify and Marshall carefully defended Chase's demeanor on the bench. Ultimately the Senate acquitted Chase by a wide margin. The outcome helped to establish the principle that judges cannot be impeached due to political disagreements, or disagreements with particular rulings—another critical and enduring principle of judicial independence.

In 1804, Americans overwhelmingly reelected Thomas Jefferson to a second term as president. He carried every state except Connecticut and Delaware. During this second term, Jefferson witnessed the successful completion of the Corps of Discovery expedition when Meriwether Lewis and William Clark reached the Pacific Ocean and safely returned East in 1806, bringing with them significant geographic, cultural, and scientific information about the vast continent which astounded and excited the American people. But the years 1805 to 1809 were not happy ones for Jefferson, who seemed to be constantly reacting to events, most often from abroad as Napoleon plunged Europe into a series of conflicts. Jefferson tried to avoid taking sides, but both the British and French interfered with American commercial shipping and the British also practiced "impressment" of American seamen—boarding American vessels and arresting and removing sailors who could be identified as deserters. When British sailors seized the *U.S.S. Chesapeake* off the coast of Virginia and killed three American sailors and wounded eighteen, Jefferson ordered all British ships to leave American ports, called for the establishment of a 100,000-man militia, and imposed a trade embargo against both Britain and France. The embargo largely failed, and just days before his term in office ended, Jefferson signed into law the Non-Intercourse Act, which repealed the embargo and replaced it with a less stringent set of economic sanctions. Two days before he left office, Jefferson wrote to a friend, "Never did a prisoner released from his chains feel such relief as I shall on shaking off the shackles of power." Jefferson returned to his bucolic farm, Monticello, where he devoted himself to his collections of books and wine, to writing, and to planning the new state university of Virginia.

James Madison, Jefferson's fellow Virginian and close friend, and the victorious but criticized defendant in *Marbury v. Madison*, followed Jefferson as president. The country became increasingly embroiled in the hostilities between France and Great Britain, culminating in President Madison's war message to Congress and then in hostilities with Britain in 1812. Domestically, President Madison adopted national economic policies similar to those of the Federalists in the 1790s. Unlike Jefferson, Madison did not believe that the courts should reflect the will of the people; he adopted a stricter constitutionalist view that the judiciary was one of the three co-equal branches of the government.

After bringing and losing his lawsuit, William Marbury continued his life as a prominent Georgetown businessman and entrepreneur. He seems to have sold everything from real estate to slaves to dry goods. Around 1806, he opened a clothing store on Bridge Street in Georgetown where he sold "the best London superfine cloths and coatings, London double milled and dress cassimeres . . . cotton, worsted and lambswool hose." That same year, he was reelected a director of the Bank of Columbia. Three decades later, the bank went broke; it would be known as "the cow" because its officers had milked it until it was dry.

The two lawyers in the case, Levi Lincoln and Charles Lee, continued to enjoy successful legal careers. President Madison nominated Lincoln to the Supreme Court in 1810. Lincoln was confirmed by the Senate, but he declined the appointment due to failing eyesight and poor health. Madison implored his old friend and colleague, telling him that "I am not unaware of the infirmity which is said to afflict your eyes, but these are not the organs most employed in the functions of a judge." Lincoln demurred and spent his remaining years at his farm in Worcester, Massachusetts.

Charles Lee continued to serve as one of Virginia's most prominent lawyers, appearing several times before the Supreme Court and his friend John Marshall. Lee served as a defense lawyer in the impeachment trial of Justice Chase in 1805 and two years later as a defense lawyer for one of the co-defendants in the Aaron Burr treason trial. In 1809, his nephew, Robert E. Lee, was born; fifty-two years later, Lee would lead the Confederate forces in the Civil War.

Aaron Burr, after the duel that killed Alexander Hamilton, became a political pariah. Burr later planned an expedition down the Mississippi River that many believed was designed to foment insurrection and possible secession from the union by Tennessee and Kentucky. When Jefferson heard of the expedition, he sent troops to stop it. Burr fled and was arrested for treason and tried in Virginia, with John Marshall presiding as trial judge.

For Jefferson, the trial of his former vice president starkly revealed everything that was wrong with the judiciary. In a series of rulings, Marshall ordered Jefferson, who bitterly objected, to produce evidence relative to the trial. In a May 1807 letter to his son-in-law, John Eppes, the president complained that the trial showed "the original error of establishing a judiciary independent of the nation and which, from the citadel of the law can turn its guns on those they were meant to defend, and control and fashion their proceedings of its own will." Although disgraced, Burr was found innocent.

John Marshall's five colleagues on the *Marbury* Court met different fates after the historic decision. Late in 1803, returning from riding circuit, William Paterson suffered serious injuries when his coach veered off a road and plunged ten feet down an embankment. Paterson never completely recovered, although he continued as a Supreme Court justice and died in 1806. Alfred Moore, the little-known justice from North Carolina, resigned from the Court less than a year after *Marbury* in January 1804, due to his continuing ill health. He died six years later at his daughter's home in his native state. William Cushing, the only one of George Washington's original appointees on the bench during *Marbury*, suffered from the accumulated pains of riding circuit. But he served on the Court until 1810, when he died at his home in Scituate, Massachusetts, at the age of 78.

After Samuel Chase's acquittal in his impeachment trial in 1805, he served on the Court for another six years. Gout continued to afflict him, and it often kept him from Court sessions. He died in Baltimore in 1811 from "ossification of the heart."

Bushrod Washington, George Washington's nephew and John Marshall's close friend, served the longest of Marshall's colleagues on the *Marbury* case. He sat with Marshall until 1829, completing thirty years on the Supreme Court before he died in November 1829 while riding circuit in Philadelphia at the age of 67. Justice Joseph Story, a Madison appointee in 1807 and a close ally of Marshall and Washington, gave Justice Washington a curiously muted eulogy: "If he was not as profound as some, he was more exact than most men."

The key figures in the debate over the judiciary in Congress had very different careers after the *Marbury* decision. John Breckinridge, Jefferson's most reliable ally in the Senate, became attorney general during Jefferson's second term, an appointment that was immensely popular in the western United States. But Breckinridge died a year later at the age of 46, leaving a widow and nine children, several of whom would grow up to become influential public servants. James Bayard, the Federalist from Delaware who had helped make Jefferson president, lost his seat in the House of Representatives but ultimately came back to Congress to serve as a senator for eight years. President Madison appointed him to negotiate the Treaty of Ghent, which eventually gave the United States full control of the Mississippi River. And the irrepressible and incorrigible Gouverneur Morris, former minister to France and former senator from New York, finally married late in life. Ironically, Morris's wife, Anne Carey Randolph, had once been involved in a scandal in Virginia and had been represented by John Marshall, who now vouched for her character to Morris and gave her a good reference. With politics and womanizing behind him, Morris settled down to the life of a country gentleman.

On March 4, 1825, Chief Justice Marshall administered the oath of office to the sixth president of the United States, John Quincy

Adams. In Braintree, Massachusetts, the health of the second president, John Adams, who had been extremely ill, seemed to improve. Now 89 years old, Adams had spent the last quarter of a century tending to his farm, working on his memoirs, reading poetry and novels, and carrying on an active correspondence with a large number of friends and former associates, including Thomas Jefferson. A decade earlier, three years before the death of his wife Abigail, Adams had written to his son that "the last fourteen years have been the happiest of my life."

Looking back over his career later that summer, Adams wrote that "the proudest act of my life was the gift of John Marshall to the people of the United States."

John Marshall finished his biography of George Washington, continued to frequent the Quoits Club, and raised six children, one of whom was expelled from Harvard for misbehavior. He suffered the loss of four other children and in 1831 his beloved wife died. Marshall also experienced deteriorating health in his later years, surviving an operation without anesthesia to remove bladder stones. But he continued to walk nearly two miles every day until one morning in 1835 when he collapsed. He was diagnosed with an enlarged liver and died a few days later.

Marshall served for thirty-four years as chief justice. While no other federal legislative act was overturned until the *Dred Scott* decision in 1857, Marshall presided over numerous landmark decisions. Seven years after *Marbury v. Madison,* the Court declared a state law unconstitutional in *Fletcher v. Peck.* And six years later in *Martin v. Hunter's Lessee,* Story wrote the decision upholding the Supreme Court's right to reverse state courts. In the 1819 *McCollough v. Maryland* decision, Marshall denied the right of a state to tax a branch of the Bank of the United States, declaring that the "power to tax" involved the "power to destroy." And finally, in the 1824 *Gibbons v. Ogden* case, the Marshall Court sided with Gibbons in arguing that a federal law was superior to a state law.

Taken together, Marshall's decisions served to strengthen the national government and firmly establish the Supreme Court as the final arbiter of the Constitution.

Although it has gone unnoticed by legions of scholars commenting on *Marbury v. Madison*, John Marshall and William Marbury ended up linked in another way besides their respective roles in the historical case. On October 6, 1857, in Alexandria, Virginia, Fendall Marbury, a descendant of William Marbury's cousin, married Kate Marshall, Chief Justice John Marshall's great niece. William Marbury and John Marshall thus ended up as family relations, decades past their deaths, though Marshall had ruled against Marbury in the most famous case in Supreme Court history. And because John Marshall also was a cousin to Thomas Jefferson, the marriage meant that Marbury, the man who spearheaded a case designed to embarrass President Jefferson, was now posthumously related to Jefferson, the man who so despised the *Marbury* opinion that he ordered it never to be cited.

This eventual intertwining of Marbury's family with Marshall's, and with Jefferson's, gives new and unexpected meaning to Jefferson's statement, on the eve of Marbury's case, that "we are all republicans, we are all federalists." Most fundamentally, the weaving together of the three families may well symbolize the role that *Marbury v. Madison* has played as a unifying fabric for Americans of all political persuasions. We remain united in the belief that we are a people governed by the rule of law, and a nation ennobled by an independent judiciary, even as we disagree about particular strands within that rich tapestry. Those are the principles bequeathed to us by the *Marbury v. Madison* decision, and that is why the decision properly lies in the national treasure room of the National Archives, flanking the Declaration of Independence, the Constitution, and the Bill of Rights.

APPENDIX 1:

MARBURY v. MADISON

SUPREME COURT OF THE UNITED STATES
5 U.S. (1 Cranch) 137 (1803)
MARSHALL, C.J., *Opinion of the Court*

At the last term, on the affidavits then read and filed with the clerk, a rule was granted in this case requiring the Secretary of State to show cause why a mandamus [p154] should not issue directing him to deliver to William Marbury his commission as a justice of the peace for the county of Washington, in the District of Columbia.

No cause has been shown, and the present motion is for a mandamus. The peculiar delicacy of this case, the novelty of some of its circumstances, and the real difficulty attending the points which occur in it require a complete exposition of the principles on which the opinion to be given by the Court is founded.

These principles have been, on the side of the applicant, very ably argued at the bar. In rendering the opinion of the Court, there will be some departure in form, though not in substance, from the points stated in that argument.

In the order in which the Court has viewed this subject, the following questions have been considered and decided.

1. Has the applicant a right to the commission he demands?
2. If he has a right, and that right has been violated, do the laws of his country afford him a remedy?
3. If they do afford him a remedy, is it a mandamus issuing from this court?

The first object of inquiry is:
1. Has the applicant a right to the commission he demands?
His right originates in an act of Congress passed in February, 1801, concerning the District of Columbia.

After dividing the district into two counties, the eleventh section of this law enacts,

> that there shall be appointed in and for each of the said counties such number of discreet persons to be justices of the peace as the President of the United States shall, from time to time, think expedient, to continue in office for five years. [p155]

It appears from the affidavits that, in compliance with this law, a commission for William Marbury as a justice of peace for the County of Washington was signed by John Adams, then President of the United States, after which the seal of the United States was affixed to it, but the commission has never reached the person for whom it was made out.

In order to determine whether he is entitled to this commission, it becomes necessary to inquire whether he has been appointed to the office. For if he has been appointed, the law continues him in office for five years, and he is entitled to the possession of those evidences of office, which, being completed, became his property.

The second section of the second article of the Constitution declares,

The President shall nominate, and, by and with the advice and consent of the Senate, shall appoint ambassadors, other public ministers and consuls, and all other officers of the United States, whose appointments are not otherwise provided for.

The third section declares, that "He shall commission all the officers of the United States."

An act of Congress directs the Secretary of State to keep the seal of the United States,

to make out and record, and affix the said seal to all civil commissions to officers of the United States to be appointed by the President, by and with the consent of the Senate, or by the President alone; provided that the said seal shall not be affixed to any commission before the same shall have been signed by the President of the United States.

These are the clauses of the Constitution and laws of the United States which affect this part of the case. They seem to contemplate three distinct operations:

1. The nomination. This is the sole act of the President, and is completely voluntary.
2. The appointment. This is also the act of the President, and is also a voluntary act, though it can only be performed by and with the advice and consent of the Senate. [p156]
3. The commission. To grant a commission to a person appointed might perhaps be deemed a duty enjoined by the Constitution. "He shall," says that instrument, "commission all the officers of the United States."

The acts of appointing to office and commissioning the person appointed can scarcely be considered as one and the same, since the power to perform them is given in two separate and distinct sections of the Constitution. The distinction between the appointment and the commission will be rendered more apparent by adverting to that provision in the second section of the second article of the Constitution which authorises Congress

> to vest by law the appointment of such inferior officers as they think proper in the President alone, in the Courts of law, or in the heads of departments;

thus contemplating cases where the law may direct the President to commission an officer appointed by the Courts or by the heads of departments. In such a case, to issue a commission would be apparently a duty distinct from the appointment, the performance of which perhaps could not legally be refused.

Although that clause of the Constitution which requires the President to commission all the officers of the United States may never have been applied to officers appointed otherwise than by himself, yet it would be difficult to deny the legislative power to apply it to such cases. Of consequence, the constitutional distinction between the appointment to an office and the commission of an officer who has been appointed remains the same as if in practice the President had commissioned officers appointed by an authority other than his own.

It follows too from the existence of this distinction that, if an appointment was to be evidenced by any public act other than the commission, the performance of such public act would create the officer, and if he was not removable at the will of the President, would either give him a right to his commission or enable him to perform the duties without it.

These observations are premised solely for the purpose of rendering more intelligible those which apply more directly to the particular case under consideration. [p157]

This is an appointment made by the President, by and with the advice and consent of the Senate, and is evidenced by no act but the commission itself. In such a case, therefore, the commission and the appointment seem inseparable, it being almost impossible to show an appointment otherwise than by proving the existence of a commission; still, the commission is not necessarily the appointment; though conclusive evidence of it.

But at what stage does it amount to this conclusive evidence?

The answer to this question seems an obvious one. The appointment, being the sole act of the President, must be completely evidenced when it is shown that he has done everything to be performed by him.

Should the commission, instead of being evidence of an appointment, even be considered as constituting the appointment itself, still it would be made when the last act to be done by the President was performed, or, at furthest, when the commission was complete.

The last act to be done by the President is the signature of the commission. He has then acted on the advice and consent of the Senate to his own nomination. The time for deliberation has then passed. He has decided. His judgment, on the advice and consent of the Senate concurring with his nomination, has been made, and the officer is appointed. This appointment is evidenced by an open, unequivocal act, and, being the last act required from the person making it, necessarily excludes the idea of its being, so far as it respects the appointment, an inchoate and incomplete transaction.

Some point of time must be taken when the power of the Executive over an officer, not removable at his will, must cease. That point of time must be when the constitutional power of appointment has been exercised. And this power has been exercised when the last act required from the person possessing the power has been performed. This last act is the signature of the commission. This idea seems to have prevailed with the Legislature when the act passed converting the Department [p158] of Foreign Affairs into the Department of State. By that act, it is enacted that the Secretary of State shall keep the seal of the United States, and shall make out and record, and shall affix the said seal to all civil commissions to officers of the United States, to be appointed by the President: . . . provided that the said seal shall not be affixed to any commission before the same shall have been signed by the President of the United States, nor to any other instrument or act without the special warrant of the President therefor.

The signature is a warrant for affixing the great seal to the commission, and the great seal is only to be affixed to an instrument which is complete. It attests, by an act supposed to be of public notoriety, the verity of the Presidential signature.

It is never to be affixed till the commission is signed, because the signature, which gives force and effect to the commission, is conclusive evidence that the appointment is made.

The commission being signed, the subsequent duty of the Secretary of State is prescribed by law, and not to be guided by the will of the President. He is to affix the seal of the United States to the commission, and is to record it.

This is not a proceeding which may be varied if the judgment of the Executive shall suggest one more eligible, but is a precise course accurately marked out by law, and is to be strictly pursued. It is the duty of the Secretary of State to conform to the law, and in this he is an officer of the United States, bound to obey the laws. He acts, in this respect, as has been very properly stated at the bar, under the authority of law, and not by the instructions of the President. It is a ministerial act which the law enjoins on a particular officer for a particular purpose.

If it should be supposed that the solemnity of affixing the seal is necessary not only to the validity of the commission, but even to the completion of an appointment, still, when the seal is affixed, the appointment is made, and [p159] the commission is valid. No other solemnity is required by law; no other act is to be performed on the part of government. All that the Executive can do to invest the person with his office is done, and unless the appointment be

then made, the Executive cannot make one without the cooperation of others.

After searching anxiously for the principles on which a contrary
opinion may be supported, none has been found which appear of
sufficient force to maintain the opposite doctrine.

Such as the imagination of the Court could suggest have been
very deliberately examined, and after allowing them all the weight
which it appears possible to give them, they do not shake the opinion which has been formed.

In considering this question, it has been conjectured that the
commission may have been assimilated to a deed to the validity of
which delivery is essential.

This idea is founded on the supposition that the commission is
not merely evidence of an appointment, but is itself the actual appointment—a supposition by no means unquestionable. But, for
the purpose of examining this objection fairly, let it be conceded
that the principle claimed for its support is established.

The appointment being, under the Constitution, to be made by
the President personally, the delivery of the deed of appointment,
if necessary to its completion, must be made by the President also.
It is not necessary that the livery should be made personally to the
grantee of the office; it never is so made. The law would seem to
contemplate that it should be made to the Secretary of State, since
it directs the secretary to affix the seal to the commission after it
shall have been signed by the President. If then the act of livery be
necessary to give validity to the commission, it has been delivered
when executed and given to the Secretary for the purpose of being
sealed, recorded, and transmitted to the party.

But in all cases of letters patent, certain solemnities are required
by law, which solemnities are the evidences [p160] of the validity of
the instrument. A formal delivery to the person is not among
them. In cases of commissions, the sign manual of the President
and the seal of the United States are those solemnities. This objection therefore does not touch the case.

It has also occurred as possible, and barely possible, that the transmission of the commission and the acceptance thereof might be deemed necessary to complete the right of the plaintiff.

The transmission of the commission is a practice directed by convenience, but not by law. It cannot therefore be necessary to constitute the appointment, which must precede it and which is the mere act of the President. If the Executive required that every person appointed to an office should himself take means to procure his commission, the appointment would not be the less valid on that account. The appointment is the sole act of the President; the transmission of the commission is the sole act of the officer to whom that duty is assigned, and may be accelerated or retarded by circumstances which can have no influence on the appointment. A commission is transmitted to a person already appointed, not to a person to be appointed or not, as the letter enclosing the commission should happen to get into the post office and reach him in safety, or to miscarry.

It may have some tendency to elucidate this point to inquire whether the possession of the original commission be indispensably necessary to authorize a person appointed to any office to perform the duties of that office. If it was necessary, then a loss of the commission would lose the office. Not only negligence, but accident or fraud, fire or theft might deprive an individual of his office. In such a case, I presume it could not be doubted but that a copy from the record of the Office of the Secretary of State would be, to every intent and purpose, equal to the original. The act of Congress has expressly made it so. To give that copy validity, it would not be necessary to prove that the original had been transmitted and afterwards lost. The copy would be complete evidence that the original had existed, and that the appointment had been made, but not that the original had been transmitted. If indeed it should appear that [p161] the original had been mislaid in the Office of State, that circumstance would not affect the operation of the copy.

When all the requisites have been performed which authorize a recording officer to record any instrument whatever, and the order for that purpose has been given, the instrument is in law considered as recorded, although the manual labour of inserting it in a book kept for that purpose may not have been performed.

In the case of commissions, the law orders the Secretary of State to record them. When, therefore, they are signed and sealed, the order for their being recorded is given, and, whether inserted in the book or not, they are in law recorded.

A copy of this record is declared equal to the original, and the fees to be paid by a person requiring a copy are ascertained by law. Can a keeper of a public record erase therefrom a commission which has been recorded? Or can he refuse a copy thereof to a person demanding it on the terms prescribed by law?

Such a copy would, equally with the original, authorize the justice of peace to proceed in the performance of his duty, because it would, equally with the original, attest his appointment.

If the transmission of a commission be not considered as necessary to give validity to an appointment, still less is its acceptance. The appointment is the sole act of the President; the acceptance is the sole act of the officer, and is, in plain common sense, posterior to the appointment. As he may resign, so may he refuse to accept; but neither the one nor the other is capable of rendering the appointment a nonentity.

That this is the understanding of the government is apparent from the whole tenor of its conduct.

A commission bears date, and the salary of the officer commences from his appointment, not from the transmission or acceptance of his commission. When a person appointed to any office refuses to accept that office, the successor is nominated in the place of the person who [p162] has declined to accept, and not in the place of the person who had been previously in office and had created the original vacancy.

It is therefore decidedly the opinion of the Court that, when a commission has been signed by the President, the appointment is made, and that the commission is complete when the seal of the United States has been affixed to it by the Secretary of State.

Where an officer is removable at the will of the Executive, the circumstance which completes his appointment is of no concern, because the act is at any time revocable, and the commission may be arrested if still in the office. But when the officer is not removable at the will of the Executive, the appointment is not revocable, and cannot be annulled. It has conferred legal rights which cannot be resumed.

The discretion of the Executive is to be exercised until the appointment has been made. But having once made the appointment, his power over the office is terminated in all cases, where by law the officer is not removable by him. The right to the office is then in the person appointed, and he has the absolute, unconditional power of accepting or rejecting it.

Mr. Marbury, then, since his commission was signed by the President and sealed by the Secretary of State, was appointed, and as the law creating the office gave the officer a right to hold for five years independent of the Executive, the appointment was not revocable, but vested in the officer legal rights which are protected by the laws of his country.

To withhold the commission, therefore, is an act deemed by the Court not warranted by law, but violative of a vested legal right.

This brings us to the second inquiry, which is:

2. If he has a right, and that right has been violated, do the laws of his country afford him a remedy? [p163]

The very essence of civil liberty certainly consists in the right of every individual to claim the protection of the laws whenever he receives an injury. One of the first duties of government is to afford that protection. In Great Britain, the King himself is sued in the respectful form of a petition, and he never fails to comply with the judgment of his court.

In the third volume of his Commentaries, page 23, Blackstone states two cases in which a remedy is afforded by mere operation of law.

"In all other cases," he says,

> it is a general and indisputable rule that where there is a legal right, there is also a legal remedy by suit or action at law whenever that right is invaded.

And afterwards, page 109 of the same volume, he says,

> I am next to consider such injuries as are cognizable by the Courts of common law. And herein I shall for the present only remark that all possible injuries whatsoever that did not fall within the exclusive cognizance of either the ecclesiastical, military, or maritime tribunals are, for that very reason, within the cognizance of the common law courts of justice, for it is a settled and invariable principle in the laws of England that every right, when withheld, must have a remedy, and every injury its proper redress.

The Government of the United States has been emphatically termed a government of laws, and not of men. It will certainly cease to deserve this high appellation if the laws furnish no remedy for the violation of a vested legal right.

If this obloquy is to be cast on the jurisprudence of our country, it must arise from the peculiar character of the case.

It behooves us, then, to inquire whether there be in its composition any ingredient which shall exempt from legal investigation or exclude the injured party from legal redress. In pursuing this inquiry, the first question which presents itself is whether this can be arranged [p164] with that class of cases which come under the description of *damnum absque injuria*—a loss without an injury.

This description of cases never has been considered, and, it is believed, never can be considered, as comprehending offices of trust, of honour or of profit. The office of justice of peace in the District of Columbia is such an office; it is therefore worthy of the attention and guardianship of the laws. It has received that attention and guardianship. It has been created by special act of Congress, and has been secured, so far as the laws can give security to the person appointed to fill it, for five years. It is not then on account of the worthlessness of the thing pursued that the injured party can be alleged to be without remedy.

Is it in the nature of the transaction? Is the act of delivering or withholding a commission to be considered as a mere political act belonging to the Executive department alone, for the performance of which entire confidence is placed by our Constitution in the Supreme Executive, and for any misconduct respecting which the injured individual has no remedy?

That there may be such cases is not to be questioned, but that every act of duty to be performed in any of the great departments of government constitutes such a case is not to be admitted.

By the act concerning invalids, passed in June, 1794, the Secretary at War is ordered to place on the pension list all persons whose names are contained in a report previously made by him to Congress. If he should refuse to do so, would the wounded veteran be without remedy? Is it to be contended that where the law, in precise terms, directs the performance of an act in which an individual is interested, the law is incapable of securing obedience to its mandate? Is it on account of the character of the person against whom the complaint is made? Is it to be contended that the heads of departments are not amenable to the laws of their country?

Whatever the practice on particular occasions may be, the theory of this principle will certainly never be maintained. [p165] No act of the Legislature confers so extraordinary a privilege, nor can it derive countenance from the doctrines of the common law. After stating that personal injury from the King to a subject is presumed to be impossible, Blackstone, Vol. III. p. 255, says, but injuries to the rights of property can scarcely be committed by the Crown without the intervention of its officers, for whom, the law, in matters of right, entertains no respect or delicacy, but furnishes various methods of detecting the errors and misconduct of those agents by whom the King has been deceived and induced to do a temporary injustice.

By the act passed in 1796, authorizing the sale of the lands above the mouth of Kentucky river, the purchaser, on paying his purchase money, becomes completely entitled to the property purchased, and, on producing to the Secretary of State the receipt of the treasurer upon a certificate required by the law, the President of the United States is authorized to grant him a patent. It is further enacted that all patents shall be countersigned by the Secretary of State, and recorded in his office. If the Secretary of State should choose to withhold this patent, or, the patent being lost, should refuse a copy of it, can it be imagined that the law furnishes to the injured person no remedy?

It is not believed that any person whatever would attempt to maintain such a proposition.

It follows, then, that the question whether the legality of an act of the head of a department be examinable in a court of justice or not must always depend on the nature of that act.

If some acts be examinable and others not, there must be some rule of law to guide the Court in the exercise of its jurisdiction.

In some instances, there may be difficulty in applying the rule to particular cases; but there cannot, it is believed, be much difficulty in laying down the rule.

By the Constitution of the United States, the President is invested with certain important political powers, in the [p166] exercise of which he is to use his own discretion, and is accountable only to his country in his political character and to his own conscience. To aid him in the performance of these duties, he is authorized to appoint certain officers, who act by his authority and in conformity with his orders.

In such cases, their acts are his acts; and whatever opinion may be entertained of the manner in which executive discretion may be used, still there exists, and can exist, no power to control that discretion. The subjects are political. They respect the nation, not individual rights, and, being entrusted to the Executive, the decision of the Executive is conclusive. The application of this remark will be perceived by adverting to the act of Congress for establishing the Department of Foreign Affairs. This officer, as his duties were prescribed by that act, is to conform precisely to the will of the President. He is the mere organ by whom that will is communicated. The acts of such an officer, as an officer, can never be examinable by the Courts.

But when the Legislature proceeds to impose on that officer other duties; when he is directed peremptorily to perform certain acts; when the rights of individuals are dependent on the performance of those acts; he is so far the officer of the law, is amenable to the laws for his conduct, and cannot at his discretion, sport away the vested rights of others.

The conclusion from this reasoning is that, where the heads of departments are the political or confidential agents of the Executive, merely to execute the will of the President, or rather to act in cases in which the Executive possesses a constitutional or legal discretion, nothing can be more perfectly clear than that their acts are only politically examinable. But where a specific duty is assigned by law, and individual rights depend upon the performance of that duty, it seems equally clear that the individual who considers himself injured has a right to resort to the laws of his country for a remedy.

If this be the rule, let us inquire how it applies to the case under the consideration of the Court. [p167]

The power of nominating to the Senate, and the power of appointing the person nominated, are political powers, to be exercised by the President according to his own discretion. When he has made an appointment, he has exercised his whole power, and his discretion has been completely applied to the case. If, by law, the officer be removable at the will of the President, then a new appointment may be immediately made, and the rights of the officer are terminated. But as a fact which has existed cannot be made never to have existed, the appointment cannot be annihilated, and consequently, if the officer is by law not removable at the will of the President, the rights he has acquired are protected by the law, and are not resumable by the President. They cannot be extinguished by Executive authority, and he has the privilege of asserting them in like manner as if they had been derived from any other source.

The question whether a right has vested or not is, in its nature, judicial, and must be tried by the judicial authority. If, for example, Mr. Marbury had taken the oaths of a magistrate and proceeded to act as one, in consequence of which a suit had been instituted against him in which his defence had depended on his being a magistrate; the validity of his appointment must have been determined by judicial authority.

So, if he conceives that, by virtue of his appointment, he has a legal right either to the commission which has been made out for him or to a copy of that commission, it is equally a question examinable in a court, and the decision of the Court upon it must depend on the opinion entertained of his appointment.

That question has been discussed, and the opinion is that the latest point of time which can be taken as that at which the appointment was complete and evidenced was when, after the signature of the President, the seal of the United States was affixed to the commission.

It is then the opinion of the Court:

1. That, by signing the commission of Mr. Marbury, the President of the United States appointed him a justice [p168] of peace for the County of Washington in the District of Columbia, and

that the seal of the United States, affixed thereto by the Secretary of State, is conclusive testimony of the verity of the signature, and of the completion of the appointment, and that the appointment conferred on him a legal right to the office for the space of five years.

2. That, having this legal title to the office, he has a consequent right to the commission, a refusal to deliver which is a plain violation of that right, for which the laws of his country afford him a remedy.

It remains to be inquired whether,

3. He is entitled to the remedy for which he applies. This depends on:

    1. The nature of the writ applied for, and

    2. The power of this court.

4. The nature of the writ.

Blackstone, in the third volume of his Commentaries, page 110, defines a mandamus to be

> a command issuing in the King's name from the Court of King's Bench, and directed to any person, corporation, or inferior court of judicature within the King's dominions requiring them to do some particular thing therein specified which appertains to their office and duty, and which the Court of King's Bench has previously determined, or at least supposes, to be consonant to right and justice.

Lord Mansfield, in 3 Burrows, 1266, in the case of *The King v. Baker et al.*, states with much precision and explicitness the cases in which this writ may be used.

"Whenever," says that very able judge,

> there is a right to execute an office, perform a service, or exercise a franchise (more especially if it be in a matter of public concern or attended with profit), and a person is kept out of possession, or dis-

possessed of such right, and [p169] has no other specific legal remedy, this court ought to assist by mandamus, upon reasons of justice, as the writ expresses, and upon reasons of public policy, to preserve peace, order and good government.

In the same case, he says,

> this writ ought to be used upon all occasions where the law has established no specific remedy, and where in justice and good government there ought to be one.

In addition to the authorities now particularly cited, many others were relied on at the bar which show how far the practice has conformed to the general doctrines that have been just quoted.

This writ, if awarded, would be directed to an officer of government, and its mandate to him would be, to use the words of Blackstone,

> to do a particular thing therein specified, which appertains to his office and duty and which the Court has previously determined or at least supposes to be consonant to right and justice.

Or, in the words of Lord Mansfield, the applicant, in this case, has a right to execute an office of public concern, and is kept out of possession of that right.

These circumstances certainly concur in this case.

Still, to render the mandamus a proper remedy, the officer to whom it is to be directed must be one to whom, on legal principles, such writ may be directed, and the person applying for it must be without any other specific and legal remedy.

1. With respect to the officer to whom it would be directed. The intimate political relation, subsisting between the President of the United States and the heads of departments, necessarily renders any legal investigation of the acts of one of those high officers peculiarly

irksome, as well as delicate, and excites some hesitation with respect to the propriety of entering into such investigation. Impressions are often received without much reflection or examination, and it is not wonderful that, in such a case as this, the assertion by an individual of his legal claims in a court of justice, to which claims it is the duty of that court to attend, should, at first view, be considered [p170] by some as an attempt to intrude into the cabinet and to intermeddle with the prerogatives of the Executive.

It is scarcely necessary for the Court to disclaim all pretensions to such a jurisdiction. An extravagance so absurd and excessive could not have been entertained for a moment. The province of the Court is solely to decide on the rights of individuals, not to inquire how the Executive or Executive officers perform duties in which they have a discretion. Questions, in their nature political or which are, by the Constitution and laws, submitted to the Executive, can never be made in this court.

But, if this be not such a question; if so far from being an intrusion into the secrets of the cabinet, it respects a paper which, according to law, is upon record, and to a copy of which the law gives a right, on the payment of ten cents; if it be no intermeddling with a subject over which the Executive can be considered as having exercised any control; what is there in the exalted station of the officer which shall bar a citizen from asserting in a court of justice his legal rights, or shall forbid a court to listen to the claim or to issue a mandamus directing the performance of a duty not depending on Executive discretion, but on particular acts of Congress and the general principles of law?

If one of the heads of departments commits any illegal act under colour of his office by which an individual sustains an injury, it cannot be pretended that his office alone exempts him from being sued in the ordinary mode of proceeding, and being compelled to obey the judgment of the law. How then can his office exempt him from this particular mode of deciding on the legality of his conduct if the case be such a case as would, were any other individual the party complained of, authorize the process?

It is not by the office of the person to whom the writ is directed, but the nature of the thing to be done, that the propriety or impropriety of issuing a mandamus is to be determined. Where the head of a department acts in a case in which Executive discretion is to be exercised, in which he is the mere organ of Executive will, it is [p171] again repeated, that any application to a court to control, in any respect, his conduct, would be rejected without hesitation.

But where he is directed by law to do a certain act affecting the absolute rights of individuals, in the performance of which he is not placed under the particular direction of the President, and the performance of which the President cannot lawfully forbid, and therefore is never presumed to have forbidden—as for example, to record a commission, or a patent for land, which has received all the legal solemnities; or to give a copy of such record—in such cases, it is not perceived on what ground the Courts of the country are further excused from the duty of giving judgment that right to be done to an injured individual than if the same services were to be performed by a person not the head of a department.

This opinion seems not now for the first time to be taken up in this country.

It must be well recollected that, in 1792, an act passed, directing the secretary at war to place on the pension list such disabled officers and soldiers as should be reported to him by the Circuit Courts, which act, so far as the duty was imposed on the Courts, was deemed unconstitutional; but some of the judges, thinking that the law might be executed by them in the character of commissioners, proceeded to act and to report in that character.

This law being deemed unconstitutional at the circuits, was repealed, and a different system was established; but the question whether those persons who had been reported by the judges, as commissioners, were entitled, in consequence of that report, to be placed on the pension list was a legal question, properly deter-minable in the Courts, although the act of placing such persons on the list was to be performed by the head of a department.

That this question might be properly settled, Congress passed an act in February, 1793, making it the duty of the Secretary of War, in conjunction with the Attorney General, to take such meas-ures as might be necessary to obtain an adjudication of the Supreme Court of the United [p172] States on the validity of any such rights, claimed under the act aforesaid.

After the passage of this act, a mandamus was moved for, to be directed to the Secretary of War, commanding him to place on the pension list a person stating himself to be on the report of the judges.

There is, therefore, much reason to believe that this mode of trying the legal right of the complainant was deemed by the head of a department, and by the highest law officer of the United States, the most proper which could be selected for the purpose.

When the subject was brought before the Court, the decision was not that a mandamus would not lie to the head of a depart-ment directing him to perform an act enjoined by law, in the per-formance of which an individual had a vested interest, but that a mandamus ought not to issue in that case—the decision necessar-ily to be made if the report of the commissioners did not confer on the applicant a legal right.

The judgment in that case is understood to have decided the merits of all claims of that description, and the persons, on the report of the commissioners, found it necessary to pursue the mode prescribed by the law subsequent to that which had been deemed unconstitutional in order to place themselves on the pension list.

The doctrine, therefore, now advanced is by no means a novel one.

It is true that the mandamus now moved for is not for the per-formance of an act expressly enjoined by statute.

It is to deliver a commission, on which subjects the acts of Congress are silent. This difference is not considered as affecting the case. It has already been stated that the applicant has, to that commission, a vested legal right of which the Executive cannot deprive him. He has been appointed to an office from which he is not removable at the will of the Executive, and, being so [p173] appointed, he has a right to the commission which the Secretary has received from the President for his use. The act of Congress does not, indeed, order the Secretary of State to send it to him, but it is placed in his hands for the person entitled to it, and cannot be more lawfully withheld by him than by another person.

It was at first doubted whether the action of detinue was not a specific legal remedy for the commission which has been withheld from Mr. Marbury, in which case a mandamus would be improper. But this doubt has yielded to the consideration that the judgment in detinue is for the thing itself, or its value. The value of a public office not to be sold is incapable of being ascertained, and the applicant has a right to the office itself, or to nothing. He will obtain the office by obtaining the commission or a copy of it from the record.

This, then, is a plain case of a mandamus, either to deliver the commission or a copy of it from the record, and it only remains to be inquired:

Whether it can issue from this Court.

The act to establish the judicial courts of the United States authorizes the Supreme Court

to issue writs of mandamus, in cases warranted by the principles and usages of law, to any courts appointed, or persons holding office, under the authority of the United States.

The Secretary of State, being a person, holding an office under the authority of the United States, is precisely within the letter of the description, and if this Court is not authorized to issue a writ of mandamus to such an officer, it must be because the law is unconstitutional, and therefore absolutely incapable of conferring the authority and assigning the duties which its words purport to confer and assign.

The Constitution vests the whole judicial power of the United States in one Supreme Court, and such inferior courts as Congress shall, from time to time, ordain and establish. This power is expressly extended to all cases arising under the laws of the United States; and consequently, in some form, may be exercised over the present [p174] case, because the right claimed is given by a law of the United States.

In the distribution of this power, it is declared that

The Supreme Court shall have original jurisdiction in all cases affecting ambassadors, other public ministers and consuls, and those in which a state shall be a party. In all other cases, the Supreme Court shall have appellate jurisdiction.

It has been insisted at the bar, that, as the original grant of jurisdiction to the Supreme and inferior courts is general, and the clause assigning original jurisdiction to the Supreme Court contains no negative or restrictive words, the power remains to the Legislature to assign original jurisdiction to that Court in other cases than those specified in the article which has been recited, provided those cases belong to the judicial power of the United States.

If it had been intended to leave it in the discretion of the Legislature to apportion the judicial power between the Supreme and inferior courts according to the will of that body, it would certainly have been useless to have proceeded further than to have defined the judicial power and the tribunals in which it should be vested. The subsequent part of the section is mere surplusage—is entirely without meaning—if such is to be the construction. If Congress remains at liberty to give this court appellate jurisdiction where the

Constitution has declared their jurisdiction shall be original, and original jurisdiction where the Constitution has declared it shall be appellate, the distribution of jurisdiction made in the Constitution, is form without substance.

Affirmative words are often, in their operation, negative of other objects than those affirmed, and, in this case, a negative or exclusive sense must be given to them or they have no operation at all.

It cannot be presumed that any clause in the Constitution is intended to be without effect, and therefore such construction is inadmissible unless the words require it. [p175]

If the solicitude of the Convention respecting our peace with foreign powers induced a provision that the Supreme Court should take original jurisdiction in cases which might be supposed to affect them, yet the clause would have proceeded no further than to provide for such cases if no further restriction on the powers of Congress had been intended. That they should have appellate jurisdiction in all other cases, with such exceptions as Congress might make, is no restriction unless the words be deemed exclusive of original jurisdiction.

When an instrument organizing fundamentally a judicial system divides it into one Supreme and so many inferior courts as the Legislature may ordain and establish, then enumerates its powers, and proceeds so far to distribute them as to define the jurisdiction of the Supreme Court by declaring the cases in which it shall take original jurisdiction, and that in others it shall take appellate jurisdiction, the plain import of the words seems to be that, in one class of cases, its jurisdiction is original, and not appellate; in the other, it is appellate, and not original. If any other construction would render the clause inoperative, that is an additional reason for rejecting such other construction, and for adhering to the obvious meaning.

To enable this court then to issue a mandamus, it must be shown to be an exercise of appellate jurisdiction, or to be necessary to enable them to exercise appellate jurisdiction.

It has been stated at the bar that the appellate jurisdiction may be exercised in a variety of forms, and that, if it be the will of the Legislature that a mandamus should be used for that purpose, that will must be obeyed. This is true; yet the jurisdiction must be appellate, not original.

It is the essential criterion of appellate jurisdiction that it revises and corrects the proceedings in a cause already instituted, and does not create that case. Although, therefore, a mandamus may be directed to courts, yet to issue such a writ to an officer for the delivery of a paper is, in effect, the same as to sustain an original action for that paper, and therefore seems not to belong to [p176] appellate, but to original jurisdiction. Neither is it necessary in such a case as this to enable the Court to exercise its appellate jurisdiction.

The authority, therefore, given to the Supreme Court by the act establishing the judicial courts of the United States to issue writs of mandamus to public officers appears not to be warranted by the Constitution, and it becomes necessary to inquire whether a jurisdiction so conferred can be exercised.

The question whether an act repugnant to the Constitution can become the law of the land is a question deeply interesting to the United States, but, happily, not of an intricacy proportioned to its interest. It seems only necessary to recognise certain principles, supposed to have been long and well established, to decide it.

That the people have an original right to establish for their future government such principles as, in their opinion, shall most conduce to their own happiness is the basis on which the whole American fabric has been erected. The exercise of this original right is a very great exertion; nor can it nor ought it to be frequently repeated. The principles, therefore, so established are deemed fundamental. And as the authority from which they proceed, is supreme, and can seldom act, they are designed to be permanent.

This original and supreme will organizes the government and assigns to different departments their respective powers. It may either stop here or establish certain limits not to be transcended by those departments.

The Government of the United States is of the latter description. The powers of the Legislature are defined and limited; and that those limits may not be mistaken or forgotten, the Constitution is written. To what purpose are powers limited, and to what purpose is that limitation committed to writing, if these limits may at any time be passed by those intended to be restrained? The distinction between a government with limited and unlimited powers is abolished if those limits do not confine the persons on whom they are imposed, and if acts prohibited [p177] and acts allowed are of equal obligation. It is a proposition too plain to be contested that the Constitution controls any legislative act repugnant to it, or that the Legislature may alter the Constitution by an ordinary act.

Between these alternatives there is no middle ground. The Constitution is either a superior, paramount law, unchangeable by ordinary means, or it is on a level with ordinary legislative acts, and, like other acts, is alterable when the legislature shall please to alter it.

If the former part of the alternative be true, then a legislative act contrary to the Constitution is not law; if the latter part be true, then written Constitutions are absurd attempts on the part of the people to limit a power in its own nature illimitable.

Certainly all those who have framed written Constitutions contemplate them as forming the fundamental and paramount law of the nation, and consequently the theory of every such government must be that an act of the Legislature repugnant to the Constitution is void.

This theory is essentially attached to a written Constitution, and is consequently to be considered by this Court as one of the fundamental principles of our society. It is not, therefore, to be lost sight of in the further consideration of this subject.

If an act of the Legislature repugnant to the Constitution is void, does it, notwithstanding its invalidity, bind the Courts and oblige them to give it effect? Or, in other words, though it be not law, does it constitute a rule as operative as if it was a law? This would be to overthrow in fact what was established in theory, and would seem, at first view, an absurdity too gross to be insisted on. It shall, however, receive a more attentive consideration.

It is emphatically the province and duty of the Judicial Department to say what the law is. Those who apply the rule to particular cases must, of necessity, expound and interpret that rule. If two laws conflict with each other, the Courts must decide on the operation of each. [p178]

So, if a law be in opposition to the Constitution, if both the law and the Constitution apply to a particular case, so that the Court must either decide that case conformably to the law, disregarding the Constitution, or conformably to the Constitution, disregarding the law, the Court must determine which of these conflicting rules governs the case. This is of the very essence of judicial duty.

If, then, the Courts are to regard the Constitution, and the Constitution is superior to any ordinary act of the Legislature, the Constitution, and not such ordinary act, must govern the case to which they both apply.

Those, then, who controvert the principle that the Constitution is to be considered in court as a paramount law are reduced to the necessity of maintaining that courts must close their eyes on the Constitution, and see only the law.

This doctrine would subvert the very foundation of all written Constitutions. It would declare that an act which, according to the principles and theory of our government, is entirely void, is yet, in practice, completely obligatory. It would declare that, if the Legislature shall do what is expressly forbidden, such act, notwithstanding the express prohibition, is in reality effectual. It would be giving to the Legislature a practical and real omnipotence with the same breath which professes to restrict their powers within narrow limits. It is prescribing limits, and declaring that those limits may be passed at pleasure.

That it thus reduces to nothing what we have deemed the greatest improvement on political institutions—a written Constitution, would of itself be sufficient, in America where written Constitutions have been viewed with so much reverence, for rejecting the construction. But the peculiar expressions of the Constitution of the United States furnish additional arguments in favour of its rejection.

The judicial power of the United States is extended to all cases arising under the Constitution. [p179]

Could it be the intention of those who gave this power to say that, in using it, the Constitution should not be looked into? That a case arising under the Constitution should be decided without examining the instrument under which it arises?

This is too extravagant to be maintained.

In some cases then, the Constitution must be looked into by the judges. And if they can open it at all, what part of it are they forbidden to read or to obey?

There are many other parts of the Constitution which serve to illustrate this subject.

It is declared that "no tax or duty shall be laid on articles exported from any State." Suppose a duty on the export of cotton, of tobacco, or of flour, and a suit instituted to recover it. Ought judgment to be rendered in such a case? Ought the judges to close their eyes on the Constitution, and only see the law?

The Constitution declares that "no bill of attainder or *ex post facto* law shall be passed."

If, however, such a bill should be passed and a person should be prosecuted under it, must the Court condemn to death those victims whom the Constitution endeavours to preserve?

"No person," says the Constitution, "shall be convicted of treason unless on the testimony of two witnesses to the same overt act, or on confession in open court."

Here, the language of the Constitution is addressed especially to the Courts. It prescribes, directly for them, a rule of evidence not to be departed from. If the Legislature should change that rule, and declare one witness, or a confession out of court, sufficient for conviction, must the constitutional principle yield to the legislative act?

From these and many other selections which might be made, it is apparent that the framers of the Constitution [p180] contemplated that instrument as a rule for the government of courts, as well as of the Legislature.

Why otherwise does it direct the judges to take an oath to support it? This oath certainly applies in an especial manner to their conduct in their official character. How immoral to impose it on them if they were to be used as the instruments, and the knowing instruments, for violating what they swear to support!

The oath of office, too, imposed by the Legislature, is completely demonstrative of the legislative opinion on this subject. It is in these words:

> I do solemnly swear that I will administer justice without respect to persons, and do equal right to the poor and to the rich; and that I will faithfully and impartially discharge all the duties incumbent on me as according to the best of my abilities and understanding, agreeably to the Constitution and laws of the United States.

Why does a judge swear to discharge his duties agreeably to the Constitution of the United States if that Constitution forms no rule for his government? if it is closed upon him and cannot be inspected by him?

If such be the real state of things, this is worse than solemn mockery. To prescribe or to take this oath becomes equally a crime.

It is also not entirely unworthy of observation that, in declaring what shall be the supreme law of the land, the Constitution itself is first mentioned, and not the laws of the United States generally, but those only which shall be made in pursuance of the Constitution, have that rank.

Thus, the particular phraseology of the Constitution of the United States confirms and strengthens the principle, supposed to be essential to all written Constitutions, that a law repugnant to the Constitution is void, and that courts, as well as other departments, are bound by that instrument.

The rule must be discharged.

APPENDIX 2:
STUART v. LAIRD

SUPREME COURT OF THE UNITED STATES
5 U.S. (1 Cranch) 299 (1803)

The Chief Justice, having tried the cause in the court below, declined giving an opinion. PATERSON, J., (Judge Cushing being absent on account of ill health) delivered the opinion of the court.

On an action instituted by John Laird against Hugh Stuart, a judgment was entered in a court for the fourth circuit in the eastern district of Virginia, in December term 1801. On this judgment, an execution was issued, returnable to April term 1802, in the same court. In the term of December 1802, John Laird obtained judgment at a court for the fifth circuit in the Virginia district, against Hugh Stuart and Charles L. Carter, upon their bond for the forthcoming and delivery of certain property therein mentioned, which had been levied upon by virtue of the above execution against the said Hugh Stuart.

Two reasons have been assigned by counsel for reversing the judgment on the forthcoming bond. 1. That as the bond was given for the delivery of property levied on by virtue of an execution issuing out of, and returnable to a court for the fourth circuit, no other court could legally [5 U.S. 299, 309] proceed upon the said bond. This is true, if there be no statutable provision to direct and authorize such proceeding. Congress have constitutional authority to establish from time to time such inferior tribunals as they may think proper, and to transfer a cause from one such tribunal to another. In this last particular, there are no words in the constitution to prohibit or restrain the exercise of legislative power.

The present is a case of this kind. It is nothing more than the removal of the suit brought by Stuart against Laird from the court of the fourth circuit to the court of the fifth circuit, which is authorised to proceed upon and carry it into full effect. This is apparent from the ninth section of the act entitled "an act to amend the judicial system of the United States," passed the 29th of April 1802. The forthcoming bond is an appendage to the cause, or rather a component part of the proceedings.

2. Another reason for reversal is, that the judges of the supreme court have no right to sit as circuit judges, not being appointed as such, or in other words, that they ought to have distinct commissions for that purpose. To this objection, which is of recent date, it is sufficient to observe, that practice and acquiescence under it for a period of several years, commencing with the organization of the judicial system, afford an irresistible answer, and have indeed fixed the construction. It is a contemporary interpretation of the most forcible nature. This practical exposition is too strong and obstinate to be shaken or controlled. Of course, the question is at rest, and ought not now to be disturbed.

Judgment affirmed.

NOTES

Some spellings and punctuation have been modernized for purposes of clarity.

PROLOGUE

King John issued the Magna Carta in 1215. The version of the Magna Carta on display in the National Archives' "Charters of Freedom" hall dates from 1297.

INTRODUCTION

An excellent biography of the underappreciated John Jay is Walter Stahr, *John Jay Founding Father* (Hambeldon Continuum, 2005).

Clare Cushman's definitive collection of essays on the Supreme Court Justices (Clare Cushman, ed., *The Supreme Court Justices* [Congressional Quarterly, 1993]) provides a valuable overview of George Washington's original appointees to the Supreme Court and their unhappy fate. Justice James Iredell complained not only of having to share a bed with a "man of the wrong sort" but also of having to "sleep in rooms where men were drinking, gambling, and swearing all night" (Cushman, *The Supreme Court Justices*, p. 30).

Justice James Wilson, an influential leader at the Constitutional Convention in Philadelphia in 1787, was imprisoned for a debt of $197,000 while still on the Supreme Court and died soon after his release in 1798. Justice John Blair, Jr., suffered from what he called "a rattling, distracting noise" in his head, which disabled him and required him to resign from the Court in 1796. John Rutledge's rejection by the Senate as chief justice in 1795 was by a 14–10 vote; it was the first Senate rejection of a Supreme Court nomination (Cushman, *The Supreme Court Justices*, pp. 6–10, 16–25).

The exchange of letters between Adams and Jay can be found in Charles Warren, *The Supreme Court in United States History, Volume One, 1789–1821* (Little, Brown and Company, 1922), pp. 172–173. Adams nominated Jay to be chief justice, and the Senate confirmed him, before Jay's letter declining the post arrived in Washington.

Adams's description of the taverns at the turn of the century is found in Richardson Wright, *American Wags and Eccentrics from Colonial Times to the Civil War* (Frederick Ungar Publishing, 1965).

CHAPTER 1

The famous dinner at Jefferson's is described in Charles A. Cerami, *Dinner at Mr. Jefferson's* (John Wiley & Sons, 2008). Other accounts of the dinner are in Joseph J. Ellis, *Founding Brothers* (Knopf, 2000), pp. 48–80, and Ron Chernow, *Alexander Hamilton* (Penguin, 2004), pp. 326–331. The dinner came about after Jefferson bumped into a disheveled Hamilton outside President Washington's house in New York. (Hamilton may well have been lying in wait for Jefferson, hoping to intercept him.) As Jefferson explained in 1792:

Going to the President's one day I met Hamilton as I approached the door. His look was sombre, haggard, and dejected beyond description. Even his dress [was] uncouth and neglected. He asked to speak with me. We stood in the street near the door. He opened the subject of the assumption of the state debts, the necessity of it in the general fiscal arrangement and its indispensable necessity towards a preservation of the Union: and particularly of the New England states, who had made great expenditures during the war . . . which were for the common cause. . . . [T]hat they considered the assumption of these by the Union so just . . . that they would make it a *sine qua non* of the continuance of the Union. . . . That if he had not credit enough to carry such a measure as that, he could be of no use, and was determined to resign.

He observed at the same time, that though our particular business laid in separate departments, yet the administration and its success was a common concern, and that we should make common cause in supporting one another. He added his wish that I would interest my friends from the South, who were those most opposed to it. I answered that I had been so long absent from my country that I had lost a familiarity with its affairs. [Jefferson had recently returned from France.] . . .

On considering the situation of things, I thought the first step towards some conciliation of views would be to bring Mr. Madison and Col. Hamilton to a friendly discussion of the subject. I immediately wrote to each to come and dine with me the next day, mentioned that we should be alone . . . and that I was persuaded that men of sound heads and honest views needed nothing more than mutual understanding to enable them to unite in some measures which might enable us to get along. (Quoted in Cerami, *Dinner at Mr. Jefferson's*, pp. 118–119)

The location of Jefferson's home is detailed in Andro Linklater, *Measuring America: How an Untamed Wilderness Shaped the United States and Fulfilled the Promise of Democracy* (New York: Walker, 2002), p. 107.

Contemporary rumors that Washington's selection of the capital location enriched him are recounted in Kenneth R. Bowling, *The Creation of Washington, D.C.: The Idea and Location of the American Capital* (George Mason University Press, 1991), pp. 213–214. As Bowling explains, the president of Dickinson College noted Washington's self-interest at the time, and Adams commented on it after he left the presidency. Washington himself frequently referred to the increase in the value of Mount Vernon resulting from the location of the new capital.

The auction of the lots and the failure of the syndicate are described in Bowling, *The Creation of Washington, D.C.*, pp. 227, 231–232; Constance McLaughlin Green, *Washington Village and Capital, 1800–1878* (Princeton University Press, 1962), pp. 14–15; and Joel Achenbach, *The Grand Idea* (Simon & Schuster, 2004), p. 183.

Jefferson's quote about having to "lodge, like cattle, in the fields" is found in Achenbach, *The Grand Idea*, p. 218.

The "sea of mud" quote is in Joseph R. Passoneau, *Washington Through Two Centuries* (The Monacelli Press, 2004), p. 35. As Joel Achenbach points out, a debate rages among historians about whether Washington was an actual "swamp" (Achenbach, *The Grand Idea*, p. 179). Kenneth Bowling is a leader of what Achenbach calls "the no-swamp school of thought" (see Bowling, *The Creation of Washington, D.C.*, pp. 237–238). Scott Berg also attacks the idea that Washington was a swamp in *Grand Avenues: The Story of Pierre Charles L'Enfant, the French Visionary Who Designed Washington, D.C.* (Pantheon, 2007). However one characterizes it, the new capital area, or at least parts of it, struck many observers as uncomfortably muddy and moist.

The Gallatin quote about the Capitol area is in Thomas Froncek, ed., *The City of Washington* (Knopf, 1977), p. 87. For descriptions of the District at this time, see Achenbach, *The Grand Idea*, pp. 217–220; Green, *Washington Village and Capital*, pp. 18–20; and Froncek, *The City of Washington*, pp. 87–91. The *Centinel* quotes are from *The Centinel of Liberty and George-Town and Washington Advertiser*, January 3, 1800, and September 12, 1800.

Oliver Wolcott's statement about "small miserable huts" and living "like fishes" may be found in Achenbach, *The Grand Idea*, p. 219. The Architect of the Capitol's "Gigantic Abortion" description is in a letter from Capitol Architect Benjamin Latrobe to Phillip Mazzei, May 29, 1806, quoted in Bowling, *The Creation of Washington, D.C.*, p. 246. Roger Griswold's "melancholy and ludicrous" description may be found in Green, *Washington Village and Capital, 1800–1878*, p. 23. Gouverneur Morris's quote may be found in

Gouverneur Morris to The Princess de la Tour, December 1800, *The Life of Gouverneur Morris, with Selections from His Correspondence and Miscellaneous Papers*, volume 3, edited by Jared Sparks (Grey & Bowen, 1832), pp. 129–130.

According to some accounts, the combined archives of the State, Treasury, War, Navy, and Justice Departments fit into seven packing cases. See, for example, John Ferling, *Adams vs. Jefferson: The Tumultuous Election of 1800* (Oxford University Press, 2004), p. 137. Two historians, however, recently reviewed long-ignored records in the National Archives and concluded that the volume of records likely was considerably larger. See Elaine C. Everly and Howard H. Wehmann, "Then Let Us to the Woods Repair," in Kenneth R. Bowling and Donald R. Kennon, eds., *Establishing Congress* (Ohio University Press, 2005), pp. 56–71.

Most accounts put the number of federal employees moving to Washington at 131 (or 134); see, for example, Green, *Washington Village and Capital, 1800–1878*, p. 17. The number may have been even less. Everly and Wehmann carefully note, "While it is always problematic to estimate the exact size of the federal government at any given time, from the report of expenditures for the removal, we know that 116 men from the executive departments, including 91 clerks and 11 messengers, came to Washington" (Everly and Wehmann, "Then Let Us to the Woods Repair," p. 57).

CHAPTER 2

The death and ensuing funeral of George Washington are recounted in a number of secondary sources, including David McCullough, *John Adams* (Simon & Schuster, 2001), pp. 532–534; Joseph Ellis, *Founding Brothers* (Alfred A. Knopf, 2000), pp. 160–161; and Jean Edward Smith, *John Marshall* (Henry Holt, 1996), pp. 255–257.

The descriptions, backgrounds, and political philosophies of Thomas Jefferson and John Adams are summarized in Arthur Schlesinger, *The Imperial Presidency* (Houghton Mifflin, 1973).

Discussions of the importance of President George Washington's life to the politics of the country, as well as personal reminiscences, are found in Page Smith, *John Adams*, volumes I and II (Doubleday & Company, 1962), and in Chernow, *Alexander Hamilton*. Explanations of the Electoral College system are based on descriptions in Ferling's *Adams Vs. Jefferson*, pp. 168–169, as well as in Edward Larson's fine book on the election of 1800, *A Magnificent Catastrophe* (Free Press, 2007), and in Donald O. Dewey's *Marshall Versus Jefferson*. The quote from Clinton Rossiter is on p. 221 of his book, *The Constitutional Convention of 1789*. The section on the rivalry between Burr and Hamilton has been pieced together from quotes and information found in Chernow's *Alexander Hamilton*, Schlesinger's *The Imperial Presidency*, and Nancy Isenberg's *Fallen Founder: The Life of Aaron Burr* (Viking, 2007). The

Republican victory in New York and ensuing Adams shake-up of his cabinet is described in Chernow's *Hamilton*, pp. 613–615. Adams's campaign and trip to Washington are discussed in Ferling's *Adams Vs. Jefferson*, pp. 137–148, as well as in McCullough's *John Adams*, pp. 341–343. Oliver Wolcott praised Marshall's skill in running the government in a letter to Fisher Ames on August 10, 1800, quoted in Smith, *John Marshall*, p. 7. Marbury's purchase of his Georgetown home in 1800 is described in Passoneau, *Washington Through Two Centuries*, p. 56.

The biographical details on William Marbury are culled from an excellent law review article by David Forte entitled "Marbury's Travail" (45 *Catholic University Law Review* 349 [Winter 1996]).

The information from the *Baltimore Gazette* was found in Schlesinger's *The Imperial Presidency*. Other information about the campaign in Maryland is gleaned from Larson's *Magnificent Catastrophe*. The section on the role of the press in the election of 1800 is based primarily on Ferling's *Adams Vs. Jefferson*, pp. 141–148. Thomas Jefferson's use of the press to advance his campaign is described in Ferling, *Adams Vs. Jefferson*, p. 140. Alexander Hamilton's role in the later stages of the campaign of 1800 is recorded in Chernow, *Alexander Hamilton*, pp. 621–623.

Information about the XYZ Affair can be gleaned from many sources: For example, David McCullough provides a helpful account in *John Adams*, pp. 495–497, and Jean Edward Smith does likewise in *John Marshall*, pp. 204–237. The impact of the Alien and Sedition Acts on the election of 1800 is described in Ferling, *Adams Vs. Jefferson*, pp. 122 and 144–146. Geoffrey Stone presents a masterful overview of the Alien and Sedition Acts in *Perilous Times: Free Speech in Wartime* (W. W. Norton, 2004), pp. 15–78.

President Adams's last speech to Congress is recounted in McCullough, *John Adams*, 544–555, and in Smith, *John Marshall*, pp. 1050–1051. Charles Adams's death is discussed in McCullough, *John Adams*, p. 555, and Adams's reaction to his defeat in the election of 1800 is noted on p. 556. Marshall's letter to Charles Cotesworth Pinckney in which he professes a desire to return to his legal practice in Richmond is found in Charles F. Hobson, ed., *The Papers of John Marshall*, volume 6 (University of North Carolina Press, 1990), p. 41.

CHAPTER 3

The Treaty of Mortefontaine is described in Smith, *John Marshall*, p. 277, as well as in McCullough, *John Adams*, p. 552. President Adams's consideration of William Paterson to be chief justice is noted in Dewey, *Marshall Versus Jefferson*, p. 3, as well as in Page Smith's *John Adams*, pp. 1063 and 1064.

President Adams's letter to John Jay nominating him to be chief justice is recounted in Smith, *John Marshall*, p. 529, n. 51. Marshall's letter to Charles

Pinckney on December 18, 1800, is reprinted in Hobson, *The Papers of John Marshall*, p. 41. The description of the relationship between Abigail Adams and Thomas Jefferson is based on information contained in McCullough, *John Adams*, pp. 558 and 559.

The quote from Fisher Ames is found in Chernow's biography, *Alexander Hamilton*, p. 633. Hamilton's campaign of letters against Aaron Burr is recounted in many sources, including in Paul F. Boller, Jr., *Presidential Campaigns* (Oxford University Press, 1984), pp. 15 and 16, and in Chernow, *Alexander Hamilton*, pp. 632 and 633. Chernow explained the reference to "Catiline" as "a powerful indictment: in ancient Rome, Catiline was notorious for his personal dissipation and treacherous schemes to undermine the republic." Hamilton's letter to Marshall is quoted in Smith, *John Marshall*, p. 14. John Jay's refusal to be renominated chief justice is noted in Smith, *John Marshall*, p. 530, n. 73. The scene depicting Adams then offering the chief justice position to Marshall is based on McCullough, *John Adams*, p. 580, as well as on Smith, *John Marshall*, p. 14. Marshall himself described the scene in a brief memoir written to Joseph Story in 1826. It is reprinted in *"The Events of My Life": An Autobiographical Sketch, by John Marshall* (Clements Library, University of Michigan and Supreme Court Historical Society, 2001).

The biographical sketch of John Marshall is pieced together from information contained in Smith, *John Marshall*, including information about the Mazzei letter on p. 14 and information about the XYZ Affair on pp. 204–233.

The Henry Adams quote is from Adams, *History of the United States of America During the Administrations of Thomas Jefferson* (Library of America, 1986), p. 132. The anecdote about Jefferson scrawling a note to Jefferson is found in Smith, *John Marshall*, p. 236. Senator Jonathan Dayton's letter to William Paterson is contained in Dewey, *Marshall Versus Jefferson*, p. 12. President Adams's description of Jefferson "in the full vigor of middle age" is quoted in many places, including McCullough, *John Adams*, p. 560. Information about locating the Supreme Court is found in Scott Berg's *Grand Avenues: The Story of Pierre Charles L'Enfant, the French Visionary Who Designed Washington, D.C.* (Pantheon, 2007) p. 238; in Robert Remini, *The House* (Smithsonian Books, 2006), pp. 68 and 80; and in Warren, *The Supreme Court in United States History*, pp. 168–171. The fire in the Treasury Department was reported in the *National Intelligencer* on January 12, 1801.

Congressional action on the Convention of Mortefontaine is described in Smith, *John Marshall*, p. 278. The description of John Marshall's swearing-in is also found in Smith's *John Marshall* on pp. 283–285.

The first meeting of the Marshall Court in the Capitol is described in Smith, *John Marshall*, p. 286.

Thomas Jefferson's farewell visit of Abigail Adams is discussed in McCullough, *John Adams*, p. 599. The description of election deadlock is provided in many sources, including Boller, *Presidential Campaigns*, p. 15, and Chernow, *Alexander Hamilton*, p. 85. The scene depicting the last conversation between John Adams and Thomas Jefferson is recounted in McCullough, *John Adams*, p. 561.

Thomas Jefferson's victory in the election of 1800 is described in Willard Sterne Randall, *Thomas Jefferson: A Life* (Henry Holt, 1993), p. 547. The mob in front of Marbury's house is described in David Forte's "Marbury's Travail."

CHAPTER 4

The definitive resource for information on Adams's midnight appointments is Kathryn Turner, "The Midnight Judges," 109 *University of Pennsylvania Law Review* 494 (1960–1961). She also provides a valuable analysis of the Judiciary Act in Kathryn Turner, "Federalist Policy and the Judiciary Act of 1801," 22 The William and Mary Quarterly 3 (1965).

Other helpful overviews of the midnight appointments and the Judiciary Act are found in Dewey, *Marshall Versus Jefferson*, pp. 49–59; Lawrence Goldstone, *The Activist* (Walker, 2008), pp. 155–169; and James F. Simon, *What Kind of Nation: Thomas Jefferson, John Marshall, and the Epic Struggle to Create a United States* (Simon & Schuster, 2002), pp. 147–150 and 173–174.

Marshall's correspondence for the first three months of 1801, including his correspondence with Oliver Wolcott, with his brother James Marshall, and with politicians recommending job-seekers, is published in Hobson, *The Papers of John Marshall*, pp. 46–93.

CHAPTER 5

President John Adams's departure from Washington, D.C., on March 4, 1801, is recounted in R. B. Bernstein's short but fine biography, *Thomas Jefferson* (Oxford University Press, 2003), p. 134, and in McCullough's *John Adams*, p. 565. Jefferson's morning rituals are described in Ferling, *Adams Vs. Jefferson*, on p. 201. The quote from Margaret Bayard Smith is contained in reminiscences of her life in Washington, D.C., circa 1800, in *The First Forty Years of Washington Society* (Frederick Ungar Publishing Co., 1965). John Marshall's letter to Charles Cotesworth Pickney and Thomas Jefferson's letter to John Marshall are both excerpted in Smith's *John Marshall*, on pp. 17 and 19 respectively.

The information on the inaugurations of Washington and Adams is found in McCullough's *John Adams*, p. 488. The description of Jefferson's inauguration is pieced together from several sources, including Ferling, *Adams Vs. Jefferson*, p. 204; Isenberg, *Fallen Founder: The Life of Aaron Burr*, p. 224; Randall, *Thomas Jefferson*, pp. 547–548, and Smith, *The First Forty Years of Washington Society*, p. 26. Gouverneur Morris's reaction to the inauguration is described by William Howard Adams in his biography of Morris, *Gouverneur Morris*, p. 273.

The first meeting of Thomas Jefferson's cabinet is described in Randall, *Thomas Jefferson*, p. 549.

An account of Jefferson's preparation for living in the President's House, as well as his postinaugural correspondence, is contained in the Foreword to the Jefferson papers, volume 33, p. xi. David McCullough points out in *John Adams* that in retirement, "Adams wrote but few letters, those mostly to friends who had written to wish him well."

The biographical sketch of James Madison is drawn largely from information contained in Cerami's *Young Patriots*, pp. 17–22. Stephen Ambrose discusses Jefferson's invitation to the Madisons to live in the President's House on pp. 62 and 63 of his book on the journey of Lewis and Clark, *Undaunted Courage: Meriwether Lewis, Thomas Jefferson, and the Opening of the American West* (Simon & Shuster, 1996).

CHAPTER 6

Jefferson's views on his future administration are discussed in Ferling, *Adams Vs. Jefferson*, as well as in Randall, *Thomas Jefferson*, p. 549. The letter to James Monroe regarding the Federalists is excerpted in a footnote on p. 610 of Smith's biography, *John Marshall*. The description of the State Department in 1801 is from a nineteenth-century State Department history. The State Department had actually grown since Jefferson held the position in 1790, when, according to Randall, the entire department "consisted of two clerks, two assistant clerks, and a translator; excluding the overseas diplomatic establishment, its entire budget was under $8,000, including his $3,500 salary." Jefferson's visit to the State Department is recounted in several secondary sources: His recollection of withholding commissions is contained in an 1804 letter to William Johnson, quoted in Smith, *John Marshall*, p. 617, n. 34; his letter to Abigail Adams is contained in Cappon, *Jefferson's Letters to Mrs. Adams*; and his letter to Thomas Randolph is found in Smith, *John Marshall*, p. 619, n. 50.

The section on Judges Cranch and Marshall is recounted in Simon, *What Kind of Nation*, p. 150. Jefferson's letter to John Dickinson is found in Smith, *John Marshall*, p. 353. Jefferson's letter to Archibald Stanton is found in Smith, *John Marshall*, p. 619, n. 50. Giles's letter to Jefferson is found in Smith, *John Marshall*, p. 303.

CHAPTER 7

Contemporary newspaper accounts in this chapter are in the *Washington Federalist*, December 8, 9, 10, 16, 22, 21, 23, 24, and 28, 1801; the *National Intelligencer*, December 7 and 14, 1801; and the *Aurora*, December 11, 13, 20, and 23, 1801.

Recent biographies exploring the life of Gouverneur Morris (including the events recounted in this chapter) are Richard Brookhiser, *Gentleman Revolutionary: Gouverneur Morris—The Rake Who Wrote the Constitution* (Free Press, 2003); James J. Kirschke, *Gouverneur Morris: Author, Statesman, and Man of the World* (Thomas Dunne, 2005); and William Howard Adams, *Gouverneur Morris: An Independent Life* (Yale University Press, 2003). Information on Gouverneur Morris's affair with the Countess de Flahut is found in Adams, *Gouverneur Morris*, pp. 182–185.

Gouverneur Morris wrote about Dolley Madison and "the shriveled condition" of her husband in his diary on January 8, 1802. Morris's original diary is preserved and available for review at the Library of Congress. James J. Kirschke explains that Morris's observation about Dolley Madison's "good dispositions" meant that Morris was "optimistic" that she was "amenable to seduction" (Kirschke, *Gouverneur Morris*, p. 257).

Information on the newspaper subscriptions of the senators in December 1801 is provided in Donald A. Ritchie, *Press Gallery: Congress and the Washington Correspondents* (Harvard University Press, 1991), p. 16.

The description of the area surrounding the Conrad and McMunn boardinghouse is contained in Margaret Bayard Smith's *The First Forty Years of Washington Society*, p. 12.

Jefferson's preparation of his State of the Union address, including the passage that he drafted and then deleted, is explained in Albert Beveridge's classic biography of Marshall, *The Life of John Marshall*, volume 3 (Houghton Mifflin, 1919), pp. 53–53 and Appendix A. Fisher Ames's response to the speech is also in Beveridge's biography at p. 53. The reactions by Hamilton and John Quincy Adams are described in Smith, *John Marshall*, p. 297.

The Supreme Court's decision regarding the schooner *Peggy* is reported at *United States v. Schooner Peggy*, 5 U.S. (1 Cranch) 103 (1801).

Information about Marbury and his fellow plaintiffs may be found in Dewey, *Marshall Versus Jefferson*, pp. 83–86, and in Smith, *John Marshall*, p. 618, n. 41. The local history files at the Alexandria Library in Alexandria, Virginia, contain interesting information regarding Hooe, Harper, and Ramsay. The Supreme Court's proceedings in the show-cause hearing on Lee's request for a mandamus are described by William Cranch in *Marbury v. Madison*, 5 U.S. (1 Cranch) 137 (1803).

Dearborn's letter to Marbury is cited in Forte's monograph, "Marbury's Travail," p. 385 and n. 188. Gouverneur Morris recorded his evening with Justice Paterson and "the Bench" in his diary entry of December 19, 1801.

CHAPTER 8

The anecdote about Senator William Plumer is recounted in Randall, *Thomas Jefferson*, p. 553. Also see John T. Morse, Jr., ed., *American Statesman*, volume 11 (Houghton Mifflin, 1883), p. 188. The description of the President's House in 1802 is based on information from the White House Historical Society. President Jefferson's work habits are described in Randall, *Thomas Jefferson*, pp. 553–555. Margaret Bayard Smith's quote about Jefferson is from a letter she wrote to Susan B. Smith on May 26, 1801, and is reprinted on p. 28 in *The First Forty Years of Washington Society*. The quote about Jefferson's control over the legislative process is from Simon, *What Kind of Nation*, p. 163.

Margaret Bayard Smith's quote about churches in Washington, D.C., is found on p. 13 of *The First Forty Years of Washington Society*.

The debate over the repeal of the Judiciary Act is drawn from the *Annals of the United States Senate,1801*, volume 11. An excellent summary of the debate is found in Simon, *What Kind of Nation*, pp. 164–168. Gouverneur Morris's observations about President Jefferson's demeanor during the debate are recorded in the entries in his diary dated January 8 and January 22, 1802. The description of Aaron Burr's role in the debate is pieced together from information found in Isenberg, *Fallen Founder: The Life of Aaron Burr*, pp. 245 and 246, and in Simon, *What Kind of Nation*, p. 166. William Branch Giles's quote about "a mandatory process" is found in Dewey, *Marshall Versus Jefferson*, p. 68, as well as in Smith, *John Marshall*, p. 621, n. 69. Giles's statement was also reprinted in the *Aurora* on March 8, 1802. The history of the Judiciary Act of 1802 is recounted in Leonard Baker, *John Marshall* (Macmillan,1974), pp. 377, 380, and 381. The meeting between Representative Bayard and Chief Justice John Marshall is cited in Simon, *What Kind of Nation*, pp. 164–168, as well as in Smith, *John Marshall*, p. 333. Gadsby's Tavern is described in "A History of Lloyd House, Part I: The Early Years, 1796–1832," *Historic Alexander Quarterly* (Fall 2003/Winter 2004). Morris's reaction to hearing Marshall's views on the Repeal Act is recorded in his diary entry dated April 29, 1802, and is also noted in Smith, *John Marshall*, p. 351.

The correspondence between John Marshall and the associate justices of the Supreme Court is found in Baker, *John Marshall*, p. 378, as well as in Smith, *John Marshall*, p. 308. The circumstances surrounding John Marshall's biography of George Washington are described in Baker, *John Marshall*, pp. 438–444. Thomas Jefferson's decision to solicit Joel Barlow to write a competing history of the United States is described in Andrew Burstein, *Jefferson's Secrets* (Basic Books, 2005), pp. 213–218, as well as in Smith, *John Marshall*, pp. 306 and 307. James Monroe's concern about the cancellation of the Supreme Court term is noted in Smith, *John Marshall*, p. 621, n. 76. James T. Callender's accusations against Thomas Jefferson are noted in Simon, *What Kind of Nation*, p. 151. The reestablishment of the circuit courts is described in Smith, *John Marshall*, pp. 310 and 311. The quote by John Marshall at the end of the chapter is found in Smith, *John Marshall*, p. 308.

CHAPTER 9

Contemporary descriptions of personalities and events are found in the *Aurora*, January 1, 3, 5, 8, 15, and 16 and February 2, 3, 5, 7, 8, 9, 12, and 14, 1803; the *National Intelligencer*, January 5, 14, 19, 21, 26, and 31 and February 2, 7, 9, and 14, 1803; and the *Washington Federalist*, January 26, 28, 31, and February 2, 4, 7, 9, 14, and 16, 1803. Elroy M. Avery describes the New Year's levee at the President's House in *A History of the United States and Its People*, volume 7 (The Burrows Brothers, 1904), p. 303.

Dumas Malone recounts the visit by Jefferson's daughters in his classic *Jefferson and His Time: Volume 4, Jefferson the President, First Term, 1801–1805* (Little, Brown and Company, 1970), p. 174. Merriwether Lewis's preparation for his trip is described in Stephen Ambrose, *Undaunted Courage* (Simon & Schuster, 1996), pp. 80–127. William Wirt, a young lawyer in Virginia at the time and later an attorney general and well-known Supreme Court advocate, provided a fascinating and entertaining portrait of Marshall in "The British Spy," his wildly popular commentary on leading Virginia personalities that purported to be the report of a British visitor; it was first published in the Richmond *Argus* and appeared in several later editions and printings as well. See, for example, William Wirt, *The British Spy: or, Letters to a Member of the British Parliament Written During a Tour Through the United States* (Newburyport, 1804).

Marshall described his "various calamities" in North Carolina in a letter to his wife Polly on January 2, 1803, reprinted in Hobson, *The Papers of John Marshall*, pp. 145–146. Jean Edward Smith recounts Marshall's circuit-riding experience in *John Marshall*, pp. 312–313.

The celebrated feud between Rutledge and Ellery is discussed in Robert K. Ratzlaff, *John Rutledge, Jr.: South Carolina Federalist, 1766–1819* (Ayer Publishing, 1982), pp. 212–216. Gouverneur Morris commented on Rutledge's attack and on his visits with Jefferson and Dolley Madison in diary entries dated December 28, 1802, and January 3, 1803, respectively.

The petitions from the judges and from Marbury and his colleagues are discussed in Smith, *John Marshall*, pp. 313–315, and in Malone, *Jefferson and His Time*, p. 147. William Cranch provides a contemporaneous summary of the *Marbury* trial in 5 U.S. (1 Cranch) 135, 135–152 (1803). Helpful accounts also are found in Smith, *John Marshall*, pp. 316–318, and in Simon, *What Kind of Nation*, pp. 178–182.

CHAPTER 10

Background on Pontius Stelle and Stelle's Hotel can be found in Maud Burr Morris, "The Life and Times of Pontius D. Stelle," *Records of the Columbia Historical Society*, volume 7 (1904), pp. 49–65; W. B. Bryan, "Hotels of Washington Prior to 1814," *Records of the Columbia Historical Society*, volume 7 (1904), pp. 110–106; and Froncek, *The City of Washington*, p. 87.

The Supreme Court minutes for February 1803 at the National Archives detail the Court's inability to meet without a quorum.

Contemporary accounts of "Doctor Fendall" and the Dancing Assembly are found, respectively, in the *Washington Federalist*, February 14, 1803, and the *National Intelligencer*, February 16, 1803. The toasts on Washington's birthday are reported in the *Washington Federalist*, March 21, 1803.

The arguments in *Stuart v. Laird* are summarized by William Cranch in 5 U.S. (1 Cranch) 299 (1803). According to Supreme Court records, the arguments in *Stuart v. Laird* took place on February 23 and 24, 1803. Bruce Ackerman suggests that Lee tailored his argument on February 24 after hearing the Court's decision in *Marbury* but notes that "[t]he court records do not make this absolutely clear" (Ackerman, *The Failure of the Founding Fathers* [Harvard University Press, 2005], pp. 182–185 and 346–347, n. 47).

CHAPTER 11

The decision in *Marbury v. Madison* is found at 5 U.S. (1 Cranch) 137 (1803) and is reprinted in Appendix 1.

The scene during Marshall's reading of *Marbury* is described in Smith, *John Marshall*, pp. 319–323; Simon, *What Kind of Nation*, pp. 185–190; and Goldstone, *The Activist*, pp. 216–223. Although some accounts describe the opinion as 11,000 words long, that total includes Cranch's account of the case in addition to the actual Supreme Court opinion.

The *Washington Federalist* first reported the *Marbury* opinion on February 25, 1803, and then published it, in installments, on March 14, 1803, and March 16, 1803. The *National Intelligencer* published it, in installments, on March 18, 1803, March 21, 1803, and March 25, 1803.

The *Washington Federalist* praised the *Marbury* decision in its introduction to the publication of the opinion on March 14, 1803. Additional commentary from the press and other observers is summarized in Charles Warren, *The Supreme Court in United States History, Volume One, 1789–1821* (Little, Brown and Company, 1922), pp. 245–267, which remains an especially valuable source for contemporary reactions to *Marbury*.

Giles's comment to John Quincy Adams is in Smith, *John Marshall*, p. 627 n. 4.

Jefferson's quotes may be found in his letters to Abigail Adams, 1804; to George Hay, June 2, 1807; to W. H. Torrance, June 11, 1815; to Spencer Roane, September 6, 1819; to William Jarvis, September 28, 1820; and to William Johnson, June 12, 1823. For information on the letters, see Merrill Peterson, ed., *Thomas Jefferson: Writings* (Library of America, 1984); Warren, *The*

Supreme Court in United States History, p. 267 n. 2; and Smith, *John Marshall*, 626 n. 65.

One contemporary example of a justice sitting on a Supreme Court case even though he had participated as a judge in the case at an earlier stage was Justice Bushrod Washington's participation in *Talbot v. Seeman*, 5 U.S. (1 Cranch) 1 (1801). See Goldstone, *The Activist*, p. 279, n. 9. Jean Edward Smith points out that Marshall recused himself in three other cases in 1804 and 1805—one because he had presided on circuit (as in *Stuart v. Laird*), one because he had represented a party, and one because he had what Smith describes as "a remote financial interest" (Smith, *John Marshall*, p. 293).

The decision in *Stuart v. Laird* is found at 5 US. (1 Cranch) 299 (1803) and is reprinted in Appendix 2.

Marshall's letter to Oliver Wolcott on March 2, 1803, is in Hobson, *The Papers of John Marshall*, p. 187. (Internal quotation marks have been omitted from the quote.)

In 1830, Marshall cryptically observed, "Nothing is unknown or can be misunderstood by intelligent men, unless it be the motives which compelled the court to give its opinion at large on the case of Marbury v. Madison" (Dewey, *Marshall Versus Jefferson*, p. vii).

CHAPTER 12

The Supreme Court's decision in *Cooper v. Aaron* is found at 358 U.S. 1 (1958). *United States v. Nixon* is at 418 U.S. 683 (1974). A compilation of every Supreme Court opinion citing *Marbury v. Madison* through 2002 is provided in Mark A. Graber and Michael Perhac, eds., *Marbury Versus Madison: Documents and Commentary* (CQ Press, 2002), pp. 383–402.

Chief Justice William Rehnquist emphasized the role of *Marbury* in William H. Rehnquist, *The Supreme Court* (Vintage, 2002), pp. 21–35. Justice Sandra Day O'Connor discussed the case's importance in Sandra Day O'Connor, *The Majesty of the Law: Reflections of a Supreme Court Justice* (Random House, 2004), pp. 242–243.

Justice John Paul Stevens reflected on *Marbury's* significance in an interview with the authors in his chambers in the Supreme Court on May 28, 2008.

Professor A. E. Dick Howard comments on *Marbury* in A. E. Dick Howard, "Toward Constitutional Democracy Around the World: An American Perspective," 9 *Issues of Democracy* 18 (2004) (testimony at the joint hearing of the U.S. Senate Committees on the Judiciary and International Relations, June 25, 2003). For the views of former Solicitor General Theodore B. Olson, see Scott Dorfman, "Olson Explores Influence of *Marbury v. Madison*," 57 *Virginia Law Weekly* 24 (April 15, 2005).

A leading example of the craftsmanship objection to *Marbury* is Susan Low Bloch and Maeva Marcus, "John Marshall's Selective Use of History in *Marbury v. Madison*," *Wisconsin Law Review* 301 (1986). The manipulation critique is provided in Goldstone, *The Activist*. Bruce Ackerman presents the capitulation argument in *The Failure of the Founding Fathers* (Harvard University Press, 2005). The exaggeration criticism, along with other criticisms, is in Sanford Levinson, "Why I Do Not Teach *Marbury* (Except to Eastern Europeans) and Why You Shouldn't Either," 38 *Wake Forest Law Review* 553 (2003). [For a response to Levinson, see Erich J. Segall, "Why I Still Teach *Marbury* (And So Should You): A Response to Professor Levinson," 6 *University of Pennsylvania Journal of Constitutional Law* 573 (2004).] Jean Smith makes the distortion objection in *John Marshall*, p. 625, n. 60.

EPILOGUE

Jean Edward Smith describes the Supreme Court as a "major social attraction" on p. 397 of *John Marshall*. President Jefferson's view of the investigation of Justice Samuel Chase is detailed in Remini, *The House*, p. 80. Congressman Giles's statement to John Quincy Adams is found in Paul W. Kahn's *The Reign of Law: Marbury v. Madison and the Construction of America* (Yale University Press, 1997), p. 14, and in Malone, *Jefferson and His Time*, pp. 472–473. The quip about Burr and Chase is reported in Simon, *What Kind of Nation*, p. 208, and in Alan Dershowitz, *Is There a Right to Remain Silent?* (Oxford University Press, 2008), p. 194, n. 82. The information on President Jefferson's second term is contained in Randall, *Thomas Jefferson*, pp. 572–583.

On March 2, 1809, Jefferson wrote to Pierres Dupont de Nemours, as quoted in Bernstein, *Thomas Jefferson*, p. 169, describing the relief he felt that his presidency was coming to a close. The discussion of William Marbury's career as a clothier is based on advertisements in the *Washington Federalist* from 1807 as well as on David Forte's law review article. The biographical information about Levi Lincoln and Charles Lee is based on Smith's *John Marshall*, pp. 399 and 352. Jefferson's letter to John Epps is also in Smith's *John Marshall*, on p. 362. The sketches of the Supreme Court justices in their later years is based on information found in Baker, *John Marshall*, pp. 537–540, and in Cushman, *Supreme Court Justices*, pp. 6–60.

Adams's quote about his years following his presidency in Quincy, Massachusetts, is found in McCullough's *John Adams*. Adams's quote about his "proudest act" is recounted in Smith, *John Marshall*, on p. 666. Adams's reaction to his son's presidency is described by McCullough in *John Adams*, pp. 637–640. The information about Marshall's later years is also in Smith, *John Marshall*, on p. 15. Jefferson referred to Marshall's biography of George Washington as "the five-volume libel."

The eventual intertwining through marriage of the Marbury family with the Marshall family (and thus with the Jefferson family) is described in William L. Marbury, *The Story of a Maryland Family* (Baltimore, private printing, 1966), p. 10, which is on file at the Maryland Historical Society in Baltimore.

SELECTED BIBLIOGRAPHY

BOOKS

Achenbach, Joel. *The Grand Idea*. Simon & Schuster, 2004.

Ackerman, Bruce. *The Failure of the Founding Fathers: Jefferson, Marshall, and the Rise of Presidential Democracy*. Harvard University Press, 2005.

Adams, William Howard. *Gouverneur Morris: An Independent Life*. Yale University Press, 2003.

Ambrose, Stephen E. *Undaunted Courage: Meriwether Lewis, Thomas Jefferson, and the Opening of the American West*. Simon & Schuster, 1996.

Arnebeck, Bob. *Though a Fiery Trial: Building Washington 1790–1800*. Madison Books, 1991

Baker, Leonard. *John Marshall: A Life in Law*. Macmillan, 1974.

Belof, Max. *Thomas Jefferson and American Democracy*. Collier Books, 1962.

Berg, Scott W. *Grand Avenues: The Story of Pierre Charles L'Enfant, the French Visionary Who Designed Washington, D.C.* Pantheon, 2007.

Bernstein, R. B. *Thomas Jefferson*. Oxford University Press, 2003.

Beveridge, Albert J. *The Life of John Marshall*. Houghton Mifflin, 1919.

Boller, Paul F., Jr. *Presidential Campaigns*. Oxford University Press, 1984.

Bowling, Kenneth R. *The Creation of Washington, D.C.: The Idea and Location of the American Capital*. George Mason University Press, 1991.

Bowling, Kenneth R., and Donald R. Kennon, eds. *Establishing Congress*. Ohio University Press, 2005.

Brookhiser, Richard. *Alexander Hamilton, American*. Simon & Schuster, 1999.

_____. *Gentleman Revolutionary: Gouverneur Morris—The Rake Who Wrote the Constitution.* Free Press, 2003.

Burstein, Andrew. *Jefferson's Secrets: Death and Desire at Monticello.* Basic Books, 2005.

Byrd, Robert C. *The Senate, 1789–1989: Addresses on the History of the United States Senate.* U.S. Government Printing Office, 1988.

Cappon, Lester J., ed. *Jefferson's Letters to Mrs. Adams.* University of North Carolina Press, 1959.

Cerami, Charles A. *Young Patriots.* Sourcebooks, Inc., 2005.

_____. *Dinner at Mr. Jefferson's.* John Wiley & Sons, 2008.

Chernow, Ron. *Alexander Hamilton.* Penguin Press, 2004.

Dewey, Donald O. *Marshall Versus Jefferson: The Political Background of Marbury v. Madison.* Alfred A. Knopf, 1970.

Ellis, Joseph J., *Founding Brothers: The Revolutionary Generation.* Alfred A. Knopf, 2000.

Ellis, Richard E. *The Jeffersonian Crisis: Courts and Politics in the Young Republic.* Oxford University Press, 1971.

Ferling, John. *Adams Vs. Jefferson: The Tumultuous Election of 1800.* Oxford University Press, 2004.

Goebel, Julius, Jr. *History of the Supreme Court of the United States: Antecedents and Beginnings to 1901.* Vol. 1 in the Oliver Wendell Holmes Devise. Macmillan, 1971.

Goldstone, Lawrence. *The Activist John Marshall, Marbury v. Madison, and the Myth of Judicial Review.* Walker, 2008.

Graber, Mark A., and Michael Perhac, eds. *Marbury Versus Madison: Documents and Commentary.* CQ Press, 2002.

Green, Constance McLaughlin. *Washington Village and Capital, 1800–1878.* Princeton University Press, 1962.

Haskins, George, and Herbert Johnson. *History of the Supreme Court of the United States: Foundations of Power: John Marshall, 1801–1815.* Macmillan, 1981.

Hickey, Donald R., and Connie D. Clark, eds. *Citizen Hamilton: The Wit and Wisdom of an American Founder.* Rowman & Littlefield Publishers, 2006.

Hobson, Charles F. *The Great Chief Justice: John Marshall and the Rule of Law.* University Press of Kansas, 1996.

————., ed. *The Papers of John Marshall,* Vol. 6. University of North Carolina Press, 1990.

Hogan, Margaret A., and C. James Taylor, eds. *My Dearest Friend: Letters of Abigail and John Adams.* The Belknap Press of Harvard University Press, 2007.

Hunt, Gaillard, ed. *The First Forty Years of Washington Society: In the family Letters of Margaret Bayard Smith.* Frederick Ungar Publishing Co., 1965.

Inaugural Addresses of the Presidents of the United States, Vol. 1. Applewood Books, 1929.

Isenberg, Nancy. *Fallen Founder: The Life of Aaron Burr.* Viking, 2007.

Johnson, Herbert A. *The Chief Justiceship of John Marshall: 1801–1835.* University of South Carolina Press, 1997.

Kahn, Paul W. *The Reign of Law: Marbury v. Madison and the Construction of America.* Yale University Press, 1997.

Kirschke, James, J. *Gouverneur Morris: Author, Statesman, and Man of the World.* Thomas Dunne, 2005.

Kramer, Larry D. *The People Themselves: Popular Constitutionalism and Judicial Review.* Oxford University Press, 2004.

Larson, Edward J. *A Magnificent Catastrophe.* Free Press, 2007.

Malone, Dumas. *Jefferson and the Ordeal of Liberty.* Little, Brown and Company, 1962.

_____. *Jefferson and His Time: Volume 4, Jefferson the President, First Term, 1801–1805.* Little, Brown and Company, 1970.

McCullough, David. *John Adams.* Simon & Schuster, 2001.

Morse, John T., Jr., ed. *American Statesmen: Thomas Jefferson.* Houghton Mifflin, 1883.

Nelson, William E. *Marbury v. Madison: The Origins and Legacy of Judicial Review.* University Press of Kansas, 2000.

Newmyer, R. Kent. *John Marshall and the Heroic Age of the Supreme Court.* Louisiana State University Press, 2002.

Oberg, Barbara B., ed. *The Papers of Thomas Jefferson.* Princeton University Press, 2006.

O'Connor, Sandra Day. *The Majesty of the Law: Reflections of a Supreme Court Justice.* Random House, 2004.

Randall, Willard Sterne. *Thomas Jefferson: A Life.* Henry Holt, 1993.

Rehnquist, William H. *The Supreme Court.* Vintage, 2002.

Remini, Robert V. *The House: The History of the House of Representatives.* Smithsonian Books in association with HarperCollins Publishers, 2006.

Rosenfeld, Richard N. *American Aurora: A Democratic-Republican Returns: The Suppressed History of Our Nation's Beginnings and the Heroic Newspaper That Tried to Report It.* St. Martin's Press, 1997.

Rossiter, Clinton. 1787: *The Grand Convention*. Macmillan, 1966.

Schlesinger, Arthur M. Jr. *The Imperial Presidency*. Houghton Mifflin, 1973.

Simon, James F. *What Kind of Nation: Thomas Jefferson, John Marshall, and the Epic Struggle to Create a United States*. Simon & Schuster, 2002.

Smith, Jean Edward. *John Marshall: Definer of a Nation*. Henry Holt, 1996.

Smith, Margaret Bayard. *The First Forty Years of Washington Society*. Frederick Ungar Publishing Co., 1965.

Smith, Page. *John Adams: Vol. I, 1735–1784*. Doubleday & Company, 1962.

_____. *John Adams: Vol. II, 1784–1826*. Doubleday & Company, 1962.

Stone, Geoffrey R. *Perilous Times: Free Speech in Wartime*. W. W. Norton, 2004.

Warren, Charles. *The Supreme Court in United States History, Volume One, 1789–1821*. Little, Brown and Company, 1922.

Winik, Jay. *The Great Upheaval: America and the Birth of the Modern World 1788–1800*. Harper Collins, 2007.

ARTICLES

Allen, William C., Architect of the Capitol. *A Political and Architectural History of Rooms s–146, s–146A, and s–145 in the United States Capitol* (April 13, 1988).

Bloch, Susan Low. "The *Marbury* Mystery: Why Did William Marbury Sue in the Supreme Court?" 18 *Constitutional Commentary* 607 (2001).

Bloch, Susan Low, and Maeva Marcus. "John Marshall's Selective Use of History in *Marbury v. Madison*." *Wisconsin Law Review* 301 (1986).

Burton, Harold H. "The Cornerstone of Constitutional Law: The Extraordinary Case of *Marbury v. Madison*." *American Bar Association Journal* 805 (October 1950).

Dennee, Timothy J. "A History of Lloyd House, Part I. The Early Years: 1796–1832." *Historic Alexandria Quarterly* (Fall 2003/Winter 2004).

Forte, David F. "Marbury's Travail: Federalist Politics and William Marbury's Appointment as Justice of the Peace." 45 *Catholic University Law Review* 349 (Winter 1996).

Nagle, John Copeland. "The Lame Ducks of *Marbury*." 20 *Constitutional Commentary* 317 (2003).

Turner, Kathryn. "The Midnight Judges." 109 *University of Pennsylvania Law Review* 494 (1960–1961).

_____. "Federalist Policy and the Judiciary Act of 1801." 22 *The William and Mary Quarterly* 3 (1965).

Van Alstyne, William W. "A Critical Guide to *Marbury v. Madison.*" *Duke Law Journal* 1 (1969).

Weinberg, Louise. "Our Marbury." 89 *Virginia Law Review* 1235 (2003).

ACKNOWLEDGMENTS

When we began to plan a book about a Supreme Court case that most Americans aren't familiar with—and, even if they are, can't explain—we knew we had an uphill climb. Mention the phrase "*Marbury v. Madison*" and many people's eyes glaze over. But we strongly believed that most Americans intuitively know, and are proud of the fact, that what sets us apart from the rest of the world is our deeply ingrained adherence to our constitutional structure.

Susan Weinberg and Peter Osnos at PublicAffairs affirmed our vision and were able to see that there is a wonderful story that explains, at least in part, how we became a nation based on the rule of law. Rafe Sagalyn also immediately grasped the potential of the two-centuries-old story and enthusiastically urged us to tell it. He served as our agent and gave us wise advice every step of the way.

Our editor at PublicAffairs, Clive Priddle, expertly guided us through the process. Always able to see the big picture, Clive also has a keen eye for detail and a strong sense of narrative flow. We benefited greatly from his collaboration. Christine Arden provided skilled (and patient) copyediting, and we are very grateful for her efforts. Daniel Bromwich, a recent University of Michigan graduate and now a Senate aide, contributed important research assistance with dedication and insight.

We also would like to thank our incomparable brain trust—Jonathan Alter, Scott Berg, Tom Gerety, Michael Janeway, Michael

Kazin, John McKean, Harry McPherson, Michael Waldman, Jacob Weisberg, and John Zentay. They read drafts at various stages and offered valuable comments and insights, and they also gave us very welcome encouragement and support.

We were honored to have the chance to talk to Supreme Court Justices John Paul Stevens and Stephen Breyer about their view of *Marbury*. We deeply appreciate their graciousness and insights.

One of the joys of historical research is immersion in the remarkable entities preserving and presenting original documents. We are especially grateful to the staff and institutions at the National Archives, the Library of Congress, The Historical Society of Washington, D.C., the Virginia Historical Society, the Maryland Historical Society, and the Alexandria Library in Alexandria, Virginia. Richard Baker and Don Ritchie of the Senate Historian's Office provided us with helpful advice and assistance. Maeva Marcus, who oversaw the Documentary History project at the Supreme Court, was generous with her time and expertise.

It is customary in acknowledgments to thank families for understanding the time away from them. In our case, both of our families—Mary Lou, Sarah, Annie, and Nick, and Kathleen, Shaw, Christian, and Kaye—were greatly amused by our enthusiasm (and occasional obsession) with life in Washington at the beginning of the nineteenth century. We're pleased that we were able to entertain them, even when we weren't intending to, and we promise to try to stop pointing out how the city looked in 1800. But we probably won't stop talking about *Marbury* and its role in American life.

INDEX

Cliff Sloan, a former Supreme Court clerk and former publisher of *Slate* magazine, is a partner at Skadden, Arps, Slate, Meagher & Flom in Washington, D.C. He has argued before the Supreme Court five times. He has also written about the Supreme Court for many publications, including *Newsweek, The Washington Post,* and *Slate.* He lives in Chevy Chase, Maryland.

KATHLEEN KAYE

David McKean is a top level Senate aide. He was chief of staff to Senator John Kerry of Massachusetts from 1999 to 2008. He is the author of two highly acclaimed political biographies—*Friends in High Places* and *Tommy the Cork.* He lives in Washington, D.C.